Remaking Kichwa

Bloomsbury Studies in Linguistic Anthropology

Series Editors:
Sabina Perrino, Paul Manning, and Jim Wilce

Presenting and exploring new and current approaches to discourse and culture, **Bloomsbury Studies in Linguistic Anthropology** examines the most recent topics in this field. Publishing contemporary, cutting edge research, this series investigates social life through everyday discursive practices, making these practices visible and unveiling processes that would remain concealed without careful attention to discourse.

The titles in this series focus on specific themes to advance the field both theoretically and methodologically, such as language contact dynamics, language revitalisation and reclamation, and language, migration and social justice. Positioning linguistic anthropology at the intersection with other fields, this series will cast light on various cultural settings across the globe by viewing important linguistic ethnographies through an anthropological lens. Standing at the frontier of this growing field, **Bloomsbury Studies in Linguistic Anthropology** offers a balanced view of the current state of the discipline, as well as promoting and advancing exciting new directions for research.

Titles in the Series:

Graphic Politics in Eastern India
Nishaant Choksi

Language and Revolutionary Magic in the Orinoco Delta
Juan Luis Rodriguez

Remaking Kichwa
Michael Wroblewski

Saying and Doing in Zapotec
Mark A. Sicoli

Remaking Kichwa

Language and Indigenous Pluralism in Amazonian Ecuador

Michael Wroblewski

BLOOMSBURY ACADEMIC
LONDON • NEW YORK • OXFORD • NEW DELHI • SYDNEY

BLOOMSBURY ACADEMIC
Bloomsbury Publishing Plc
50 Bedford Square, London, WC1B 3DP, UK
1385 Broadway, New York, NY 10018, USA
29 Earlsfort Terrace, Dublin 2, Ireland

BLOOMSBURY, BLOOMSBURY ACADEMIC and the Diana logo are trademarks of
Bloomsbury Publishing Plc

First published in Great Britain 2021
This paperback edition published 2022

Copyright © Michael Wroblewski, 2021

Michael Wroblewski has asserted his right under the Copyright, Designs and Patents Act, 1988, to be identified as Author of this work.

For legal purposes the Acknowledgments on p. viii constitute an extension of this copyright page.

Cover design: Ben Anslow
Cover image © MB Photography / Getty Images

All rights reserved. No part of this publication may be reproduced or transmitted in any form or by any means, electronic or mechanical, including photocopying, recording, or any information storage or retrieval system, without prior permission in writing from the publishers.

Bloomsbury Publishing Plc does not have any control over, or responsibility for, any third-party websites referred to or in this book. All internet addresses given in this book were correct at the time of going to press. The author and publisher regret any inconvenience caused if addresses have changed or sites have ceased to exist, but can accept no responsibility for any such changes.

A catalogue record for this book is available from the British Library.

Library of Congress Cataloging-in-Publication Data
Names: Wroblewski, Michael, author.
Title: Remaking Kichwa: language and indigenous pluralism in
Amazonian Ecuador / Michael Wroblewski.
Identifiers: LCCN 2020037940 | ISBN 9781350115552 (hardback) | ISBN 9781350212817 (paperback) | ISBN 9781350115569 (ebook) | ISBN 9781350115576 (epub)
Subjects: LCSH: Quechua Indians–Ecuador–Languages. | Quechua language–Ecuador–Revival. | Language revival–Ecuador. | Bilingualism–Ecuador.
Classification: LCC F2230.2.K4 W76 2021 | DDC 986.6/01–dc23
LC record available at https://lccn.loc.gov/2020037940

ISBN: HB: 978-1-3501-1555-2
PB: 978-1-3502-1281-7
ePDF: 978-1-3501-1556-9
eBook: 978-1-3501-1557-6

Series: Bloomsbury Studies in Linguistic Anthropology

Typeset by Deanta Global Publishing Services, Chennai, India

To find out more about our authors and books visit www.bloomsbury.com and sign up for our newsletters.

Contents

List of Illustrations	vi
Acknowledgments	viii
Notes on Orthography and Transcription	x
Introduction: Language, Indigeneity, and Pluralism in Amazonian Ecuador	1
1 The Tena Kichwa Sociolinguistic World	35
2 Language Revitalization, Nation-Building, and Code Choice	53
3 Bilingualism, Racialization, and "Poorly Spoken Spanish"	83
4 Intercultural Memories: Ritual Activism in Discourses of the Past	111
5 Intercultural Futures: Urban Media and the Predicaments of Translation	135
Conclusion: Discourse and the Remaking of Indigeneity in Amazonia	165
Notes	175
References	177
Index	194

Illustrations

Figures

1	Mateo and Camila walking through their family's **chakra**	2
2	Camila and Mateo demonstrating the medicinal use of **kalulu**	4
3	Mateo and an *ayawaska* vine	6
4	Map of Ecuador	18
5	Photo of central Tena in 2015	22
6	Map of Napo Kichwa dialect regions	66
7	Spanish *ll* allophone frequency according to generation	99
8	Spanish *ll* allophone frequency according to level of education	99
9	Spanish *ll* allophone frequency according to residence history	100
10	Spanish *rr* allophone frequency according to generation	104
11	Spanish *rr* allophone frequency according to level of education	104
12	Spanish *rr* allophone frequency according to residence history	105
13	Spanish *rr* allophone frequency according to gender	105
14	Screenshot of Patricia, Native beauty pageant contestants and Lorenzo on *Telediario* news, **Ally** TV Channel 34, Napo Province public television, 2015	136
15	A tiara for a Native beauty pageant designed by a Kichwa artisan in Tena	145
16	Vicki demonstrates proper sorting of waste during her performance, the **Ñusta Yutsullakta Warmi** pageant	146
17a–b	Vicki reveals her *traje típico*	147–8
18	Dance group **Inti Wayra** performs "The Harvest"	154

Tables

1	Kichwa Orthographic Conventions	xi
2	Transcription Conventions	xi

3	Examples of Phonological Differences between Tena Kichwa Dialect and Unified Kichwa	71
4	Examples of Lexical Differences between Tena Dialect and Unified Kichwa	75
5	Examples of Morphological Differences between Tena Kichwa Dialect and Unified Kichwa	78

Acknowledgments

I am grateful for the support of countless people who made the completion of this book possible. It would not have happened without the generosity of the people of Napo who guided my research, let me record their words and wisdom, and allowed me to share their knowledge with others. I am deeply indebted to Ricardo Grefa, Jr., for his endless contributions to my fieldwork, guidance through complicated intercultural interactions, and concerns for my well-being in Tena. I would like to thank the Grefa and Licuy family, Juan Ricardo Sr., Maria, Ireni, Amalia, Liveya, Guillermo and Nancy for their boundless generosity in supporting my research, teaching me Kichwa, welcoming me into their home, and keeping me well fed. I am grateful to Galo Grefa Andy and his family for inviting me into their homes and workplaces, talking with me for hours on end and teaching me patiently about Napo Runa life. I would like to thank Victor Cayapa, Jr. for his incredibly astute contributions to my understanding of Kichwa culture and language in Tena. Dr. Fabian Espinosa guided me through my first, transformative semester in Ecuador as an undergraduate and helped me negotiate the bureaucratic hurdles of beginning dissertation fieldwork. Dr. Rubén Calapucha has provided me with continuous support, deep knowledge, and vital local contacts in the Napo Runa community over the years. I will always be indebted to him, Carlos Grefa, and Jorge Shiguango for teaching me Unified Kichwa and sharing their visions of a revolutionary indigenous future.

No one else has contributed more to the shaping of this book than Thea Strand, through her numerous careful readings and insightful comments on chapter drafts and the endless inspiration she has given me over our many years of intellectual discussions. I cannot even imagine what this project would have been like without her confidence and counsel.

I am indebted to many others who have shaped my work as a researcher and scholar, including Jane Hill and Norma Mendoza-Denton for their wisdom, exemplary leadership, and continued mentorship throughout my academic career. I am grateful for the intellectual guidance of Ellen Basso, who introduced me to the discourse-centered study of native Amazonia and supported my early graduate studies.

This book has benefited immeasurably from my discussions with colleagues in the Anthropology department at Grand Valley State University, the thoughtful comments of Grand Valley Anthropology students, whom I subjected to reading early chapter drafts, and the shrewd observations of various readers and discussants at academic conferences. It would not be what is without the editorial support of Sabina Perrino, Paul Manning, Andrew Wardell, Becky Holland, and anonymous reviewers at Bloomsbury Press, who helped me clarify and strengthen my message with their enthusiastic suggestions and incisive critiques.

Ethnographic research for this book was funded by generous grants from the Wenner-Gren Foundation (grant #7827), the University of Arizona, and Grand Valley State University, the latter of which provided an essential sabbatical period that allowed me to get this book off the ground. I am grateful to the Experimento de Convivencia Internacional of Ecuador for sponsoring the visa for my dissertation fieldwork and to the administrators and staff at the Dirección Provincial de Educación Intercultural Bilingüe de Napo for assisting me in my early research and study of Kichwa language.

Finally, I would like to thank my parents, Deborah and Edmund, sisters, Andrea, Katherine, and Meredith, and daughters, Elisabeth and Clara, for their constant support and encouragement throughout my research and my academic career.

Notes on Orthography and Transcription

Kichwa (also known as *Quichua*) words and morphemes in the text and transcripts included in this book are in **bold italic text**, while Spanish words and morphemes are in *regular italic text*. All Kichwa words are spelled using Unified Kichwa orthography. Alternative orthographies are used only when a prior spelling is already established, as in the case of proper nouns such as personal names, place names, and names of organizations. All words in Tena Kichwa dialect are spelled using Unified Kichwa graphemes in a way that reflects the dialect's systematic phonological and morphological characteristics. Tena Kichwa dialect words have not been respelled according to prescribed phonological or morphological norms of Unified Kichwa.

For example, voiced allophones [b], [d], and [g] are spelled with Unified Kichwa graphemes *p*, *t*, and *k* respectively, since these are the only available Unified Kichwa graphemes for these obstruents, meaning variable pronunciations like [kanda] and [kanta] are both spelled ***kanta***. Nonstandard morphological forms unique to Tena Kichwa dialect are spelled as they sound, according to Unified Kichwa orthography. For example, the Tena Kichwa accusative suffix is spelled using the Unified Kichwa grapheme *r* as -***ra*** (e.g., [yayaɾa] = ***yayara***), rather than being respelled as -***ta*** (as in ***yayata***), as Unified Kichwa orthography prescribes. Similarly, [ɾiksiŋgak] is spelled ***riksinkak***, not as it would be, following Unified Kichwa morphological prescriptions, as ***riksinkapak***. For more information on the distinctive morphological features of Tena Kichwa dialect, see Chapter 2 and Wroblewski 2010. The Unified Kichwa orthographic conventions used in this book are outlined in (Table 1).

The transcription conventions used in the book are outlined in (Table 2).

Notes on Orthography and Transcription

Table 1 Kichwa Orthographic Conventions

Grapheme	Description
Vowels	
a	low central vowel, similar to Spanish *a*
i	high-front vowel, ranges in realization from Spanish *i* to Spanish *e*
u	high-back vowel, ranges in realization from Spanish *u* to Spanish *o*
Consonants	
ch	post-alveolar affricate that can be realized as a voiceless [tʃ], similar to English *ch*, or as voiced [dʒ] in post-nasal position, similar to English *j*
h	voiceless glottal fricative, similar to English *h*
k	velar obstruent that can be realized as voiceless [k], as voiced [g] in post-vocalic, intervocalic, and post-nasal positions, or sporadically as voiceless [x]
l	voiced alveolar lateral approximant
ll	voiced palatal lateral approximant
m	voiced bilabial nasal
n	voiced alveolar nasal
ñ	voiced palatal nasal, similar to Spanish *ñ*
p	bilabial obstruent that can be realized as voiceless [p] or as voiced [b] in post-vocalic, intervocalic, and post-nasal positions
r	voiced alveolar liquid that is usually realized as tap [ɾ] and also infrequently as either a trill [r], similar to Spanish *rr*, or as a voiced palatoalveolar fricative [ʒ], similar to Spanish *rr* as it is pronounced in much of the central Ecuadorian highlands
s	voiceless alveolar fricative
t	alveolar obstruent that can be realized as voiceless [t] or as voiced [d] in post-nasal positions
w	voiced labial velar approximant, similar to English *w*
y	voiced palatal approximant, similar to English *y*

Table 2 Transcription Conventions

Symbol	Description
(( ))	speech or commentary inserted by the author
…	speech that has been omitted by the author
[text]	overlapping speech
-	truncated word or morpheme or interrupted utterance
=	closely latched utterance
?	rising terminal intonation
.	falling terminal intonation
,	grammatical pause
:	elongation of a vowel
#	inaudible or unintelligible syllable
#text	transcribed words are uncertain
text	marked emphasis or stress
TEXT	marked raise in speech volume

Introduction

Language, Indigeneity, and Pluralism in Amazonian Ecuador

Tena, Ecuador, is a picturesque Amazonian city of approximately 23,000 inhabitants. It sits at the confluence of two rivers and multiple worlds. Situated in the forested lowlands east of Ecuador's central Andean cordillera, Tena serves as the capital of Napo Province and a gateway to the Amazonian *Oriente*, or eastern lowlands. On a recent trip there, I met up with an old Kichwa friend at his family's home in the peri-urban *barrio* of San Carlos. Like Tena's other peripheral *barrios*, San Carlos occupies an in-between place geographically and culturally. Dense city neighborhoods of a predominantly *Colono* (the local Spanish word for White and Mestizo) population cross-fade with a sparsely populated zone of forest hamlets, home to a mostly Indigenous Kichwa citizenry. The foreign traveler to San Carlos, who usually goes by bus or pickup-truck-taxi via Tena, senses arrival in this liminal space by way of a jolt, which happens when Tena's paved streets give way to bumpy gravel paths where motor vehicles are obliged to slow. As the terrain changes under foot, the greyness of the city dissolves in the rearview as the greenery of the Amazonian lowlands reemerges ahead. The vegetation in San Carlos is a mixture of young, second-growth forest and lush cultivated patches of **chakrakuna**, or family garden plots, that adjoin cleared parcels with modest homes made of cinderblock walls and corrugated metal roofs. Mateo's is one of the many Kichwa families that continues to occupy the multiethnic barrio of San Carlos, which used to be a forest **ayllulakta**, or Indigenous Kichwa community, before it began its transitional absorption into Tena's expanding and ethnically diversifying urban sector.

Mateo and I spent the morning trekking through his family's **chakra**, checking on the health of his plants, clearing overgrowth, and taking breaks in the shade to replenish with water and vine-ripened bananas. Mateo was eager to show me how his piece of the garden was coming along since I last saw it years earlier, just after he and his father had wrested it back from the forest. Though at the time he was working as a security guard in Tena, Mateo's passion has long been teaching others about his native culture and ecology. He has a knack for approaching wayward foreigners and quickly making friends with them, which is how we met eight years prior. We walked among the diverse ornamental and edible plants that packed the garden as we had done numerous times before, Mateo acting as an instructional guide and anticipating my many questions. Still a young man in his mid-twenties, Mateo is a self-educated, hobby ecologist, and a *heritage speaker* of Kichwa, meaning he has a family connection to the language but is not a fluent speaker himself. While his parents and older siblings speak Kichwa as their first language, his education in a Spanish-monolingual school system in urban Tena was stressed at the expense, as he sees it, of being taught to speak Kichwa effectively in his home. As a result, he understands Kichwa when his relatives and friends speak it, but when he responds, he laments, his words come out "*por tramos, por partes*," in stretches and bits.

We passed through a wall of vegetation into a wide grove of plantain trees where Mateo and I stumbled upon Camila, his middle-aged mother, resting in the shade after a long morning of gardening (Figure 1). Without a word

Figure 1 Mateo and Camila walking through their family's *chakra*.

she decided to join us on our educational walk through Kichwa eco-culture. Unlike Mateo, Camila is a Kichwa-dominant bilingual—more comfortable speaking Kichwa but fully capable of conversing in Spanish. She is also a traditional healer and possesses an even broader working knowledge of edible, medicinal, and otherwise useful flora than Mateo. So, I pestered her with my questions too.

It was a relatively wet morning in the garden, and I noticed that there were plentiful fruitings of fungi on felled tree limbs that scattered the ground. We came across a cluster of rubbery lobes of a brown jelly fungus sprouting from a log, which I recognized right away from my walks in the temperate woods of the Northeastern United States as wood ear mushroom (*Auriculara auricula*). I asked Camila in Spanish if it had a Kichwa name.

> "What is it called, *mami*?" Mateo reiterated, always eager to help me with my research, and in this case, eager to learn the word for himself.
> "**Kalulu**" (pronounced [kalolo]), Camila told us.
> "**Kalulu**," Mateo repeated, mirroring Camila's pronunciation, and apparently working to catalogue the word into his still expanding repertoire of Kichwa. "People used to eat it," Camila explained. "My grandfather liked it."
> "You peel it," Mateo interjected, "and it is good for cuts."

Camila carefully extracted one of the lobes from the wood. "When you want to put it on a cut you peel it slooowly," she explained, as she delicately removed the rubbery outer layer of the fruiting body, exposing its sticky, gelatinous center. "And you stick it, like this, onto your cut." Mateo offered his own demonstration, adding, "It dries like that, and it starts to shrink." "Mhm," Camila concurred. "They are pretty, aren't they?" (Figure 2).

We continued walking through the garden led by Camila, who periodically slashed at low hanging branches and vines in our path. Camila and Mateo offered more demonstrations of harvesting the useful and edible plants we passed, including **lisanpapa** (*Carludovica palmata*) whose fibers are used to make baskets and the famed "Panama Hats" in the Andes, and whose stems bear pods with an edible heart.

> "You peel it like this," Camila explained in Spanish while demonstrating with a pod in her hand, "and you take out this part."
> "And it's like noodles," Mateo offered. "It's delicious."
> "It's like noodles." Camila agreed, "You cook them in a leaf, with a bit of salt."

"Do you like to eat it?" I asked her.

"Sometimes," she said. "But this one is *pasado* (past its ripe stage)." Then she smiled, evidently recalling something fondly. She turned to Mateo,

"*Stefan* **mikuka**," she reminded him by switching into Kichwa in an inquisitive tone, meaning "Stefan used to eat it [remember?]"

"Mhm," he agreed.

"*Stefan sabía comer, no?*" she reiterated in Spanish.

"*Sí*," Mateo reaffirmed.

Figure 2 Camila and Mateo demonstrating the medicinal use of **kalulu**.

I had heard numerous references to the enigmatic Stefan, a German tourist who settled for a couple of years in a rented house near San Carlos when Mateo was a young boy. Mateo's parents took Stefan in as a kind of surrogate family member, as his sudden plunking down in the Ecuadorian *Oriente* without any family or friends seemed to both puzzle and worry them. Their years visiting with Stefan, an energetic joker who evidently always indulged opportunities to sample Camila's traditional Kichwa cooking, was their first close relationship with a **Rancia** (a curious Kichwa-fied version of the Spanish word *Francia*, "France," which has come to mean "White foreigner"). Their close relationship with Stefan was also a lasting source of grief. One day, after sharing countless meals and stories and laughs with them, Stefan packed up his house and left Ecuador with little explanation, returned to his home country, and has not sent word to them since. Camila often reminded me, with tears in her eyes, that she still thinks of Stefan every time a plane passes overhead.

I always took stories of Stefan as indirect, grave reminders of my own responsibility as a privileged **Rancia**. Here I was, again, suspiciously and unpredictably entering into and out of the lives of this family at whim. In my case, I was not only visiting and sharing experiences but also benefiting in invaluable ways, professionally as much as personally, from their generosity with knowledge. The sound of Stefan's name pierced through the sensory splendor of the garden as a sobering reminder that I had better not let them down too.

I was shaken from my thoughts about ethical responsibility when Mateo unexpectedly veered from our path into a small clearing, where a thick, woody bow of a vine bent out into view. It formed a massive living arc from the muddy duff below our feet up into the canopy where it joined the trunk of a tree and then coiled around it, upward and eventually out of sight. It was ***ayawaska*** (*Banisteriopsis caapi*), a visually unexceptional South American liana with exceptional visionary properties as an ingredient in a psychoactive brew. This garden vine has a long history of use by myriad Native Amazonian peoples, including the Napo Runa, or Kichwa-speaking people of Napo, as both a medicine and source of metaphysical knowledge. While we took in the impressive girth and determination of the mature ***ayawaska*** specimen, Mateo began an instructive explanation about the *"señor"* who lives in the vine and teaches those who ingest it new forms of understanding and vital healing knowledge (Figure 3).

Figure 3 Mateo and an *ayawaska* vine.

After we returned to his family's house on the edge of the garden, Mateo and I sat and chatted over bowls of **chunta aswa**, a mild beer made from the fruit of the **chunta**, or Peach Palm tree (*Bactris gasipaes*) that Camila had prepared earlier. We talked about Mateo's plans for cultivating his section of the garden and his job as a security guard. I asked if he still had any interest in his former dream of working as an independent Native guide to international tourists. It was a business venture I watched him work tirelessly, but unsuccessfully, to get off the ground during the year when I first met him as an idealistic eighteen-year-old. The question reminded him of something he had been meaning to show me. He produced from a nearby cabinet a file folder in which he kept a document he referred to as his "Native certificate." I was expecting a plastic photo identification card like the ones I had seen in the wallets of certified Native ecotourism guides in Ecuador before. Instead, on a sheet of white legal paper was a typed memorandum, printed on letterhead bearing the seals of the Ecuadorian Ministry of Education and the national and provincial directorates of Bilingual and Intercultural Education (BIE). It read:

COUNCIL OF THE KICHWA LANGUAGE

CERTIFICATE OF HONORABILITY

I, the undersigned, Lic. Manuel Romero Mamallacta, Coordinator of the Provincial Directorate of Bilingual and Intercultural Education, in due and legal form,

CERTIFY:

That Mr. Calapucha Andy Mateo José, carrier of the citizenship number XXXXXXXXXX, is a person that has demonstrated impeccable character, superior responsibility, and recognized moral solvency, qualities that accredit him with our esteem and consideration, **at the same time is part of the Kichwa Nationality of this Province.**

I can certify all of the above in full truth, and I empower the use of this document for all ends necessary, except judicial procedures.

Tena, March 27, 2013

Centered toward the bottom of the form, below the date line, was Romero Mamallacta's signature and stamped insignia as the coordinator of the Provincial Directorate of BIE.

Understanding Complexity

My experiences in the urban and rural Kichwa communities of Napo have often been like this one, full of lessons in complexity—of practices, identities, histories, and webs of meaning in the Tena Kichwa world. For an uninitiated outsider, the events described earlier would likely raise several questions, including the following: What is the cultural significance of Amazonian land to urban Kichwas? Is urban Amazonia still Indigenous Amazonia? What does it mean to be "Indigenous"? What does it mean to speak an "Indigenous language"? Why does Camila speak fluent Kichwa and Mateo does not? How important is speaking Kichwa to being "Kichwa"? What about speaking Spanish? How can people see plants as both utilitarian objects and as people who teach us things? Why would an Indigenous person want or need a "Native certificate"? Who is this "Council of the Kichwa Language" and why are they giving out such certificates? What is the "Kichwa Nationality"? Answering these questions and making sense of experiences like the ones described above requires a full ethnographic account. In other words, it takes a book.

This is a book about Indigenous words, about how they reflect and configure Indigenous worlds and about the diverse ways Indigenous people express knowledge and experience through them. I have been conducting ethnographic research in Napo's Amazonian communities, from rural forest villages to urban and peri-urban neighborhoods in the Tena region since 2008, attempting to answer research questions like the ones mentioned earlier from the experiential point of view of self-defining Indigenous Kichwas. I draw primarily on two phases of ethnographic research: a year-long visit to Tena from 2008 to 2009, when there was still a "Council of the Kichwa Language" directing local language revitalization, and a shorter fieldwork period in the spring of 2015, two years after local language revitalization lost its centralized planning body. My sources of data for this book include recorded metalinguistic interviews, recorded speech in social interaction, and public media texts, which I use to shed light on what it means to be and to speak Kichwa in contemporary Amazonian Ecuador. This book offers a glimpse at an Indigenous people, reflecting on and remaking their history, through their own words.

The first main goal of this book is to provide ethnographic context for my experiences of Tena Kichwa life and discourse. Using ethnography, I aim to trace links between Indigenous language, identity, and politics in a time of intense public self-reflection and remaking. The historical period I focus on is one marked by transition. Unchecked twentieth-century generational language shift was met with an early twenty-first-century era of institutionalized "interculturality" and language revitalization. In the current era, the future of language and identity is again back in the hands of everyday citizens like Mateo, Camila, and other protagonists of this book.

The second main goal of this book is to demonstrate the importance of linguistic anthropological analysis of discourse as it unfolds. My aim in this regard is to go beyond the simple referential meanings of Indigenous words and make sense of them in context—linguistic, cultural, political, and historical—to illuminate their evolving and contested interpretations. Previous studies of Amazonian Kichwa peoples have decisively shown that their lifeways, worldviews, and forms of expression are not *commensurate*—equivalent and easily translatable—to those of others. I continue this tradition in my effort to show how Indigenous Tena Kichwa life and language are uniquely complex, heterogeneous, and adaptive, despite many outsiders' expectations of them as static, homogeneous, and disappearing.

Mateo, Camila, and the language council coordinator who signed Mateo's "Native certificate" are all, in different ways, exemplary of a Tena Kichwa experience of living at the confluence of worlds. Experience, identity, and language in this part of Amazonian Ecuador, as in many regions of Indigenous Latin America, are composite, fluid, and changing. Throughout this book, I argue that being Indigenous in a postcolonial, globalizing world implies a pluralistic experience. By *pluralistic*, I mean that Indigenous people regularly and knowingly engage with multiple and distinct languages, knowledges, histories, and ways of experiencing the world. *Discourse*—conventional, culturally rooted, and ideologically charged forms of talk—is the focus of my analysis. Following an established linguistic anthropological tradition, I treat discourse as simultaneously shaped by social interaction and constitutive of social life and show how its various expressions are historically patterned and best understood in sociocultural contexts of use (Philips 2013; Wortham & Reyes 2015). The discourse of Tena Kichwas like Mateo and Camila at once reflects and shapes a unique sociolinguistic world, a world that is *polycentric* (Blommaert 2007), or characterized by multiple centers of authority, to which everyday speakers orient. This Indigenous discourse reveals Indigenous pluralism in its routine juxtaposing of contrasting languages, perspectives, voices, styles, and intellectual traditions. This book illuminates this pluralistic Indigeneity, tracing the links between Indigenous words and Indigenous perspectives on, or *ways of knowing*, the world. Tena Kichwas like Mateo and Camila commonly mix languages and experiential ways of speaking; they mix bodies of knowledge and ways of knowing. As they switch between signs from multiple *semiotic*, or sign-making, systems, they weave together diverse discourse genres, contrasting voices, and seemingly incongruous intellectual traditions from multigenerational and multicultural experiences. And very often, they do this knowingly, exposing their own refractions of the words of "others" for political purposes. Through their discourse, a picture emerges of Tena Kichwas as immersed in a phase of radical reinvention, of their languages, identities, and social categories.

Indigeneities, Plural

In this book I aim to contribute to the ongoing redefinition of *Indigeneity*, or the qualities of being Indigenous, building on recent ethnographic works that centralize Indigenous Peoples' own critical, contested, and multiple understandings on this concept (e.g., Ball 2018; Graham & Penny 2014; Halbmayer 2018; Jackson 2019; Shulist 2018). Like others, I see Indigeneity as defined by mixture, eclecticism, and dynamism (De la Cadena & Starn 2007), as internally heterogeneous and fluid (Canessa 2007), and as exhibiting selectivity and strategy (Warren & Jackson 2002). Like previous scholars working in Latin America, throughout the book I call attention to Indigenous discourse forms as multilingual and multivocal (Graham 1995; Hill 1995), including contrasting idioms (Gow & Rappaport 2002), styles, registers, formulaic content (Graham 2002), and exhibiting multiple experiential perspectives, epistemologies (Cepek 2016), and cosmologies (Halbmayer 2018; Vilaça 2015). I seek to expand common notions of Indigenous discourse to show its inherent pluralism—the coexistence of multiple, conventionalized ways of speaking and ways of knowing in single utterances. Discourse will be the channel for presenting an anatomy of Tena Kichwas' uniquely complex sociolinguistic world and for exploring Indigenous Latin American pluralism more generally.

In characterizing Tena Kichwa Indigenous discourse as pluralistic, I build on previous studies that challenge simplified notions of Indigenous *hybridity* in Latin America as an inherently unstable state of being simultaneously and incompletely pulled toward tradition or modernity (Canclini 2005). Following the work of previous Amazonianist scholars who have centralized

Indigenous hybridity as defining cultural practice, I see Tena Kichwa cultural adaptation not as evidence of acculturation, as some earlier anthropologists, non-Kichwas, and even some older Kichwas in Tena would have it, but rather as a process of change rooted in and according to Indigenous principles. Tena Kichwas' appropriations of exterior, modern elements of culture do not simply happen at the expense of Native, traditional ones; rather, adaptation is generated by Native processes of change, and according to Native conceptions of self and other. As Santos-Granero (2009) points out, openness to understanding the ways of "others" has long been a defining characteristic of Native Amazonian societies in anthropological accounts, where the persistence of society is seen as dependent on an ability to incorporate "dangerous foreign entities and forces" (see also Gow 2007; Halbmeyer 2018; Vilaça 2007; Viveiros de Castro 1998). While Westerners may view such hybrid forms of expression as inherently contradictory, for many Indigenous Peoples, contradiction is not in itself problematic. As Vilaça (2015) notes, many non-Western societies, including Indigenous Amazonian ones, "base their inventive process on creating alternatives to convention . . . creating a dialectical process between convention and invention that enables the coexistence of diverse alternatives" (12).

Scholars working among Amazonian Kichwa communities have already identified a Native theory of cross-cultural engagement as a driving mechanism for cultural maintenance and change. Uzendoski (2005) refutes earlier ethnographers' description of Amazonian Kichwas as a "transitional" culture on a path toward assimilation to Mestizo lifeways, arguing instead that Amazonian Kichwa social processes are defined by fluid boundaries and continuous identity transformation, or, in a word, *transculturation*. Whitten and Whitten (2008: 2011) similarly argue that being Runa implies an ability to be critically minded and attuned to the experiential and cultural knowledge of non-Runa others. They highlight Amazonian Kichwas' ongoing moves toward achieving an "alternative modernity," which involves appropriating "modern accoutrements of life through counterhegemonic and transformative systems of Indigenous meaning" (2011: 184).

In other words, unidirectional notions of Indigenous "acculturation," singular understandings of "modernity," and simplified depictions of hybridity as a clash between "traditional" and "modern" cannot account for productive Native Amazonian processes of knowledge gathering, identity transformation, and cultural maintenance. Nor can they account for the complex practices that result from these processes—for example, composite belief systems, notions of self, forms of material culture, and ways of speaking—which do not fit into stale dichotomies of "Indigenous" and "non-Indigenous." The reproduction of Indigeneity, rather, often involves actively reflecting on and absorbing multiple, alternative models of practice and forms of knowledge and creating innovative new forms of expression that selectively mix and juxtapose these.

Building on these challenges to outdated notions of acculturation and hybridity, I look to Indigenous discourse as a dynamic set of practices where intercultural processes are laid bare. Tena Kichwas' discourse practices are plural in that they are derived from various source materials, forms, conventions, and histories. They are plural*istic* in that they follow a logic of openness to multiplicity rooted in ancestral intellectual traditions while also in dialogue with nationalistic multiculturalist ideologies. Hybridity, in the nuanced sense espoused by Santos-Granero (2009), thus refers in this book to a defining Tena Kichwa cultural practice—a merging and coexistence of "clashing traditions," as well as an "enduring openness" to others. Pluralism refers to a way of engaging this coexistence of ideas, but more specifically according to recognized Latin American political ideologies. Pluralism is hybridity with an established ethos, one that is drawn from both Native and non-Native ideological traditions. Tena Kichwas regularly weave together distinct sets of knowledges and practices in self-conscious ways, mirroring the multiculturalist ideals espoused in contemporary Latin American policy. Sometimes implicitly and other times explicitly, the voices and traditions of "self" and "other" are kept separate in these pluralistic discourses. This follows a contemporary Latin American ideology of promoting diversity without acculturation, of cultural exchange without cultural displacement. Change is certainly experienced by some as "loss" and displacement, since the making of pluralistic discourse naturally operates in socially oriented fields of asymmetry and power, where certain practices become normal and prestigious, and others marginal and stigmatized. But Tena Kichwas' appropriation of others' ways, as I will explain in more detail throughout the book, tend to redirect the power over representation into Indigenous hands.

Throughout this book, I highlight pluralistic discourse as a display of a pluralistic Indigeneity that has become commonplace in Latin America, where self-determination and cultural continuity require absorbing and mastering the ways of recognized others. I suggest pluralism as a next-step concept for characterizing hybridity in Indigenous Latin America, as both a state of being and a form of cultural practice with an established ethos, drawn from the common ground created by Indigenous social movements and accommodating nationalist and global policies. In the chapters that follow, I illuminate this pluralism in the words of Tena Kichwas and trace the links between Indigenous discourse and a changing Latin America.

Remaking Indigeneity

The defining historical moment that takes shape through the words of Tena Kichwas in this book is an ongoing *intercultural* experiment—a dynamic exchange between Indigenous and dominant cultural systems, knowledges, and values that has come to frame Ecuadorian nationalism and drive local political initiatives. While the intercultural experiment in Napo is directed at a broad Amazonian territory and people, where rural forest communities still serve as the cradles of Kichwa culture, the intellectual and administrative locus of interculturality is urban Tena, which Kichwa activists are working to remake as Indigenous space. This study therefore also seeks to present an inclusive picture of Native Amazonia by emphasizing urban-orienting Indigenous people and their globally orienting discourses, in keeping with an expanding ethnography of urban Amazonia (see Alexiades & Peluso 2015).

Indigenous takes on a specific meaning in this era of global Indigenous politics and Ecuadorian plurinationality and interculturality. In 2008, the year I first met Mateo and Camila, Ecuador had rewritten its constitution and ushered in a new era of multiculturalism in policy and nationalist rhetoric. Scholars have been pointing to ongoing radical transformations in the political order throughout Latin America since the 1960s, largely due to the work of Indigenous social movements that reached a period of intensified protests in the 1990s and 2000s against neoliberal globalization and exclusive governing structures, in favor of autonomy, self-representation, and cultural recognition (Hale 2005; Sieder 2002; Van Cott 2005; Warren and Jackson 2002, 2005). Twenty-first-century Latin America has so far been distinguished by a responsive shift, referred to as the "pink tide," to leftist governments and policy transformations that align with grassroots social movements (Cameron &

Hershberg 2010; de la Torre 2010; Stahler-Sholk et al. 2014), notwithstanding very recent returns to right-wing populism in the administrations of certain countries.

In the case of Ecuador, vocal and powerful Indigenous organizations and "ethno-political parties" (Warren & Jackson 2005; see also Jameson 2011) have redirected national policymaking toward new considerations of minorities' claims to distinctive political organizations and cultural identities. The administration of President Rafael Correa, in power from 2007 to 2017, originally ran on a platform of radical reform, a so-called Citizens Revolution, meant to bring an end to neoliberal policies, economic inequality, and the marginalization of minority peoples. The progressive 2008 constitution, with its radical inclusion of environmental rights and the official recognition of Ecuador's constituent Indigenous nationalities, was rewritten under Correa's direction during his first term in office. It is important to note, as Becker (2014) does, that many of the reforms Correa sought to include in the new constitution were already recognized Indigenous demands, which leaders viewed as being hijacked by Correa in his pursuit of power.

Ultimately, the Correa administration and its "Citizens' Revolution" were largely rebuked by activists for keeping the language of plurinationality intentionally vague, excluding established Indigenous social movements in favor of emphasizing individual rights and centralizing power (Becker 2014), as well as for glaring reversals on anti-neoliberal and environmentalist policies (Davidov 2013; Martinez Novo 2014) that fomented destruction in Indigenous territories. Still, the new constitution and its mandate for constitutionally guaranteed multiculturalism (cf. Garcia 2005) remain bright spots in the policy changes of the last decade, as potential new spaces have been opened up for Indigenous decolonization of government, economy, and culture. While current Ecuadorian president Lenín Moreno has so far worked to reverse many of his predecessor's policy reforms, this multiculturalist legacy of the pink tide is still strong and still evolving through the work of localized Indigenous leaders.

Under Article 1 of the 2008 constitution, Ecuador is defined as both a "plurinational" and "intercultural" state. The principle of *plurinationality* was first proposed for inclusion in official discourses in the late 1980s by the Confederation of Indigenous Nationalities of Ecuador (CONAIE) and intended as both a restructuring of political representation and a shift away from a history of assimilation and monoculturalism that began with the Spanish conquest and continues in the postcolonial era (CONAIE 1997; Jameson 2011; Walsh 2009). Rather than acting as an argument for political separatism, as had been suggested by its early critics, the plurinational label is seen as an official recognition of fourteen Indigenous nationalities and other diverse social collectivities existing within the Ecuadorian nation (Ayala Mora 1992; Walsh 2009). Like multiculturality (as opposed to multicultural*ism*), "plurinationality" thus officializes a descriptive term used to characterize an already-existent state of affairs, in which a multiplicity of Indigenous, Afro-Ecuadorian, and Mestizo peoples, along with their established worldviews, belief systems, values, practices, and political entities coexist under a unified state.

As Thomas (2016) notes, Ecuador has always been multicultural in its composition, but has only recently begun to recognize pluralism politically and legally. Policymakers continue to struggle with how to translate this recognition into practice. The Native concept of *interculturality* is often appropriated in state rhetoric as a vague reference to strategies for creating community among Ecuador's variously recognized peoples. Interculturality is intended as an undoing of colonial hegemony, through the development of peoples and practices that have been historically subjugated and marginalized (Whitten 2003). It is meant to operate through locally determined projects of exchange between peoples on equal terms. It involves, as Walsh (2009: 41) explains, "permanent communication and learning" between holders of different "values, traditions, logics," and "rationalities," and designed to promote "mutual respect and a development of individual and collective capacities." Interculturality is hailed by progressive policymakers as the social ingredient for achieving **Sumak Kawsay**, a Kichwa phrase that translates to "good living" and that has been used throughout Andean nations in South America to signify an ideal state of ecological and social affairs, including responsible government, proactive environmental laws, welfare programs, and the sharing of distinct cultural knowledges (Acosta 2012; Hidalgo-Capitan 2013; Macas 2010; Radcliffe 2012).

From 1989 to 2013, interculturality in Ecuador's Amazonian Province of Napo, whose majority population is Indigenous Kichwa, was under the institutional guidance of the Provincial Directorate of BIE in Napo (DIPEIB-N), the self-proclaimed "Council of the Kichwa Language" on Mateo's Native certificate. DIPEIB-N was an independent, Indigenous-run administrative office funded by the Ecuadorian state and a self-appointed front for the revitalization of Native Kichwa language and culture. DIPEIB-N's mission was to reverse a history of forced Indigenous assimilation. Its leaders worked to revitalize and revalue ancestral Indigenous languages, cosmologies, and values in order to achieve self-respect and a harmonious coexistence (*convivencia*) between Napo's resident peoples (DIPEIB-N 2009). DIPEIB-N's rural community-based BIE centers promoted revitalization through a curriculum that integrated Kichwa language, traditional knowledge, and social practices with classic academic teaching in Spanish. During its period of leadership, DIPEIB-N activists spread their goal of "rescuing and revaluing" Kichwa through a combination of holistic, rural education, and urban exhibitions of Native culture, sometimes in partnership with Tena's municipal government. While the DIPEIB-N office in Tena closed permanently in 2013, when bilingual education was expropriated by the Ecuadorian Ministry of Education under the direction of the Correa administration, it has left an enduring model for language and culture revitalization that is still being followed by current BIE administrators, teachers, students, and affiliates. DIPEIB-N activists and their successors have long stressed that successful intercultural exchange is predicated on a viable and politically mobilized Kichwa *nationality*—a people with its own territory, history, culture, and language (Becker 2014). According to DIPEIB-N's model, linguistic unification is paramount; to be Kichwa means to be symbolically linked by language. More specifically, this unification requires a grammatically standardized and linguistically purified *Unified Kichwa*, a now-pervasive Indigenous power code (Hill & Hill 1986) that will be a central focus of this book.

To be *Indigenous* in this historical milieu thus means to be of a recognized *people*, to have cultural and political rights that are affirmed by broader national society. It means being linked to other Indigenous individuals and peoples who are apart from dominant society in terms of history, practices, values, and cosmologies. At the same time, it means occupying a minority ethnic and racial status position, one that comes with constant work at combating marginalization, appropriation, and political disempowerment.

Beyond these basic principles, the local meaning of *Indigenous* is variable and complex among Tena Kichwas. Being Indigenous means being simultaneously *Runa* and *Kichwa*, two distinct but overlapping states of consciousness. While the moniker **Runa** tends to be glossed in English as "human" or "person," Uzendoski (2005) offers a more contextualized understanding of the term to mean a "completed person" and "'the product of a whole life' in which moral worth is not individual but resides in 'the social form,' which includes as a vital element the maintenance of continuity" (26). When used by the Napo Runa, Runa thus at once means "human," or subjectively conscious (Kohn 2007), fully socialized into a shared set of Indigenous lifeways and practices, and a recognized Indigenous ethnic group. Runa is thus the preferred moniker used by Kichwa speakers to refer to themselves when speaking Kichwa. In interethnic and multilingual social interactions, including my own ethnographic encounters, self-reference tends to shift from Runa to *Kichwa*. Being Kichwa means being part of a constitutionally recognized nationality, unified by shared symbols that cut across regional geographic and ethnic divisions. For many activists, community leaders, and members of Indigenous federations, Kichwa-ness is foregrounded in daily life. "Kichwa" thus takes on a double function among Napo Runa. It is a term of convention for talking to outsiders who have limited situated understanding of what it means to be Runa. Its use is also a signal of self-awareness of White-Mestizo/Indigenous oppositions. Self-identification as "Kichwa" implies being self-consciously "Indigenous," an extraneously imposed ethno-racial category that implies a minority status within colonial and postcolonial social hierarchies as well as a shared, non-dominant (or *counterhegemonic*) worldview (cf. Jackson 1991; Ramos 1995, 1998).

Who Are the Tena Kichwa?

The people I refer to as "Tena Kichwa" are a subset of Indigenous Napo Runa, who are themselves a subset of a people ethnographers collectively label the Amazonian Kichwa, an ethnolinguistic complex of approximately 150,000 Native inhabitants (Uzendoski & Whitten 2014) of the contemporary Ecuadorian provinces of Napo, Pastaza, and Orellana (see Figure 4). The language of the Amazonian Kichwa, referred to by its speakers as **Runa Shimi**, or "human speech," includes several dialects of Ecuadorian Kichwa that belong to the greater Quechua language family also spoken in Colombia, Peru, Bolivia, and Argentina. Many linguists and ethnographers believe that Kichwa emerged

Figure 4 Map of Ecuador (D-Maps 2014, with alterations).

in the Amazonian region of Ecuador prior to Spanish conquest, through contact between the lowland Omagua-Cocama inhabitants and highland Kichwa-speaking traders (Muysken 2011; Torero 1984; Uzendoski & Whitten 2014). Despite dismissive historical labels of the Amazonian Kichwa as a diasporic Andean people (Whitten & Whitten 2008) and as "acculturated" Natives (Oberem 1970; Uzendoski 2005), several decades of ethnographic research have demonstrated their "unquestionable Amazonian identity" (Muratorio 1991), rooted in a distinctive tropical rainforest culture and cosmology and reflected in a similarly distinctive set of language and discourse practices.

The Napo Runa are one of four ethnic groups that comprise this larger Amazonian Kichwa complex. They are defined linguistically by their use of the Tena and Loreto-Ávila dialects of Kichwa (Muysken 2000; O'Rourke &

Swanson 2013; Orr & Wrisely 1965) and by their ancestral connection to the forest environments surrounding the upper Napo River. The Napo Runa, following Uzendoski (2005), include a continuum of identities, with Whites and Mestizos at one extreme and *auca*, or savage, at the other (see also Reeve 1985). **Runapura**, or "humans among themselves," fall in the middle of this continuum and include various Indigenous affiliations, such as Shuar, Pastaza Runa (Kichwa speakers from Pastaza Province), and *Otavaleños* (Kichwas from the highland Otavalo region) (Uzendoski 2005: 15). Whites and Mestizos, referred to collectively as *Colono/as* in Spanish (essentially meaning "colonist") and as **Mishus** in Kichwa, tend to occupy the most salient opposing racial and ethnic category, though their identities and practices at times overlap with those of Indigenous Runa, as I will explain throughout this book.

The moniker used to describe the people of this book, *Tena Kichwa*, is my own. It is a product of my experiences conducting ethnographic fieldwork among a diverse population of Kichwa speakers and heritage speakers, who are concentrated in and around the urban sector of Tena. Some of my informants in this book live in the city of Tena proper. Many have family homes in Tena's peri-urban *barrios*, like Mateo and Camila, while others live in rural forest communities at distances up to an hour or more from Tena by bus, car, or boat. All of the people in this book are *of* Tena, though, in the sense that they engage regularly with its inhabitants, institutions, economy, history, and discourses, as much as they are *of* the surrounding Amazonian forest environment (cf. Whitten & Whitten 2008). I have chosen to use the term "Tena Kichwa" for three reasons. First, the use of "Tena" acknowledges the central role of the city in identities and practices. Second, I use "Kichwa," as opposed to "Runa," because this is the ethnic self-descriptor I hear most often in the intercultural interactions of my ethnographic fieldwork, which are conducted in Kichwa and Spanish (and also very infrequently in English). Third, all of my Indigenous informants share a heritage connection to what linguists refer to as the *Tena Kichwa* dialect, which is connected to an upper Napo River regional culture that is distinct from that of other Amazonian Kichwa groups and Kichwas in the Andean highlands.

While the Tena Kichwa represent only a small sector of the highly diverse Amazonian Kichwa and Napo Runa ethnolinguistic complexes, their composite rural-urban lifeways and Runa-Kichwa double consciousness are characteristic of contemporary global Indigenous experiences, where mobility, culture contact, and change have become normal states of affairs. Runa-ness and Kichwa-ness are not mutually exclusive identity traits, but rather poles on a wide spectrum of Indigenous identities. Shifting claims to different aspects of Indigeneity are signified through Tena Kichwas' shifting engagements with rural and urban practices, distinct languages and language varieties, and diverse political ideologies.

Being Kichwa in Tena: Weekend *Macheteros* and Urban Intellectuals

The distinctive culture, cosmology, language practices, and social life of Amazonian Kichwas in the rural **ayllullaktakuna**, collectively referred to as "*las comunidades*" ("the communities") by Spanish-speaking residents of Napo, have already received extensive ethnographic documentation that goes back several decades (e.g., Muratorio 1991; Nuckolls 1996, 2010; Uzendoski 2005; Uzendoski & Calapucha-Tapuy 2012; Whitten 1976). These scattered rural, kin-based forest communities of the Upper Napo River region are still seen by contemporary Tena Kichwas as the cradles of "traditional" ethnolinguistic identity and practice. Social life and language in Tena and its demographically Kichwa *barrios*, however, have so far received scant attention in the ethnographic literature, one of the reasons why I have chosen to make these central foci of this book.

Amazonian cities have been noted in many previous ethnographic studies as important centers for short-term participation in economic exchange and high-profile political activism (e.g., Graham 1995, 2005; High 2015; Oakdale 2005; Uzendoski 2005; Whitten 1985), typically for select members of an economic and political elite or for participants in specialized ethnic folklore markets who make periodic, long-distance commutes to perform and/or sell cultural material. Recently, though, increasing numbers of Indigenous Amazonians are being incorporated into these cities, through the urbanization of their rural forest communities, short-term commutes, and long-term relocations in order to form new political alliances, take advantage of jobs, schools, and services, and to be closer to other urban migrant kin. As a result, there is now a growing body of ethnographic literature on the regional urbanization of Indigenous Amazonia. These studies have tended to focus on the resulting adaptations that have occurred within Indigenous Amazonian cultures, languages, and forms of social organization, including the rise of cities as staging grounds for Indigenous Amazonian political mobilization (e.g., Alexiades & Peluso 2015; Eloy & Lasmar 2012; Espinosa 2012; Imilán 2010; McSweeney & Arps 2005; Shulist 2018; Virtanen 2010).

As the administrative capital of Napo Province and due to its proximity to the headwaters of the Napo River (a major tributary of the Amazon River), Tena has been reimagined as a "familiar" place for the Tena Kichwa (cf. Whitten & Whitten 2008 on the Puyo Runa). Tena sits in the middle of Indigenous Amazonian territory, in a province where Kichwas constitute a demographic majority.[1] Tena is currently a center of activity for local Indigenous organizations and an economic hub for Kichwa workers and students. It has also become a nucleus of Ecuador's thriving eco-cultural adventure tourism industry, a growing source of income for rural Kichwa forest communities and urban-based Native guides and a key medium of intercultural exchange between Kichwas and (inter)national visitors. Along with biodiversity, Kichwa culture has become a main attraction for travelers passing through Tena to other parts of Napo Province, and considered by the municipal government to be part of the "principal wealth" of the region. Offering experiences of both biodiversity and Indigenous community life, ecotourism became a driving economic force for planned development in Tena in the twenty-first century, as it allows for capitalization on the region's "natural riches" while promoting their "rational utilization" (Gobierno Municipal 2000), thereby promising sustainable economic income in a way that historical natural resource extraction projects have not been able to do (Figure 5).

In Ecuadorian legal and everyday local discourses, there is a conceptual opposition between rural communities, depicted as islands of cultural tradition, subsistence horticulture, and sustainable living, and cities, imagined as "non-Indigenous" zones of economic development and the incorporation of Indigenous citizens into national culture. Napo's Indigenous communities are, in fact, legally recognized as cultural patrimony, where autonomous development, forms of social organization, sustainable use of biodiversity, teaching of ancestral knowledge, and the use of Indigenous languages are protected by the constitution (Asamblea 2008). Low-impact subsistence practices and cultural vulnerability are often illustrated by Tena Kichwas as

Figure 5 Photo of central Tena in 2015.

exemplary of rural community life, which is opposed to life in the city, a center of noise, contamination, materialism, unchecked development, environmental destruction, and, as I will discuss in more detail in subsequent chapters, experiences of language and culture "loss."

For many young and middle-aged Tena Kichwas, "home" tends to be a composite place defined by urban and rural practices, including weekday work in the city and weekend time laboring and socializing with kin in forest communities. In my ethnographic interviews, I often found that the seemingly simple question "Where are you from?" is actually a complicated one. Patricia, a 23-year-old Tena Kichwa, explained it this way:

> I am from many places. Well, I am from the Community of La Paz ... I say that I come from there because my family is rooted there, namely, my mother and father. And we have a farm there. And I say that I am from there because, even though I wasn't born there, on the other hand, most of the time my family has lived there.

For Tena Kichwas like Patricia, life and identity are pluralistic. While migration to Tena ensures economic survival, city time is often balanced with weeknight and weekend participation in rural community social life as means of ensuring cultural continuity. In visiting their rural home communities or those of their relatives, Tena Kichwas reassert their place within **unay**, or "mythical space-time" (Uzendoski 2005), while reconnecting with the empowering forces, or **samay**, of the forest. Thus, visits to rural heritage communities are not only an escape from the city but acts of cultural maintenance. They are returns to one's rightful, Indigenous metaphysical place, and they often involve emblematic cultural practices, such as drinking *chicha*, bathing in rivers, trekking through the forest and unselfconsciously speaking Kichwa.

One of the primary activities associated with return migration to the communities is work on family **chakrakuna**, often referred to in Spanish as *fincas* ("farms"), like Mateo and Camila's, which are typically small plots used for subsistence harvesting and animal husbandry, small-scale raising of fruits and vegetables such as plantains, cocoa, and vanilla for sale in local produce markets, and the cultivation of timber for family construction projects. For city-dwellers, working on the family **chakra** allows for an escape from urban life and an opportunity to revisit with kin.

Many Tena Kichwas who work, study, or live in the city claim to do so as a temporary measure that affords a certain amount of economic security for their families. It also prepares them for interactions with institutions of dominant, mainstream culture, as liaisons for kin living in the communities who have not been afforded similar opportunities. As forty-year-old Diego, an independent ecotourism operator, explained:

> I live in the city for my work in tourism. If I go to live in the community, then I am not engaging in my career, right?... So, I go to the *finca*, and I raise chickens, cattle, and plant cocoa, all that stuff. So ... for that reason, I always go to my home. Every weekend I go to my house to visit my dad, my mom ... in the community. And I am always planting yuca, plantains, trees, like that ... I live in Tena for tourism ... and my children are in school here in Tena. For those reasons I am here.

While many Tena Kichwas view urban living as a necessary evil, like Diego, they also recognize its valuable resources for economic empowerment, formal education, and exposure to extra-local discourses. In a 2009 interview on a local talk radio show, Nicolás, an aspiring Kichwa politician running for office in provincial government, reflected on his own socioeconomic climb from being the son of a rural *machetero*, or "machete farmer," to being an educated, self-determined professional:

> When I was a boy my father ... said, "Nicolás, you must be a great professional. When you are a professional, I will be filled with satisfaction ... I don't want ((my children)) to be like me, *macheteros*" ... I am a professional that has worked, I have gotten ahead with education ... it has changed ((my)) destiny. Because if I had not been prepared, I would have been out in the country, ignoring certain things. My preparation has allowed me to share with the communities ... Many times, our fellow Kichwas have been exploited by intermediaries. So, we must go on changing. This training means leadership, it means creating schools ... so that our fellow citizens can better the quality of their lives.

Echoing this sentiment, Tomás, a young Kichwa father of two, urged for education and exposure to dominant discourses and media, of being, as he put it, "in contact with *el pueblo,*" or "people," including urban Kichwas:

> People from the communities are not prepared. Sometimes they don't listen to the radio, they don't watch television, they don't see the news, which is a priority. We should be in contact with *el pueblo*, what is happening, is it progressing, is it not progressing ... In that way, I become quickly prepared.

Many of my Tena Kichwa informants similarly stress the value of urban exposure, formal education, and the acquisition of Spanish, in learning to negotiate interethnic contact. They believe that the social sacrifices they make by moving to the city will ultimately pay off in an improved quality of life for all Kichwas. Like Tomás, many are enrolled in professional programs so that they can serve their heritage communities and ensure their continued autonomous development. Tomás went on to explain:

> With education we don't want to say that our identity is being lost. Instead, with what we learn, our cultural identity is fortified. In the communities, they know absolutely nothing about how to do official business. Because of this, parents sometimes have a problem with their land, family problems ... So, when one learns, when he or she is prepared, then I can go defend my father and my family. So, I step forward and I say "Dad, I am going to help you ... I prepared for this and you educated me." And now we can do official documents with lawyers, conduct formalities at the municipal office ... With this, the family is strengthened. And, meanwhile, we are valuing our cultural identity and we continue rising above.

Not surprisingly, Tomás is a product of the Indigenous-run BIE system. A growing sector of Kichwa intellectuals—representatives of Indigenous federations, former BIE administrators, teachers, and students—see in community-based BIE the promise of new generations of educated, politically mobilized, empowered Kichwa citizens. Following the model created by DIPEIB-N, they see formal education as a crucial step toward fortifying Indigenous cultural values for successful intercultural living.

Discourses of Loss and Revitalization

While pluralistic identities have become embraced by members of multiple generations, it is important to note that not all Tena Kichwas share such progressive outlooks toward urbanization and formal education. In fact, many middle-aged and senior Kichwas see these as threats to Indigenous Amazonian lifeways. A Kichwa municipal government worker I interviewed in 2008 bemoaned urban acculturation using what I eventually learned to be a familiar refrain. "If you go to a community," Ignacio explained to me,

> You will see people speaking Kichwa, drinking *chicha*, eating *yuca*, plantains. But in the city they do not. They drink cola, eat canned products, and speak Spanish. They do not want to drink *chicha* and eat traditional food. The problem is that Kichwas are ashamed to speak Kichwa and to practice Kichwa customs in Tena.

Many elder Kichwas I have interviewed over the years similarly describe the city as a space of cultural vulnerability, where young Kichwas are pulled toward abandoning the heritage practices they learned growing up in rural communities in order to more successfully blend in with their *Colono* peers. For these critics, being Indigenous, as Ignacio put it, is exemplified by "drinking *chicha* and speaking Kichwa." *Chicha*, or **aswa** in Tena Kichwa, is a mildly fermented beer most often made from mashed *yuca*, or cassava, a starchy root that is a staple of the Napo Runa diet.

Some middle-aged and senior Kichwas are particularly preoccupied with a perceived loss of traditions they have experienced in their own lifetimes. No doubt influenced by academics' predictions about the inevitable assimilation of Amazonian Kichwas to national, White-Mestizo culture (Uzendoski 2005), the fear of ceasing to exist as a people still pervades discussions of Kichwa culture in Tena. Readily apparent changes in the direction of adopting *Colono* culture, such as the current pattern of language shift among the youth to Spanish monolingualism and the ongoing abandonment of traditional diets, residence patterns, and material practices, have caused some older Kichwas to adopt disturbingly fatalistic attitudes about the future of Kichwa culture. Santiago, a middle-aged Tena resident, explained language and culture loss as a lamentable, though inevitable, process, in which

> A powerful culture is going to consume the weak cultures. And we are part of this weak culture. Uh, in sociological terms it is called 'cultures in danger of extinction.' And that's where we're heading. And soon, soon we, as Kichwas, only the name will remain, but the language will have disappeared completely.

Older *Colonos* make dire predictions too, often citing what they see as apparent evidence of ethnic disappearance that has already occurred in and around Tena. When asked if he thought Kichwa culture was at risk of disappearing, Simón, a sixty-year-old *Colono* municipal worker, matter-of-factly responded:

> Obviously. It already has. You look at an Indigenous girl, you don't distinguish the Indigenous girl from the *Colona* because she dresses in fashion. She dresses with better clothes than the *Colonas*. ... I would like to see them wearing their beautiful dress that they have ... the **makikutuna** and the **kumpalina**. That's beautiful, right? But they don't wear it. They ... walk around in shorts up to here, with low-cut blouses and all. They walk around in fashion.

Similarly, when discussion turned to urban-dwelling Kichwas, Valeria, a 62-year-old *Colona* and long-term resident of Tena, lamented:

> What shame they must feel because their identity is ending ... They can talk of 'our customs, our identity,' but where is it? It's not there.

Thus, while development and modernization are viewed as positive and inexorable signs of progress in Tena, deeply rooted academic and popular separations between "tradition" and "modernity" (Halbmeyer 2018) still persist among Tena Kichwa populations, as has been noted by previous scholars (e.g., Muratorio 1998; Uzendoski 2005). Such lamentations of "loss" are especially common among urbanizing Indigenous Peoples in global contexts who, as Colloredo-Mansfield (2003) explains, have "tenuous claims on urbanity and citizenship." For them, "the accelerated, crime-ridden, globally connected millenial city can be especially problematic" for both "countrified" theories of Indigenous Peoples and for the empowerment of ethnic identities that are founded on connections between people and place (275–6).

My discussions of urban and intercultural living among Tena Kichwas thus tend to turn toward calls for "rescuing," "preserving," and "revitalizing" Indigenous Kichwa language and culture. Exactly what defines these, and what aspects of them should be revitalized, however, have become major sources of contention. Studies of Indigenous activist movements in Latin America have demonstrated that revitalization can create conflicting ideas about traditional identity, (dis)continuity and change, resulting in identity discourses that vary greatly according to generation (Hervik 2001; Warren 1998, 2001) and among distinct resident communities (Cojtí-Cuxil 1996; Gow & Rappaport 2002; Nagel 1996; Warren and Jackson 2002). This is certainly the case among Tena Kichwas, as I will show, where members of different generations and resident communities distinctly conceptualize and "moralize" continuity and discontinuity (Warren 1998), resulting in competing definitions of Indigeneity.

Contemporary Tena Kichwa lifestyles and identity practices, though, exhibit clear challenges to these historical either/or logics of tradition versus modernity (Halbmayer 2018). Along with urban *macheteros* and progressive intellectuals, there is currently a growing population of youth who have been raised as Spanish speakers and pushed into urban schools and jobs, who expressly blend modern lifestyles with ancestral Indigenous values. These youth have become dedicated to teaching themselves Tena Kichwa dialect, learning about the medicinal properties of forest plants, visiting shamans, becoming experts on Indigenous material culture, eating only "natural" products, and advocating forest conservation and sustainable lifestyles. Mateo is exemplary of this young traditionalist community of practice. When he was still a teenager in 2008, I conducted one of my first recorded interviews with him in the shade of a plywood cabin on the edge of his family's **chakra**. It was then that he first told me of his plans to become an independent forest guide. I asked him if he planned to live in Tena, since doing so is often necessary to generate business with foreign tourists. As he saw it,

> I could live in the city, but I would like to practice the culture of my grandparents ... I like the things of my culture, to eat plantains, to eat fruits from here, that is maintaining culture ... I prefer being right here, natural, like this ... *yuca*, bananas, all the time ... ((City kids)) are more interested in

... partying, having friends around all the time ... I do that one or two times a month, but always I am here at my **chakra**. I like my culture.

I have met many young traditionalists like Mateo who are reclaiming their grandparents' practices in the creation of new urban-rural Indigenous identities. These revivalists assert that taking an active interest in learning about and protecting their ancestors' way of life can make one "Indigenous," even if heritage linguistic and cultural practices have not always been part of their everyday, urban experience. Many of these Kichwas are recently turning to paid and volunteer jobs in ecotourism and international forest conservation projects as a way of maintaining urban living and study while preserving ancestral practices and increasing their international visibility.

Remaking Discourse

So, if this is what it means to be Indigenous for Tena Kichwas, then what is *Indigenous discourse*? While certain subjects of this book—for example, urbanization, modernity, globalization, interculturality, bilingualism, politics, and ethnogenesis—may not seem to fit the classic picture of Native lowland South America, I submit them, as other scholars have before me, as central topics of concern for twenty-first-century Amazonian ethnography. This book is meant to contribute to and redirect an established tradition of Amerindianist fieldwork that goes back to the early twentieth century. I offer Indigenous words through collections of *Native texts*, direct evidence of a culture's "cosmology and reflexive historical consciousness, its members view of their sociocultural universe" (Silverstein 2017: 23). Like my predecessors, I subject these examples of Indigenous discourse to close linguistic and broad sociocultural analysis. Expanding notions of what qualifies as a "Native text," I include a range of expressions, from monologic, single-speaker narratives in Kichwa, to bilingual conversations between speakers of multiple generations, to Spanish-language interviews, urban media performances, and even formal written documents, like Mateo's "Native certificate." Like other Native texts, as Silverstein (2017) points out, the ones in this book are the product of power-laden interaction, involving Native speakers and me, a non-Native recorder-transcriber-translator-analyst. These texts must therefore be read critically, as "precipitated in and pointing to ('indexing') a complex and multilayered interactional context" (Silverstein 2017: 23) of assymmetrical power relations. While I recognize that, like my academic predecessors, I have a great deal of say in how these Native texts are selected, reproduced, and interpreted here, I try to present them as undisguised and accurately as possible, in the hope of challenging the unquestioned dominance of Western intellectual frameworks. I use the tools of linguistic anthropological analysis to offer an, albeit limited, ethnographically grounded insight into the ways my Tena Kichwa informants have already mastered multiple ways of knowing and communicating about the world.

As the form and content of Native Amazonian texts continue to adapt to changes in both Indigenous lifeways and the interactional context of ethnography, I believe the focus of ethnographers' attention should be redirected in kind. According to early twentieth-century anthropological accounts, which have left a lasting mark on academic and popular understandings of Latin American Indigeneity, individuals like Mateo, Camila, and others quoted earlier—that is, educated, bilingual, and bicultural citizens—typify marginality and contradiction. Such "marginal" individuals have served an important historical role as go-betweens for early ethnographers, missionaries, explorers, and other foreign visitors to Latin America, often as interpreters and cultural translators. At the same time, they have been cast as unstable, uncomfortable, and incompletely "civilized" or partially "modernized" figures (Wong 2019, see also Park 1928). An entire population of Kichwas in Amazonian Ecuador has been historically dismissed in this way, as an ethnographically "lackluster" people, misplaced speakers of a diasporic "Andean" language, and "semi-civilized" hybrids (Whitten and Whitten 2008). Such misguided labels, as five decades of ethnography among Amazonian Kichwas has shown (e.g., Whitten 1976; Uzendoski and Whitten 2014), conceal a far more complicated experience, one that can be both stressful and productive, of having a foothold in multiple worlds. In my own interactions, I have found that Tena Kichwas show a multicultural sensibility that is aptly suited for living in contemporary Latin America: they are an Indigenous people at once prepared to defend their cultural and linguistic heritage and eager to adapt to a rapidly changing world on their terms. Some Amazonianist scholars have noted that straddling multiple worlds in this way, regularly engaging "disparate social institutions" and "positions in which social fields collide," can cause emotional strain and cognitive dissonance (Oakdale & Course 2014b). Meanwhile, others have shown how educated and mobilized Indigenous Peoples can capitalize on their alternative ancestral beliefs as forms of resistance and "counterpower" (Turner 1991; Uzendoski & Calapucha-Tapuy 2012), strategically wielded to challenge their marginalization, upend structural inequalities, and forge "alternative modernities" (Whitten & Whitten 2008, 2011) that involve appropriating global technologies while holding fast to Indigenous value systems (see also Halbmayer 2018; Rappaport 2005).

We must continue to update academic understandings of Indigenous discourse in light of such ongoing adaptations. Contact, change, and reinvention have become recent focal points in *discourse-centered* ethnographies (Sherzer 1987) of lowland South America, which have long shed light on Native speech practices that do not fit neatly into aesthetic or intellectual categories presumed by Westerners. While this effort began as a quest to document "traditional" forms of Native discourse, such as narrative, ritual, and music, "still occurring" despite destructive encroachments from "the outside world" (Urban and Sherzer 1986; see also Basso 1987, 1995; Hill 1993, 1988; Sherzer 1983, 1990; Urban 1991), many ethnographers have turned their attention to the ways Indigenous speakers transform the form and content of their words to reflect ongoing changes brought by culture contact, engagement with national economies and polities, and reconfigured notions of history (e.g., Ball 2018; Basso 1995; Graham 1995; High 2015; Oakdale 2005; Oakdale & Course 2014a; Rubenstein 2002). Scholars highlight the apparent hybridity, or blending together of contrasting semiotic systems, values, models of personhood, of Indigenous intermediaries who simultaneously inhabit conflicting roles and identities (Oakdale & Course 2014b) in a transforming Amazonia.

In parallel with this rich body of inwardly focused ethnography of Indigenous communities, anthropological studies of Indigenous activism have also turned attention to hybrid forms of discourse, where signs of Indigeneity are strategically used as platforms for enacting broad political reform. Activists blend discursive traditions in high-profile venues in order to forge political middle grounds (Conklin & Graham 1995) between Indigenous spokespeople and powerful, non-Indigenous allies. In so doing, Indigenous agents seek to indigenize global political discourses, forcing non-Indigenous audiences to engage with their distinctive languages and ways of speaking (Graham 2002; Shulist 2018), philosophical frameworks (Rappaport 2005), values (Greene 2009) and cosmologies (De la Cadena 2010). A new body of literature has begun to take shape around documenting the complex semiotics of now commonplace, public, self-conscious performances, which many argue are essential to articulating Indigeneity in contemporary Latin America (e.g., Conklin 1997; Graham 2002, 2005; Graham & Penny 2014; Wroblewski 2014, 2019b). According to anthropologist Laura Graham, a founding figure in this area of research, "a full analysis of the creative and unique ways Indians are blending languages, discourse forms, semantic content, and other performance genres," necessitates further documentation of hybrid performances, of the speech practices of "cultural mediators." "Precise documentation" of such performances, she suggests, "is certain to provide rich material for future analyses" (2002: 211).

While responding to this call, I hope to show in this book that the "cultural mediator" is no longer an exceptional Indigenous figure, and performances of Indigeneity happen through a wide range of practices on- and off-stage. High-profile Indigenous leaders have already caught the attention of Amazonianist scholars as "skillful interethnic negotiators and transculturites" (Oakdale & Course 2014b) who are finding adaptive ways to fight for their "existential recognition" (Graham 2005) before a global public and ensure ethnic survival. In the chapters to come, I will show that interethnic negotiation and transcultural adaptation are not the exclusive domains of respected orators and political leaders, and that they happen through the words of everyday Indigenous citizens. While high-profile public performances will certainly be featured in this book (in fact, they are central in Chapters 1 and 5), lower-profile discourse genres, such as conversations, interviews, oral histories, and even written texts, display *interdiscursive* connections—that is, links in form, content, relevant tokens, and types—with the more conspicuous events. Tena Kichwa discourse is always in dialogue with politicized twenty-first-century versions of Indigeneity, and is never about "untouched reality" (De La Cadena & Starn 2007), even when it is directed at reclaiming precolonial ways of being. This book thus represents a continuation of a rich tradition of discourse-centered study of Native Amazonia, in which I bring this approach into dialogue with the study of Indigenous Latin American activism, language and identity (Bucholtz & Hall 2004), ethnographic sociolinguistics (Eckert 2012) and the sociolinguistics of globalization (e.g., Blommaert 2007, 2010; Blommaert & Rampton 2011). I present reconsiderations of established academic notions such as *Native texts, verbal art, language, discourse, and performance*.

Structure of the Book

Throughout the book I attempt to paint a detailed picture of a pluralistic Tena Kichwa sociolinguistic universe by foregrounding the words and experiences of its inhabitants. Each chapter begins with Indigenous words as they occurred during the course of my fieldwork, sometimes in unexpected forms and places. The initial chapters provide an ethnographic overview of contemporary Tena, Tena Kichwa Indigeneities, and ways of speaking. In later chapters I explore specific genres of Tena Kichwa discourse, tracing the semiotic links between them.

Chapter 1 begins with a description of a Kichwa-language urban media text—a morning greeting to a diverse, bilingual audience of a Kichwa-language TV news show—which demonstrates the polycentric character of the Tena Kichwa sociolinguistic world. I analyze this Native text within the ethnographic context sketched earlier, showing the importance of everyday language choices in the remaking of history, identity, and territorial rootedness in a time of ecological, demographic, and cultural change. In so doing, I offer an introduction to several key theoretical concepts that will be used throughout this book in order to understand the links between language choices and emergent Tena Kichwa ethnolinguistic identities. I offer an inclusive view of Tena Kichwas as made up of multiple, heterogeneous communities of practice, and regularly engaging with multiple languages, bodies of knowledge, and centers of ethnolinguistic authority.

In Chapter 2, I focus on language revitalization and the dissemination of the national written standard, Unified Kichwa, pointing to the emergence of Tena Kichwa dialect in discourse as a contrasting marker of local ethnicity. I contextualize Tena Kichwa discourses about language choice within recent global language revitalization movements and then turn to an analysis of local Kichwa-language revitalization. I present an overview of contemporary linguistic pluralism, highlighting two newly enregistered and competing codes—Tena Kichwa dialect, and a spoken form of Unified Kichwa that I refer to as the *intercultural code*. This chapter will underline the use of these codes as choices between ideological stances, demonstrating competing values for Kichwa nation-building or protecting local Amazonian Runa identity.

In Chapter 3, I return to the discussion of code choice to shed light on understudied areas of Indigenous discourse: foreign-language acquisition and bilingual identity. The chapter opens with bilingual Kichwas' reflections on their own linguistic insecurity, in which my questions about local Spanish were met with lamentations about "*Castellano mal hablado*," or "poorly spoken Spanish." I combine linguistic anthropological frameworks of language ideologies and raciolinguistics with detailed sociolinguistic analysis of two Spanish phonetic variables to show the effects of Spanish-Kichwa language contact and Tena Kichwas' attitudes about bilingualism. Challenging perscriptivist depictions of isolatable dialects in Latin America, I show how the ongoing racializing of Indigenous-sounding phonemes precludes them from gaining status as features of dialect or "accent."

While the first few chapters deal with explicit talk about code choices, Chapter 4 is about implicit experiences of culture contact through linguistically mixed oral narratives of the past. Elders' oral histories have become highly valued among younger Kichwas as important repositories of local history and cultural continuity. As such, their retellings have been reframed as forms of *ritual activism* or politically oriented ritual speech. Through a detailed analysis of two oral histories of life on the late colonial frontier, I expose narrators' interweaving of Kichwa and Spanish in order to evoke a key Tena Kichwa *chronotope*, or imagined field of time-space. I build on linguistic anthropological studies in discourse-centered ethnography and interdiscursivity to show the effects of culture contact, political activism, and enduring struggles for agency on Kichwa autobiographical narrative discourse.

In Chapter 5, I zoom back out to the broader Tena Kichwa sociolinguistic sphere and examine how speakers selectively mix multiple discourses and visions of Indigeneity in urban public media. I start by examining a televised promotion of an anniversary celebration of a peri-urban Native community and its Native beauty pageant. I then move into a broader discussion of forms of *intercultural media,* where Indigenous actors blend Napo Runa verbal traditions, material culture, dialect and Unified Kichwa, and technologies of global media, in an attempt to re-indigenize historically "non-Indigenous" urban space. I explore the creative ways Kichwas use media to translate across distinct semiotic systems, focusing on the challenges they face in adapting their visions to the constraining interpretations of non-Indigenous audiences.

In the Conclusion, I summarize contemporary sociohistorical developments in the Tena Kichwa sociolinguistic world and present a vision of the future of language revitalization and Indigenous remaking. I resituate this inclusive picture of Tena Kichwa cultural and linguistic heterogeneity as a case study for understanding diverse and composite discourse practices of Indigenous Latin Americans more generally. I offer a proposal for renewed ethnographic focus on pluralistic discourses as key forms of Indigenous culture in contemporary Latin America, and argue for the importance of such analyses in creating alliances between Indigenous Peoples and outsiders in projects of language preservation, culture maintenance, and rights struggles.

In addition to offering a detailed picture of the Tena Kichwa sociolinguistic world through its discourse, this book has two additional pedagogical objectives. First, in each chapter I work to introduce readers to essential theoretical concepts in linguistic anthropology, explaining them in accessible language while demonstrating their explanatory power in analyzing Tena Kichwa discourse. Second, I try to provide the reader with an intimate look into the ethnographic process. Bringing the voices of Tena Kichwas to the fore, I hope to convey a sense of what it is like to do anthropological fieldwork on behalf of an Indigenous people who are already quite capable of speaking for themselves. In doing so, I offer potential new directions in forging common ground between anthropologists and our critically aware Indigenous informants, as we work together to promote Indigenous autonomy and self-determination.

1

The Tena Kichwa Sociolinguistic World

On weekday mornings from a small transmitter station in Tena, **Ally** *TV—*Napo Province's public television channel—broadcasts a one-man Kichwa-language news program called ***Rayu Shinalla***, Kichwa for "Lightning Fast." The show is hosted by Eladio Tapuy, a late 30s local celebrity, former radio host and emcee of urban Native beauty pageants. ***Rayu Shinalla*** airs at 5:30 a.m. on screens throughout Tena, nearby towns, and rural forest communities. The show opens with the serene sounds of stringed instruments, drums, flutes, and twittering jungle birds. Transient images of rainforest fauna, Kichwa women in ceremonial face paint, men in feathered headdresses, and scenes of city people walking through central Tena cross-fade beneath superimposed Kichwa and Spanish text that reads:

Speech Sample 1. *Rayu Shinalla* opening credits

1 *Karantutamantallakankunawakallarinchi,*
2 *Rayushinalla*
3 *Ñukanchikawsay, ñukanchiyuyay, kankunawamikan*
4 *Rayushinalla, ñukanchirunakichwakikinshimipi.*
5 *Todas las mañanas inciamos con ustedes, **Rayushinalla***
6 ***Rayushinalla**, en nuestro propio idioma Kichwa* ((sic))

1 ((In Kichwa:)) Each morning we begin with you,
2 ***Rayu Shinalla***
3 With you, our way of life, our knowledge
4 ***Rayu Shinalla***, in our own Kichwa people's language.
5 ((In Spanish:)) Every morning we begin with you, ***Rayu Shinalla***
6 ***Rayu Shinalla***, in our own Kichwa language

A sheeny ***Rayu Shinalla*** logo hovers briefly above a grove of digitally rendered trees before the camera opens on Eladio, typically in a button-down collared shirt and holding the cell phone he uses to field live text messages from his viewers. He greets his audience in **Napu Marka**, which is in Unified Kichwa, the national standard variety, for "Napo Province." He addresses them as **mashikuna**, the Unified Kichwa word for "friends." Sometimes he offers another, more traditional, salute to **mamakuna, yayakuna,** and **maltakuna** ("mothers, fathers, and young people"). Eladio announces the day's date and time in Unified Kichwa, usually translating these into Spanish, and he thanks his viewers for tuning in using the Unified Kichwa idiom **yupaychani**, or "I am grateful." For the next thirty minutes, he delivers announcements about local happenings with classic newscaster inflection. In between segments of prerecorded Spanish-language news stories and his own bilingual commentaries, Eladio reads aloud live text messages, relays happy birthday messages to local residents, and airs Kichwa-language music videos by Ecuadorian artists from Amazonia and the Andes.

At the beginning of a typical episode of **Rayu Shinalla** that I recorded in the spring of 2015, Eladio switched back and forth between Kichwa and Spanish to extend a welcome to his culturally and linguistically diverse audience:

Speech Sample 2. Eladio's greeting on **Rayu Shinalla**

1 *Chasnami kan, mashikuna ... Kushi shunkuwan, kushi ñukanchiraykunawa uraspika*
2 *Allimi kanta ñawpakma rinkapak mashikuna. Allimi kan, karan ayllullaktakunapi,*
3 *chimpachikunchi* barrioskuna kay Tena llaktapi, Archidona **llaktapi,** Arosemena
4 *Tolapurapi, alli puncha. Kankunawami kanchi karan punchalla atarisha kuintarisha*
5 *apankapak mashikuna.* A ustedes la más cordial bienvenida amigos y amigas a esta,
6 su programación **Rayu Shinalla**, a través de la televisión pública Ally TV canal 34.
7 Hoy es miércoles, seis de mayo ... Así es, todas las mañanas siempre nos amplifican a
8 través de nuestra programación en los diferentes sectores en nuestra provincia de
9 Napo ... Saludos muy cordiales a todos los amigos visitantes quienes están aquí
10 radicados, o prácticamente vienen de turismo, no? Saludamos a todos los amigos
11 turistas quienes también nos ven a través de la pantalla chica en los diferentes
12 sectores, en los barrios, comunidades, caseríos. Allí, donde nosotros llegamos todas
13 las mañanas a partir de las 5:30 ... para compartir lo mejor de la información, a
14 través de nuestra programación **Rayu Shinalla**. Recuerde, hoy es miércoles, seis de
15 mayo. Ustedes tienen la posibilidad de enviar sus mensajes respectivos a 099 ...
16 **Chasnami kan mashikuna, yupaychanchi. Kankunawami katiran munakunchi**
17 *imasnara tuparankichi rukumamakuna, rukuyayakuna.*

1   ((In Kichwa:)) So it is, friends ... With a happy heart, we are happy to be with you this
2   time as before, friends. Very well, in all of the communities, over to the *barrios* of
3   Tena, in Archidona, in Arosemena Tola, good morning. We are with you each
4   morning, we wake up with you, friends. ((In Spanish:)) A most cordial welcome to
5   you, friends, to your program, **Rayu Shinalla**, on Ally TV channel 34 public television.
6   Today is Wednesday, May 6th ... So it is, every morning we grow via our program in
7   the different sectors of Napo Province ... Very cordial greetings to all of the visitors
8   spread out there ... to all of our tourist friends that also watch us on the small screen
9   in the different sectors, in the *barrios*, the communities, the rural villages. Out there,
10 where we arrive every morning at 5:30 ... to share the best information on our
11 program, Rayu Shinalla. You can send text messages to 099 ... ((In Kichwa:)) So it is,
12 friends, we thank you. We want to continue meeting with you as well, grandmothers
13 and grandfathers.

Continuing in Kichwa, Eladio introduced his first prerecorded Spanish-language news story, an on-the-scene piece about new *tuberías petroleo***kunata**, a mixed Spanish-Kichwa phrase meaning "oil pipes," which had recently been donated to the government of Napo to be used as culverts in provincial road development projects.

Each weekday morning Eladio delivers the news like this, as line 4 of the aforementioned opening credits affirms, "*ñukanchi* **Runa Kichwa kikin shimipi**," "in our own Kichwa people's language." As Eladio adeptly demonstrates, this "language" challenges mainstream monolingual ideas about what "a language" is supposed to look and sound like. Speaking "our own Kichwa people's language" involves constant mixing and shifting between *codes*, or what Hill and Hill (1986: 100) define as "set[s] of principles for selecting variants from a range of possible choices, in order to construct an utterance." For Eladio, these codes include what would usually be defined as multiple languages and language varieties. However, his discourse is characterized by frequent *code switches* or shifts between codes at phrasal and clausal boundaries. It also contains numerous *code mixes* or free-form blending of morphemes of multiple codes into single words and phrases. Because of this, Eladio's codes are difficult to separate and classify. Even the show's title, **Rayu Shinalla**, is a linguistic admixture: **rayu** (pronounced with a tap [ɾ] and a high-back [u] vowel) is a phonetically Kichwa-fied borrowing of the Spanish word *rayo* (pronounced with a trilled [r] and a mid-back [o] vowel), which means "lightning," while **shinalla**, which literally means "just like" and in this phrase implies "fast," is Kichwa.

Like his language, Eladio's audience is mixed. His viewers include bilingual Kichwa urbanites in Tena, nearby towns, peri-urban *barrios*, and rural forest communities, and Ecuadorian and international tourists. Just as **ñukanchi Runa Kichwa kikin shimi** refers to a language made up of multiple codes, **ñukanchi** ("we"), **Runa** ("people"), and **Kichwa** together refer to a heterogeneous community of speakers who engage regularly with non-Indigenous "others." Given a proper ethnographic examination, as I plan to show in this chapter, it turns out that Eladio's low-tech, one-man-show is, like most examples of Tena Kichwa discourse, rich in linguistic, cultural, and political complexity. It also reveals the contested notions of what it means to be Indigenous, Runa, and Kichwa, as outlined in the Introduction. From the linguistically mixed content to the composite identity of its host, **Rayu Shinalla** is perfectly suited for a contemporary audience of diverse Tena Kichwas and their *polycentric*, or multicentered, sociolinguistic environment.

Captivating an Audience

Eager to learn more about how he came to host Tena's only "Kichwa-language" news show, I convinced Eladio to take a brief break from his scheduled editing duties to sit down with me for a recorded conversation. On a hallway bench just outside the newsroom where he records **Rayu Shinalla**, I began our *metalinguistic interview*, an open-ended, interviewer-guided talk-about-talk, as I usually do, with questions about his linguistic background—"What languages do you speak?" "Where did you learn them?" "When and where do you speak [language X]?" Eladio began his account with a familiar lament among Kichwas of his generation: "When I was little, my parents didn't instruct me very well in Kichwa." Though he spent his early home years speaking Kichwa, he was sent to Spanish-monolingual schools, where, as he recalled, he began to "lose" his Kichwa. Despite this shift to Spanish as his dominant language, Eladio continued to identify with his Indigenous heritage and sought out roles where he could act as a community leader. He found his way into grassroots community media, which he saw as an emerging arena for promoting endangered Kichwa language and culture. He got his first foothold as a co-host of a Kichwa-Spanish *radio revista* ("radio revue") program directed by Napo's local Indigenous *Federación de Organizaciones Nacionales Kichwas de Napo* ("Federation of Indigenous Kichwa Organizations of Napo"), or FONAKIN. He worked for several years as a Kichwa music DJ and talk-show host covering cultural, political, and economic issues affecting Indigenous Napo communities. As part of his training for the position, he relearned Kichwa through the help of FONAKIN and DIPEIB-N instructors who taught him to read and write in Unified Kichwa, the standardized Ecuadorian variety. "For that reason," he recounted,

Speech Sample 3. Metalinguistic interview with Eladio

1 I was better at Unified Kichwa than my friends who speak the other Kichwa, the
2 one from here. There was a conflict too. When they listened to the radio, they
3 said "Why?" The grandparents, for example. Because ((Unified Kichwa)) changes
4 the meaning of what is being said ... So now I try not to speak too much Unified
5 Kichwa, although sometimes, I get lost. So, I try to explain it, you know? What is
6 said commonly and what it means in Unified Kichwa ... Before, they used to urge
7 us to speak Unified Kichwa. For example, in the Native beauty pageants they
8 urged us to speak in Unified Kichwa. But now, no, they say speak however you
9 can.

Throughout our conversation, Eladio kept coming back to this struggle to appeal to different Kichwa-speaking audiences. And there always seemed to be two opposing sectors: (1) his dialect-speaking kin and friends in rural communities and peri-urban *barrios* and (2) his Unified Kichwa-literate colleagues working in Tena. In order to have a successful career as a Kichwa spokesperson, Eladio has to constantly check in with both of these subsets of his audience to make sure his TV performances are being favorably received. One particularly interesting example of this ongoing struggle was revealed in his story of searching for the show's title. "Choosing a title was difficult," he recalled,

10 I mean, to capture the public I needed a title ... that would have an impact.
11 'Information' means giving knowledge of day-to-day occurrences
12 to the community, right? So, I mean, I wanted something from nature. I looked
13 for a name of a bird that- fast, something like a parrot. I thought, I imagined. I
14 went almost three months without a name ... And, well, I thought of ***rayu***

15   (('lightning')). It's *rayo*, right? *Chuta*, okay. I went with that, **Rayu**. Information
16   that is fast ... So, at that time there was the Directorate of Bilingual Education.
17   They never used **rayu** like *rayo*. Here, with the changes in the intercultural-
18   bilingual education system, it changed a lot from *el idioma Kichwa propia*
19   *nuestra* (('our own proper Kichwa language')) that we spoke before, and now to
20   Unified Kichwa ... So, I asked my friends at the Directorate of Bilingual Education,
21   "*Chuta*, how do you say, instead of saying **rayu**, in Unified Kichwa?" "No," they
22   said, "you should use onomatopoetic sounds." I said, "What?" We, here, *rayo*,
23   when we hear that, the onomatopoetic sound would be **tulum**. **Tulum**, and it is
24   fast, right? **Tulum shinalla**, or, like real fast. Like *rayo* (('lightning')) and *rápido*
25   (('fast')), the information that moves quickly. But it didn't agree with me, I
26   mean, **tulum shinalla** didn't convince me. It doesn't stick, it doesn't have an
27   impact here. So, I said, no, **rayu** is better. Like we say here, **rayu**. **Rayu** is *rayo*.
28   **Rayu**, you just change the *u*. I had to pass on the advice of the Directorate. Well,
29   then I asked my friends in the communities. They said, "It's good. No, it's good."
30   They supported me ... It took me some time to come up with that name. But I settled
31   on **rayu** and **shinalla**.

Indexing Diversity

Eladio's on- and off-screen discourse is replete with complex *indexes* that link him to a diverse community of Tena Kichwas, identities, experiences, and practices. An *index*, following the theoretical proposition of logician and semiotician Charles Sanders Peirce, is a kind of sign-making relationship in which the sign vehicle, often referred to more simply as the "sign," co-occurs in the same context as the object to which it refers, linking the two together in a natural, causal, or existential relationship. Like other types of signs, an index can take any form—for example, a word, an action, a thing, and a concept—in representing its object. The English word "tree" is a sign that stands to represent an actual "tree" in the world or the abstract concept. The word "tree," however, acts as what Peirce refers to as a *symbol*, in that it has a completely arbitrary connection to its object of reference. English speakers have learned to effortlessly make the connection between the word "tree" and its referent object through repetitive use, just as Spanish speakers have done with the semantically equivalent word *árbol* and Tena Kichwa speakers have with the word **yura**.

An index, however, is not arbitrarily connected to its object of reference in the way that a symbol is. The word "here," while symbolic for English speakers of "a location in relatively close proximity to the speaker," also has a more specific, indexical meaning once it is uttered by a speaker to refer to a field of objects in a real speech situation. While it still usually refers to a point or general location relatively proximal to the speaker uttering the word, its specific meaning in the context of speech becomes linked to the specific time and place of its utterance. As I type these words, *here* may refer to my office, my university campus, and my home state of Michigan. When you, the reader, utter the word "here," it refers to an entirely different set of locations proximal to you. Thus, the word "here" functions as a *referential index*, a kind of sign whose referential meaning is linked to a specific context of use. When Eladio uses the Spanish word *aquí* (which I have translated to *here*) in lines 17 and 22 of Speech Sample 3, he is referring to a specific Tena Kichwa sociolinguistic environment at a specific time in history. And his concept of *here*, as a Tena Kichwa in that environment, will always be somewhat different from mine, as a foreign observer.

In the same way that a footprint in the sand is an unmistakable index of the person that made it, linguistic indexes, like words, pronunciations, and grammatical constructions, can also act as *non-referential indexes*, or signs that point to previous social contexts of use. By *social context*, I mean the backdrop of social interaction—individual speakers, their respective social groups, and their cultural systems of meaning. Non-referential indexes, also called *indirect indexes* (Ochs 1992) or *social indexes*, inevitably carry with them the traces of previous interactions and all of this social stuff that surrounds them. When speakers speak, listeners hear social identities ("woman," "politician," "young person"), imagine typical practices (clothing, behavior, activities of interest), and ascribe associated qualities (warmth, intelligence, youth) and relative values (good, bad, normal, strange) to their words. We link these things with words because we have learned to notice them through previous experiences with real speakers and shared cultural ideas about them (i.e., types and stereotypes). From these experiences we develop preconceived models about who people are based solely on the way they speak. Every word choice (saying "y'all" vs. "you"), pronunciation (saying "gonna" vs. "going to"), or grammatical construction (saying "I don't got none" vs. "I don't have any") thus signals social things to listeners about the speakers who utter them. When Eladio pronounces the word **uraspika** as "uraspiga" (in line 1 of Speech Sample 2), listeners know he is a speaker of the local Tena Kichwa dialect. When he says **rinkapak**, instead of the more local **rinkak** (in line 2), they can also tell that he knows Unified Kichwa.

Every community of speakers or members of "a culture" shares a basic set of understandings about which signs are linked with other signs, objects, and ideas. And yet, at the same time, every individual community member's understanding will be slightly different based on their unique perspective on the world. Moreover, since our understandings are the result of endless reinterpretations, the meanings and functions of signs are in a constant state of change. So, when Eladio uses Unified Kichwa words, or Tena Kichwa dialect words, or Spanish words, he indirectly (i.e., indexically) communicates to his audience aspects of his social identity—where he comes from, what social circles he might be part of, and generally what kind of person he seems to be. While some general qualities of this social identity will be recognized by all Tena Kichwas who watch his show and understand his words, each audience member will have a slightly different interpretation and attitude about the various signs that comprise his total semiotic self.

Certain social indexes may even become *iconized*, meaning they take on an additional function of displaying the inherent nature or essence of a group of people by way of resemblance to it (Irvine & Gal 2000: 37; later referred to as *rhematization,* see Gal 2013; Gal & Irvine 2019). Along with symbols and indexes, Peirce lists *icons* as a third type of sign-object relationship, in which the icon resembles or shares qualities with the object it represents, in the way that a map of a location resembles the physical properties of that location or the word "meow" resembles an English speaker's approximation of the sound made by a cat. Certain indexes come to take on such a strong link to their objects of reference that they transform into icons, or natural seeming emblems of the essences of things. Babel (2018) has highlighted the iconization process in the construction of Indigenous identities in multiethnic settings, showing how Quechua speakers in highland Bolivia form enduring iconic links between highly salient categories of Indigenous practice. Like speaking Quechua for highland Bolivians, speaking Kichwa in Ecuador is an iconic sign of Indigenous identity, such that doing so makes Eladio sound unmistakably "Indigenous" on his show.

Language and Indexical Order

Through his collective performances on **Rayu Shinalla**, Eladio indexes a particular kind of Indigeneity, one among many kinds of Indigeneity recognized by Tena Kichwas. Linguistic Anthropologist Michael Silverstein (2003) has expanded Peirce's concept of the index to the study of social interaction, arguing that, though their meanings are variable and constantly shifting, indexes do not simply circulate randomly. Instead, the meanings of indexes are ordered and predictable according to cultural patterns of use and interpretation. As Silverstein puts it, indexes come in integral, ordinal degrees. While a *first-order* index signals aspects of the context in which it is normally used, this index may also be understood via an overlapping *second-order*, or ideological, relationship, to expected contexts of use. Silverstein explains that there is always "transcendent and competing overlay" (2003: 194) of contextualization involved in any indexical relationship, in which there are multiple orders of meaning at play, and a single index can take on novel meanings in new contexts. This means that language forms that convey meaning for a social group (a first-order index) may become a naturalized index of qualities associated with speakers in that group (a second-order index). The dropping of /r/ after a vowel (as in saying "cah" instead of "car"), for example, may act for many American English speakers as a first-order index of New York City, since speakers, particularly working-class White ones, from New York City are known to drop their /r/s as a normal feature of their language. At the same time, the dropping of /r/ may signal, via a second-order index, stereotypical qualities of New Yorkers—"fast-talker," "rude," or "street smart." The dropping of /r/, then, becomes a typified way of speaking, such that it can be deployed even by non-New Yorkers, say a character in a movie, to sound specifically "New Yorky" or generally "urban" and "street smart." Similarly, when Eladio refers to his audience members as **mashikuna**, he signals to them that he is both a Unified Kichwa speaker and "educated." The use of an index in social interaction, then, simultaneously communicates referential information and ordered ideas about people, their practices and their associated values. This indexical order serves to produce, as Blommaert (2007) explains, social categories, recognizable individual and group emblems, and a "more or less coherent semiotic habitat" (117). Through a close analysis of Eladio's language choices, we can see aspects of the Tena Kichwa semiotic habitat coming into relief.

Understanding the processes of indexical ordering is important to linguistic anthropological study of communication in any given context, in which indexes and icons may become deployable features of a speaker's social identity and unique experiences with language. Indigeneity, as I will demonstrate throughout this book, may be understood as a construct that is built largely via pluralistic indexes and icons that are communicated in recognizable ways to audiences. Laura Graham (2002) has shown how language, with its simultaneously referential and non-referential indexical functions, "holds a unique status among the signs that Indians can invoke to express Indianness" (190). In performances before a global public sphere, particular kinds of message content—mythological themes, for example—can index Indigenous perspectives even when uttered in non-Indigenous languages. Meanwhile, language choice, discourse practices, and discourse styles all can convey Indigenous identity via multiple orders of indexicality as languages are taken as emblems of Indigeneity. "Use of a language," Graham argues, "which happens to signal membership in a particular Indigenous group (first-order indexicality) becomes a deployable 'naturalized index' of a general 'Indian essence' (second-order indexicality) as a function of emerging performance expectations of audiences for 'Indianness'" (2002: 190).

On **Rayu Shinalla**, Eladio signals a specific brand of pluralistic Indigenous Kichwa identity. His strategic use of icons, such as Kichwa language, sounds of forest birds, and images of face paint and headdresses, readily evokes a traditional Native Amazonian identity. His use of Spanish, his cell phone, and his professional attire, meanwhile, brings to mind a global modernity that he participates in daily. More often, Eladio reveals his pluralistic social identity through referential and social indexes, namely his choice of language features. Some of his words, pronunciations, and discourse styles are especially *marked*, meaning they are highly recognizable to others as linking him with social groups that are different from the locally default, or "normal" ones (Bucholtz & Hall 2004). Particularly noteworthy here is his conspicuous and regular use of Unified Kichwa, which in Speech Sample 2 includes highly marked neologisms such as **mashikuna** (lines 1, 5, and 17) and **yupaychani** (line 17) and pronunciations like **rinkapak** (line 2) and **kanchi** (line 4) (as opposed to *rinkak* and ***anchi***, as these are respectively pronounced in Tena Kichwa dialect). In using Unified Kichwa, he aligns himself, by way of first-order indexicality, with an elite sector of Unified Kichwa speakers, including his Indigenous activist mentors and colleagues. By way of second-order indexicality, he further aligns himself with ideologies of language standardization, Kichwa nation-building, and a political consciousness that some Kichwas tout as the future of Indigenous identity.

And yet, just as telling as his use of Unified Kichwa words are his deliberate attempts to "try not to speak too much Unified Kichwa," as he explained in our interview. His codeswitches into dialect and Spanish index his simultaneous orientation toward those who speak "the other Kichwa"—that is, dialect. It was only with their blessing that he settled on ***Rayu Shinalla***, a code-mixed title for his show, as opposed to ***Tulum Shinalla***, the title suggested by bilingual education administrators, as he explained Speech Sample 3. It is for the speakers of "the other Kichwa" that he uses marked dialect words like ***uras*** (Speech Sample 2, line 1, meaning "hours," or "time," from Spanish *hora*) and *barrioskuna* (line 3), in place of available Unified Kichwa neologisms. His rhetorical move to single out ***rukumamakuna*** and ***rukuyayakuna***, grandmothers and grandfathers, in lines 16–17 of Speech Sample 2, is further indexical of his need to bridge the growing divide between urbanizing Kichwas like himself and older Kichwas who see urbanization as a threat to their ancestral ways of life. In our interview, Eladio conveyed his keen awareness of his own high-profile role in this conspicuous historical "conflict" over language planning, bilingual-intercultural education, and the rise of Unified Kichwa.

Polycentricity and Tena Kichwa Communities of Practice

In order to understand Eladio's indexes in Speech Samples 1, 2, and 3, we must therefore take into consideration the polycentric nature of the Tena Kichwa sociolinguistic world. Building on Silverstein's theory of indexical orders, Blommaert (2007) elaborates that such orders are not singular within a social system. Instead, they operate on an additional higher plane of structuring, in which multiple indexical orders relate to each other in terms of mutual valuation—higher/lower, better/worse. Some sign-making practices are perceived as valuable and others as less valuable, and some are not taken into account at all. But all patterns of indexicality are also "patterns of authority, of control and evaluation, and hence of inclusion and exclusion by real or perceived others" (117). This is especially important to note in the context of globalization, culture contact, and multilingualism, where speakers routinely orient toward multiple semiotic systems. All texts should therefore be addressed as expressions of inherent linguistic variation, and the analysis of discourse should presume a "non-nativeness in language usage" that is characteristic of late modernity (116). All contemporary communicative environments, in other words, are always polycentric. Speakers recognize multiple centers of authority that offer different ideal types, norms, and criteria for appropriateness for language and behavior. Authority emanates from these centers, telling speakers how "good" discourse about particular topics is made, and speakers orient toward them. We are always taking into consideration the idea of some evaluating authority during our interactions with addressees, and these centers of authority are multiple, guiding our language choices in different directions in different social contexts.

What is so interesting about Eladio is that, in his role as a Kichwa spokesperson, he is critically aware of this polycentricity and strategically appeals to multiple authorities in single strings of discourse. He does this explicitly when he salutes audiences in multiple locales. He does it implicitly when he switches between his audience members' various codes: Tena dialect, Unified Kichwa, and Spanish. In these ways, he indexes his own membership in multiple *communities of practice* that make up his wider *speech community*. By *communities of practice*, I mean aggregates of people who are linked by distinctive ways of speaking and active engagement in shared sets of *practices*, or socially oriented, socially structured activities (Bourdieu 1991; Eckert & McConnell Ginnet 1992; Lave & Wenger 1991). Kichwas in Amazonian Ecuador together form what linguistic anthropologists have traditionally referred to as a *speech community*, or a group of people who share a set of linguistic and semiotic resources and knowledge of their uses, meanings, and values. However, ethnographic investigation shows that they, like members of any speech community, orient to and use these resources in different ways across geographic and social divides. The Amazonian Kichwa speech community is thus better understood as a patchwork of various, overlapping communities of practice, each with their own sets of language and identity resources. Mary Bucholtz (1999) has argued that the community of practice model, which has become highly influential in the linguistic anthropological study of language and identity, presents a more nuanced alternative to the speech community model. Instead of identifying a "community" based on their perceived linguistic similarities, archetypal members, and points of consensus, the community of practice approach emphasizes participants' own definitions of community. Group internal differences, conflict, and constant change are assumed as guiding principles of identity formation. This fittingly characterizes the Tena Kichwa, whose multiple groupings, as we have already seen, demonstrate various understandings and expressions of what it means to be "Indigenous," "Amazonian," and speakers of "Kichwa." Eladio's success as a Kichwa spokesperson depends on being keenly aware of this.

Through detailed ethnographic study and description, linguistic anthropologists can expose the active linking of signs, social identities, and cultural models. Making sense of signs requires deep understanding of the cultural contexts in which they operate. Interpreting the complicated semiotics of Eladio's discourse requires both a detailed linguistic analysis of his words and a full ethnographic account of the setting in which he communicates them. Who are the members of Eladio's audience? How do they use the various languages and varieties he employs? What cultural ideas guide their interpretations of his messages? While we have already begun to sketch a picture of the ethnographic context of Indigenous Tena Kichwa lifeways, in this and subsequent chapters, I aim to paint the broader sociolinguistic backdrop. Foregrounding the voices of Kichwas, like Eladio, from a broad spectrum of identities and experiences, I hope to bring the contemporary Tena Kichwa sociolinguistic world into view. I argue that this world can best be characterized as polycentric, with three major poles of ethnolinguistic authority: (1) rural, horticultural, dialect-speaking, (2) urban, upwardly mobile, Unified Kichwa-speaking, and (3) global, Spanish-speaking. In their discourse, Tena Kichwas display their orientations toward these centers of authority through constant and complex code choices. Like Eladio, they often appeal to multiple centers of authority by mixing their codes in single strings of speech.

Pluralism in Discourse

Eladio's use of **Runa Kichwa Shimi**, as opposed to **Runa Shimi**, in Speech Sample 1 reflects his own pluralistic identity and double consciousness as Runa and Kichwa. He is Napo Runa and a heritage speaker of Tena Kichwa dialect. He is a proud representative of the Kichwa nation and a speaker of its representative code of Unified Kichwa. He is also a self-consciously Indigenous citizen of Ecuador and well versed in Spanish-dominant mainstream culture and politics. As such, throughout his discourse on **Rayu Shinalla**, Eladio skillfully shifts orientation between (1) Napo's rural and peri-urban communities, where Tena Kichwa dialect is the unmarked speaking norm, (2) globally orienting, Unified Kichwa-speaking intellectuals concentrated in urban Tena, and (3) a global Spanish-speaking public, which is also often conceptually linked with the urban sphere. Eladio indexes this polycentricity through both direct addresses to members of a mixed rural-urban audience and through more subtle shifts between their respective codes.

In lines 8–10 of Speech Sample 2, for example, Eladio opens with a Kichwa greeting of **alli puncha** ("good morning") to residents of the **ayllullaktakuna** ("communities"), **Tena llakta** ("urban Tena"), and its *barrioskuna* ("neighborhoods"). Switching to Spanish, in lines 15–18, he adds a further greeting to *los amigos visitantes* ("visiting friends") and *los amigos turistas* ("tourist friends"). While he repeatedly addresses his collective audience using the Unified Kichwa term **mashikuna** ("friends"), he also makes a special point, in line 17, to acknowledge the largely Kichwa monolingual **rukumamakuna** and **rukuyayakuna** ("grandmothers" and "grandfathers").

As a high-profile Tena Kichwa representative, Eladio recognizes the key role of the **ayllullaktakuna** ("kin-based communities"), which for him include rural forest villages and Tena's Kichwa predominant peri-urban neighborhoods, as the core of what he refers to in lines 3–4 of Speech Sample 1 as **ñukanchi kawsay, ñukanchi yuyay** ("our way of life, our knowledge"). He explained to me in our interview that the residents of these communities are his primary target audience. But he also understands the importance of making alliances with powerful urban agents of global culture, such as Kichwa intellectuals working for Indigenous organizations, *Colono* media makers, and "*los amigos turistas,*" in the pursuit of cultural maintenance. In order to help his community "achieve cultural identity," as he put it during our interview, he must become a skilled "transculturite," one who moves regularly between cultures (Oakdale & Course 2014b), rural and urban cultural locales, and multiple linguistic codes. Though he lives a high-profile life of moving between cultures and languages, Eladio's experience as a transculturite is hardly unique among Tena Kichwas, as we have already seen.

Thus, by looking closely at the semiotics of this series of brief Native texts, it becomes apparent that the Tena Kichwa sociolinguistic environment, like all sociolinguistic environments, is a polycentric one that is defined by complex variation and constant transformation. Tena Kichwas include heterogeneous and composite urban and rural communities of practice, among which circulate competing discourses, ideologies, and expressions of Indigeneity. As a product of this environment and as an acting representative for his diverse people, Eladio's discourse is a pluralistic mix of intersecting codes and corresponding appeals to multiple centers of ethnolinguistic authority. Eladio's work as a Kichwa media celebrity is primarily geared toward, as I have heard him state in many venues, "rescuing" and "revitalizing" Kichwa language and culture. ***Rayu Shinalla***, as he states in line 4 of the opening credits in Speech Sample 1, is his effort to keep his people informed, "in our own Kichwa people's language." ***Rayu Shinalla*** is therefore not just a news show, it is also a political statement, intended to call attention to threatened Indigenous language and practice, a project that we will see take various forms in the chapters to come.

Eladio's performances on TV directly reflect his own pluralistic experience of Indigeneity and his vision for language revitalization. One cannot help but notice, for example, that just after the credits declare, in Kichwa, that ***Rayu Shinalla*** is broadcast "in our own Kichwa people's language," in line 6 this phrase is translated into Spanish as *"en nuestro propio idioma Kichwa."* Reviving Kichwa, as is often the case in contexts of Indigenous language revitalization, also depends on getting the attention of a globalized Spanish-speaking public. It is important to remember here that Eladio's show is hosted by ***Ally TV***, a public access station funded by the provincial government of Napo. As such, he is able to engage in creative, hybrid, and anti-normative language practices (cf. Urla 1995) like codemixing, but he is also never entirely free from the constraining expectations of Spanish-speaking producers, Kichwa prescriptivists, and multiethnic audiences. His chosen strategy for negotiating this contradiction involves a self-conscious straddling of his imagined publics, as he openly embraces mixtures of disparate linguistic systems, simultaneously appealing to multiple centers of authority.

Promoting Indigenous revitalization, as we see in this case and will see again in later chapters, also depends on appropriating historically "non-Indigenous" practices, such as broadcast media technology, styles, and associated modern values for global interconnectedness (Spitulnik 1999) and "lightning fast" communication. Eladio's particular brand of revitalization—broadcasting in Kichwa from central Tena while wearing Western, professional attire and fielding live text messages from his audience—aligns him with upwardly mobile, modernized generation of Kichwas, discussed in the Introduction, who are working to remake Tena as an Indigenous center of self-determination. According to progressively minded Kichwas like him, self-determination involves embracing the benefits of global interconnectedness, urban educational and media resources, and the economic affordances of engagement with wage labor, while never being fully dominated by the logics of Western intellectual traditions or the capitalist world system (cf. Halbmeyer 2018). Being Indigenous for Eladio and his peers means mastering the ways of others in order to protect ancestral values, strengthen heritage communities, and present alternative modernities. As Tena Kichwas become more mobile and their communities more connected, they are more able to achieve what Colloredo-Mansfeld (2003) calls "relational autonomy," a "potent, situational capacity to engage powerful others according to one's values" (2003: 276). For Tena Kichwas, the centrality of the city affords not only the high-profile exposition of traditional Indigenous practices but also the potential for new, globally conscious identities to take shape. Eladio's work thus exemplifies a vision of an alternative modernity that involves the simultaneous appropriation of modern, Western practices and the indigenizing of them.

Moreover, Eladio's discourse reveals a somewhat tense coexistence between distinctive Tena Kichwa ways of speaking and their associated social and political indexes. While he has clearly mastered the art of speaking to and for his people, his own reflections demonstrate that he must often do so with careful consideration, in order to acknowledge their diverse, contrasting experiences and opinions. As we will see, Eladio's life experiences and deliberations about language choices are typical among Tena Kichwas, who draw from a pluralistic pool of linguistic and cultural resources that always come with social and political baggage. His story is also a telling example of the challenges that Kichwa community leaders like him face in straddling disparate worlds in order to plan the future of Napo Runa language and identity. This project, as well as the controversies it stirs, will be the subject of Chapter 2.

2

Language Revitalization, Nation-Building, and Code Choice

Just a few days into my first fieldwork trip to Amazonian Ecuador in the fall of 2008, I stumbled upon an artful speech performance in an unlikely form and place—a municipal worker's tirade in a downtown office building. As is often the case in the course of ethnographic fieldwork, my illuminating interview with Santiago, a Kichwa nonprofit administrator in his mid-fifties, was entirely unplanned. I had been directed to his office in central Tena on the recommendation of one of his colleagues, whose acquaintance I had just made that morning. As his colleague suggested, Santiago quickly proved to be an ideal interviewee. He was full of knowledge and strong opinions about Kichwa language and culture and seemed eager to share his insights. Following some preliminary questions about his linguistic background, he began a lengthy lament about acculturation, which began with that familiar refrain—how the kids today have forgotten how to "speak Kichwa and drink *chicha*." When I eventually redirected the conversation to the related, presumably more positive, topic of language revitalization, Santiago launched into a surprisingly (to me, at that time) bitter polemic on the "failure" of bilingual education. The focus of his broadside was the teaching of Unified Kichwa. Santiago, like many others as I would later find out, saw Unified Kichwa as a menace to the local dialect of Tena Kichwa and to Napo Runa identity. He indulged my questions on the topic for almost two hours.

When I listened to the recording of the interview later that day, I was struck by how artful and complicated Santiago's critique was. Although this was an interview, his long, monologic responses fit the pattern of narrative, as he weaved together multiple speaking personalities. In one memorable string of speech, captured in Speech Sample 4, he described the process of language shift from Kichwa to Spanish by assuming the voices of its various stakeholders—an intellectual critic, a speaker of the threatened local Kichwa dialect, an uninvited speaker of Unified Kichwa, and a confused and exasperated student trying to make sense of it all. Lines 35–53 of the speech sample include numbers in subscript to mark implied switches in voice, which I will explain later.

Language shift to Spanish continues to happen, Santiago explained, because BIE, which was designed to revive Kichwa use among youth, has failed. In Amazonia, he elaborated, teachers promote a "foreign" language variety, Unified Kichwa, which "comes from the *sierra*" (Andean highlands).

Speech Sample 4. Santiago's critique of bilingual-intercultural education

1	*Les enseñan otros códigos,*	They teach other codes,
2	*entonces, ese código que aprenden en la escuela,*	so, that code that they learn in school
3	*jamás utilizan en la casa porque en la casa,*	they never use at home because at home
4	*el papá y la mamá le hablan de otra manera.*	dad and mom speak another way.
5	*Entonces, mire, aprende una cosa en la escuela*	So, look, they learn one thing at school
6	*y en la casa les dicen otra cosa,*	and at home they tell them something else,
7	*entonces hay un conflicto* ((hits fists together)).	so there is a conflict ((hits fists together))
8	*Eso dicen los psicólogos, no cierto?*	That's what the psychologists say, right?
9	*Eso produce un conflicto,*	That produces a conflict,
10	*y dentro de nuestro cerebro,*	and in our brain,
11	*en que es la computadora,*	in which is the computer,
12	*también se produce un confli- un choque.*	it also produces a confli-, a clash.
13	*De la final no aprendan ni lo uno ni lo otro.*	In the end they neither learn one nor the other.
14	*Queda allí un, e,*	There remains a, uh,
15	*u::n, como un especie de corto circuito nada más.*	a::, like a type of short circuit.
16	*Y no produce aprendizajes.*	And it does not produce learning.
17	*Entonces, esa- e- eso es lo que yo defiendo,*	So, that- th- that is what I defend,
18	*Los maestros, la educación bilingüe,*	the teachers, bilingual education,
19	*los que enseñan lenguas*	those that teach languages
20	*deben partir primeramente de lo local.*	should start with the local.
21	*Y más no con cosas que han sido copiadas*	And not with things that have been copied
22	*o impuestos por otro organismos.*	or imposed by other organisms.
23	*Lo de lo local y*	That which is the local and
24	*de esta manera, como nos entendemos nosotros,*	in this way, as we understand it,
25	*y se debe manejar nuestros códigos lingüísticos.*	we should manage our own linguistic codes.
26	*Yo hablo con una persona y le digo, e,*	I talk to a person and I say, uh,
27	**Riki wawki, kanta ashka**	Hey brother,
28	**Ilakishkawa kuna tutamanta salurani.**	I greet you this morning with much love.
29	*Ya?*	Okay?
30	*Y él me entiende.*	And he understands me.
31	*Pero, en cambio, el otro dice*	But, on the other hand, the other says
32	**Mashi,**	Friend,

33	*dice, e,*	he says, uh,	
34	**kanta ashka llakishkawa kuna mushkun.**	I ((unknown word)) you today with much love.	
35	*No no.*₁	No no.₁	
36	*Hablan cosas,*₂	They say things,₂	
37	*y cosas que me confunden.*₂	and things that confuse me.₂	
38	*Yo digo, en que, yo digo en que quedamos?*₁	I say which, I say which do we go with?₁	
39	*No le entiendo.*₂	I don't understand.₂	
40	*Al otro le entiendo clarito.*₂	I understand the other clearly.₂	
41	*Pero lo que me dice el otro, no.*₂	But what the other says to me, no.₂	
42	*Entonces viene aquí la confusión.*₁	So herein lies the confusion.₁	
43	*Entonces, no se da ni lo uno, ni lo otro.*₁	So neither one works nor the other.₁	
44	*Con cuál me comunico?*₂	With which one do I communicate?₂	
45	*Con la- con el código lingüístico de mi comunidad*₂	With the- with the linguistic code of my community₂	
46	*con el código lingüístico de la comunidad*₂	or with the linguistic code of the₂	
47	*extraña?*₂	foreign community?₂	
48	*No- no se da nada.*₁	It doesn't work.₁	
49	*Entonces es- si hay ese conflicto,*₁	So, that- if there is this conflict,₁	
50	*entonces por último,*₁	in the end,₁	
51	*santos,*₂	Jesus,₂	
52	*no hablo nada.*₂	I won't speak at all.₂	
53	*Mejor aprendo el Castellano.*₂	I'm better off learning Spanish.₂	

Through early conversations like these, I was quickly made aware that language revitalization, the seemingly well-reasoned response to language shift to Spanish that was meant to benefit all Kichwas, was apparently a controversial project. In this short speech, Santiago also invoked several key words that, I realized later on, had highly specific meanings for him: "language," "code," "local," "foreign," "community," and "we." I have spent years since that interview unpacking the rich and politically loaded meanings of these words for Tena Kichwas.

Voicing the Politics of Language

Like other Tena Kichwa speakers I have introduced in previous chapters, Santiago is a template for a complicated, multilingual, and pluralistic sociolinguistic environment. He is also an exceptional informant. He holds a high-status job as an office administrator and professional intellectual. Like Eladio in Chapter 1, Santiago is a gifted orator and public spokesperson for his people. While engaging in this kind of talk-about-talk is not unusual among Kichwas in Amazonian Ecuador, Santiago shows a keen self-consciousness of the composite nature of his bilingual Indigenous identity and a rare capacity for incisive political critique. He has an educated grasp of the complexity of Kichwa "heteroglossia," literary theorist Mikhail Bakhtin's (1981) term for the coexisting, conflicting varieties of language within a language, and an artist's ability to play with this heteroglossia for dramatic effect.

In Speech Sample 4, Santiago performs Tena Kichwa sociolinguistic pluralism through shifts in voice. Linguistic anthropologist Jane Hill (1995) defines *voice* as the site of speaking consciousness and subjectivity, or the "speaking personality." This speaking consciousness is characterized by a particular will, desire, timbre, and overtones (Holquist 1981). Linguistic anthropological research on voice details the construction, performance, and evaluation of distinct social personae (Keane 2001) and their respective perspectives on the world through discourse. Voices in discourse are expressed and distinguished from each other through language features such as word choice, intonation, variations in fluency, pronunciation, grammar, and choice of referential indexes, importantly including personal pronouns. While voices tend to be understood by listeners as linked to individual speakers, particularly through the performance of dialogue, they can also index social identities, such as gender, race, age group, status, and political stance.

The *voice system*, according to Hill (1995), is the complete picture of interacting forms of consciousness that exist in discourse. It is a field of dialogue and conflict between different speaking personalities that are interpreted through the dominant voice of an author. In our interview, Santiago created a multilingual voice system by reanimating the voices of his world. He strategically plays with his role as a speaking *author*, carefully selecting words to communicate an argument, which he illustrates by repeatedly "changing hats," as Goffman (1981) puts it, between various speaking characters or *principals*, each with their own moral and political stances. By looking more carefully at his voice system, we can see how Santiago paints a detailed picture of political conflict within the Tena Kichwa sociolinguistic world.

In the beginning of his critique of bilingual education, in lines 1–7 of Speech Sample 4, Santiago establishes his author voice as a concerned Kichwa community member, describing the "clash" that occurs when Indigenous students bring Unified Kichwa—the "other code"—into the homes of their dialect-speaking parents. In lines 8–16, he offers the voice of an educated critic, his professional role and his anchoring persona throughout our interview, referencing psychology and using technological metaphors (the brain as "computer" and the educational "short circuit") to explain how this conflict inhibits effective language learning. In lines 17–25, he argues his case for private, community-based (rather than public, administrative) management of "linguistic codes" and renewed support for what he, in line 20, refers to as *lo local* ("the local"), a colloquial expression for the Tena Kichwa dialect.

In lines 26–34, Santiago performs the linguistic discordance he is describing by channeling hypothetical speakers of contrasting language varieties through *direct reported speech*, or quoting through grammatical and lexical shifts. First, he quotes himself as a narrated character and a speaker of Tena Kichwa, grammatically marking himself with the first-person pronoun "I" and using familiar dialect words that, he explains, his hypothetical interlocutor "understands." Next, he quotes a speaker of the "other code," shifting to third-person pronoun *he*, and altering his reported speech style to incorporate features of Unified Kichwa, which engender an apparent "confusion." The linguistic composition of each of these quoted voices is artfully complex, as I will explain in a more detailed analysis later in this chapter.

In the remaining section of the performance, lines 35–53, Santiago continues his theatrics, by employing what Bakthin (1973) calls "double voiced" discourse. This time, he alters between speaking perspectives through indirect, or indexical, shifts and without grammatical marking of any kind. He is still the "I" of his discourse, but his "I" has a compound meaning: he is both (1) "I," an expert, critiquing bilingual education from an educated position (2) "I," a novice, receiving bilingual education and becoming exasperated at its conflicting messages. This latter "I," which Urban (1989) calls the "de-quotative I," is still Santiago, of course, but it is not Santiago's ordinary, current speaking self. He assumes the position of an "other" self, who is being exposed to Unified Kichwa for the first time. In order to demonstrate these switches between voices more clearly, I have marked lines of speech performed in voices (1) and (2) with these respective numbers in subscript at the end of lines 35–53.

While Santiago shows an ability to conjure up multiple voices of a multilingual and conflict-ridden world, his compound Indigenous identity and his self-conscious understanding of it, as we have already seen, is defining of his time and place. Like many other Kichwas of his age, Santiago has experienced cultural marginalization and watched generational language shift to Spanish, and he is consumed with worry about the ethnolinguistic disappearance of his people. Though he fights daily for ethnic survival, directing a nonprofit that promotes Kichwa cultural maintenance, his fatalism about the future of Kichwa is evident in Speech Sample 4. "If BIE has failed," I asked Santiago, "what might be a better plan for the future of Kichwa language and culture?" "Linguistic variation must be respected," he said, "because that is the identity of a people." When I asked for clarification on what language variety he felt best represented his people, he responded, matter-of-factly, "our own thing" (*lo propio,* literally "that which is proper"). He later qualified "our own thing" to mean "dialect," which he referred to as "the Kichwa that *we* speak, that our grandparents spoke here in Amazonia."

A New Ethnolinguistic Consciousness

Santiago's use of terms like "the other Kichwa," *lo propio,* and *lo local* to describe a language that is typified by the speech of "grandparents" (just like Eladio did, in Chapter 1) signals an important historical turning point in Napo Runa identity formation. Tena Kichwas frequently refer to their unique way of speaking as *lo propio,* indexing a collective recognition of dialect as the protected language variety of a distinctive ethnic group. Santiago's defense of "dialect" represents a claim to an oppositional Indigenous Runa identity in a time of Kichwa nation-building. It also signals a divide between ideologies of language revitalization versus language maintenance, respectively revealed through the choice to use Unified Kichwa versus Tena Kichwa dialect.

For Tena Kichwas, this reclaiming of dialect is part of a larger, ongoing process of Napo Runa *ethnogenesis,* or reawakening and reconfiguring of ethnic group identity. This ethnogenesis is a direct response to the ethnically fusing forces of pan-regional Kichwa nation-building and language standardization, which are perceived by many Tena Kichwas as threats to Napo Runa identity and cultural continuity. The Napo Runa ethnolinguistic region, long recognized as distinctive by linguists and anthropologists, is becoming reclaimed by Tena Kichwas as what I refer to as an *ethnolinguistic domain,* or a protected territory of ethnolinguistic identity. Discourse about linguistic differentiation, namely between Tena Kichwa dialect and Unified Kichwa, has become a site for enacting *pachakutik*, the voluntary "destroying, recuperating and transforming" (Uzendoski 2005: 165) of Napo Runa Indigenous identity, society, and history.

In this chapter, I draw on metalinguistic interviews among Tena Kichwas like Santiago to trace Napo Runa ethnogenesis and rising linguistic consciousness in progress. Specifically, I examine the identification of Tena Kichwa dialect in discourse as a distinct linguistic object, which happens through its differentiation from Unified Kichwa. I argue that this objectification of dialect is a direct declaration of a redefined Napo Runa ethnic identity that is territorial, class-based, politically factional, and distinctly "Indigenous." Discourses of linguistic difference among Tena Kichwas highlight Unified Kichwa's perceived foreignness, artifice, and unintelligibility. Through differentiation, Tena Kichwa dialect comes into relief as the linguistic representation of an Indigenous Napo Runa identity that is contrastingly Native, authentic, and meaningful. Napo Runa ethnogenesis is fueled by Kichwa *nation-building*, or the creation of a Kichwa nationality. This latter project is predicated on a philosophy of *pan-indigenism*, or the building of solidarity between disparate Indigenous ethnic groups in order to resist domination. Many Tena Kichwas show their opposition to this proposed fusing of diverse Kichwa ethnic groups and their respective ways of speaking by deliberately choosing to use Tena Kichwa dialect and sometimes outright refusing to speak, learn, or even understand Unified Kichwa.

Tena Kichwa dialect is in the process of becoming an icon, or defining emblem, of local Indigeneity. It is emerging in discourse as Indigenous Napo Runa culture and identity made manifest, as it is by definition Native, domestic, and historically rooted. Santiago's declaration of *lo propio,* as the representative Napo Runa variety is thus a bold one. It signals an emergence of Tena Kichwa dialect as an object of Tena Kichwa ethnolinguistic consciousness. It also signals a direct challenge to the contradictory tactics taken by Indigenous activists who promote language revitalization through linguistic unification, standardization, and purification as opposed to ancestral language maintenance. Within this contentious discourse surrounding the politics of language, Kichwa ways of speaking have become separated into three recognized codes: (1) the *proprietary code* of Tena Kichwa dialect, (2) the *intercultural code*, a spoken variety that blends Tena Kichwa dialect and written Unified Kichwa forms and is often referred to inaccurately as "Unified Kichwa" (see Wroblewski 2014), and (3) the *plurinational code* of Spanish.

As shown in Chapter 1, while these codes are imagined and talked about by Tena Kichwas as separate "languages," they are not clearly discrete, bounded entities. They overlap in structure and are frequently mixed in single strings of discourse. Tena Kichwa dialect, despite its conceptual link with local Amazonian Indigeneity, is actually a linguistically mixed variety that has been shaped by a long history of contact with Spanish. Unified Kichwa, meanwhile, which is intended to be a "pure" Indigenous code, is actually structurally engineered to be commensurate with Spanish. And Spanish, usually conceptualized as a "non-Indigenous" code by Tena Kichwas, is actually a defining feature of Tena Kichwa bilingual identity and daily practice. In this chapter, I will focus on discourses surrounding the first two Indigenous codes, Tena Kichwa dialect and its ideological opposite, Unified Kichwa, in an effort to show their respective roles in shaping Napo Runa ethnogenesis. Spanish and related discourses of bilingualism will be the subjects of Chapter 3.

Language Revitalization and the New Indigenous Order

Kichwa nation builders in Napo are exemplary of an era of global language revitalization movements, and in many ways exhibit contentious ideologies of language revitalization that have been documented by ethnographers working in Indigenous communities in Latin America (e.g., England 2003; French 2010; Hornberger & King 1996; King 2001; Shulist 2018) and elsewhere (e.g., Austin & Sallabank 2014; Avineri & Kroskrity 2014; Davis 2018; Goodfellow 2009; Granadillo & Orcutt-Gachiri 2011; Hornberger 2008; Kroskrity 2012; Kroskrity & Field 2009; Meek 2010; Nevins 2013; Reyhner & Lockard 2009). My use of "language revitalization" to describe these processes in Amazonian Ecuador has been carefully arrived at. Following a linguistic anthropological understanding of language as a non-neutral medium and a system of social differentiation (Duranti 2011), a disciplinary concern with language ideologies (Kroskrity 2000; Schieffelin et al. 1998; Woolard & Schieffelin 1994), and a commitment to the ethnographic documentation of language in situ and in progress (Woolard 2008), I approach language revitalization as a complex political and social project that involves various agents with overlapping and competing interests, visions, and ideological orientations toward language (see Hinton et al. 2018). I view Kichwa-language revitalization as inextricably bound to a larger project of cultural, ethnic, and political redefinition that engages with global trends in language shift, and endangerment (e.g., Crystal 2000; Eisenlohr 2004; Fishman 1991; Grenoble & Waley 2006; Hinton & Hale 2001; Nettle & Romaine 2000), and minority language planning, language policy, and ethnic nation-building (Costa et al. 2017; French 2010; Jaffe 1999; Romaine 2002; Urla 2015). I align with critical considerations of authoritative rhetoric on language endangerment, highlighting the complex power dynamics involved between Indigenous and non-Indigenous agents, including between language documentation scholars and their informants, in promoting language revitalization movements (e.g., Ahlers 2006; Errington 2003; Heller & Duchene 2007; Hill 2002; Rice 2009; Shulist 2018; Whitely 2003).

The term "language revitalization" also closely captures the way this complex project is conceptualized and talked about by both Indigenous activists and their critics in the ethnographic context of Tena, all of whom agree that Kichwa must be revived and reanimated (cf. Shulist 2018). Where they disagree, is on the critical issue of whether ethnic reconfiguration requires linguistic reconfiguration. Like many of their activist contemporaries in parallel Indigenous movements, pan-indigenist Kichwa activists differ from their critics in their assumption that language standardization is fundamental to language revitalization. They believe in the multiculturalist goal of openly celebrating cultural and linguistic heterogeneity, but they see internal ethnic divisions as threats to the stability of a unified Indigenous popular base. Unification, they believe, promotes national cultural legitimacy, economic mobility, and political empowerment and, ultimately, will enable the political restructuring of the nation-state. The merging of regional Kichwa dialects into a Unified Kichwa, following a pan-indigenist model that has been used throughout Latin America, is seen as a crucial step toward codifying ethnic solidarity in linguistic practice while also establishing Kichwa as a legitimate, "modern" language of literacy that can stand up to Spanish (cf. Costa et al. 2017).

Language revitalization and standardization have been principal concerns for Indigenous activists since the rise of Ecuador's first Indigenous organizations in the 1960s, and these goals were central to DIPEIB-N's mission since its inception. In order to protect territorial rights, ensure ethnic survival, and establish regional autonomy, Indigenous organizations throughout the highlands and Amazon promoted institutional recognition of Indigenous languages as part of national culture. Localized literacy education initiatives eventually created the foundation for a national system of BIE, which became a constitutionally recognized and protected entity that had active administrative branches in all of Ecuador's twenty-one provinces.

King (2001) claims that the first major precursor to the legal institution of bilingual education in Ecuador was the unification and standardization of the Kichwa language, the "major Indigenous language in the country" (39). With the help of linguists at the Catholic University in Quito, a group of Kichwa-speaking language planners and educators met in 1981 in order to create a standardized variety of Ecuadorian Kichwa, known as Unified Kichwa. Unified Kichwa was intended as an Indigenous replacement for Spanish-language-based orthographies for written Kichwa, a previously nonliterate language, that had been used since the conquest and still continue to be used by lay speakers of Kichwa and some scholars today. In addition to the standardization of Unified Kichwa orthography, pan-indigenist language planners promote the purification of Kichwa lexicon, an ongoing process that involves the replacement of widely used Spanish borrowings with available regional Kichwa words or invented neologisms. The goal, again, is to make Kichwa words equally expansive and expressive as Spanish. Grammatical prescription, through the creation of standardized morphemes and syntax, is further intended to make Kichwa ordered, stable, and as prestigious as Spanish. New, and constantly changing, morpho-syntactic rules are periodically published in brief sections in Unified Kichwa dictionaries (e.g., Ministerio de Educación 2009) and bilingual education instruction manuals (e.g., Jerez 2008). Linguistic unification, standardization, and purification are meant to reverse ongoing language shift toward Spanish while developing Kichwa into a legitimate national literary language.

The advancement of literacy in Unified Kichwa was made official educational policy in 1993 by the National Directorate of Bilingual and Intercultural Education (DINEIB), which, from the late 1980s until very recently, autonomously directed much of primary and select secondary education in Ecuadorian provinces with majority Indigenous populations (see Limerick n.d.). According to the Model of Bilingual and Intercultural Education (MOSEIB), the duties and functions of DINEIB included the following:

(1) The construction of bilingual and intercultural curricula and didactic materials in accordance with the needs of local Indigenous populations,
(2) The development of teacher-training programs,
(3) The promotion of educational and cultural material in conjunction with Indigenous organizations,
(4) The development of Indigenous communities through the development of bilingual education programs and resources, and
(5) The application and advancement of unified writing systems (Ministerio de Educación y Cultura 1993: 7).

MOSEIB further recognizes the importance of participation of families and communities in the education of children and the promotion of "intercultural" curricula. Previous educational systems, the document states, have promoted the disintegration of family and community, as well as "acculturation and de-culturation," the "the abandonment of native languages," and the "loss of identity" (Ministerio de Educación y Cultura 1993: 9–10).

For DINEIB, a democratic, intercultural society in Ecuador is one that is expressly "communitarian," "plurinational" and also "multilingual" (Ramírez 2008). In bilingual or multilingual contexts, language becomes the "principal vehicle" through which values are transmitted reciprocally between groups. Due to the inextricability of language from culture, it follows that "without language, culture does not exist, let alone intercultural relations" (Ramírez 2008: 10). "Primordial and fundamental" in DINEIB's pursuit to teach cultural values for the purpose of intercultural exchange in Ecuador is thus the teaching and learning of Indigenous languages, alongside Spanish, both as practical means of communication and as technical languages in scientific study. Indigenous languages are to be used as the "principal languages of education, with Spanish as the language of intercultural relations" (Ministerio de Educación y Cultura 1993: 11).

From 1989 to 2013, DINEIB's local branch in Napo, the Directorate of Provincial Bilingual and Intercultural Education of Napo (DIPEIB-N), administered the education of over 6,000 students annually in its mostly rural community-based "education centers" in Napo's three Amazonian counties. These predominantly Kichwa-run primary, secondary, and trade schools promoted the revitalization of Kichwa culture through a curriculum designed to integrate Indigenous language, knowledge, and social practices with conventional academic teaching in Spanish. Since the shuttering of the DIPEIB-N office in Tena in 2013 under the direction of the administration of the then president Rafael Correa, Indigenous education is now under the purview of the Ecuadorian Ministry of Education, which has appropriated the intercultural-bilingual education system. Many of my key informants in this book include former administrators, teachers, and students of DIPEIB-N. While no longer a centralized linguistic authority, DIPEIB-N has left an enduring legacy on current language planning efforts in the region, including the continued use of Unified Kichwa in educational settings, formal institutional gatherings, and various public media.

Though Indigenous empowerment has been the expressed goal since the beginning of Kichwa nation-building and language planning in Napo, political factionalism and social division have been unavoidable by-products. As many anthropological studies of Indigenous activism elsewhere in Latin America have shown, several decades of organizing have given rise to an elite sector of Indigenous leaders who serve as a professional activist intelligentsia (Conklin & Graham 1995; Graham 2002; Montejo 2002; Warren 1998; Warren & Jackson 2002). Former and current BIE administrators, teachers, and their students have come to represent a minority Indigenous elite in the upper Napo who tend to align politically with pan-indigenist activists working in the Ecuadorian highlands. Unified Kichwa, as an ordered, elevated register, has become the shared hallmark of pan-indigenist activism and their chosen symbol of triumph over Indigenous minority status. Meanwhile, the majority of Napo Runa, most of whom live in rural communities, have not received higher education and have not been trained in Unified Kichwa. Members of this majority Indigenous base are not convinced that the abstract national goals of professional activists will bring about promised prosperity and empowerment in any tangible form for struggling local communities. Furthermore, while Kichwa nation builders see integration and uniformity as empowering, their opponents, as Santiago explained earlier, see these projects as threats to cultural distinction and local ethnic survival. Tena Kichwa dialect has become the hallmark of their version of territorial ethnic identity and traditional Indigenous culture. The very use of Tena Kichwa, once the unquestioned way of speaking in Napo, can now be a political act, as the protection of an Indigenous way of life that is doubly threatened by Spanish and Unified Kichwa. The use of Unified Kichwa is therefore policed by these critics, and those who use "too much" Unified Kichwa may be viewed as ideologically oriented toward the dissolution of a local identity. This is precisely why Eladio, in Chapter 1, explained that he "tr[ies] not to speak too much Unified Kichwa" on TV, and why Santiago outright refuses to use it at all.

King (2001) has documented similar social divisions brought about by the introduction of Unified Kichwa into bilingual education in the Southern Ecuadorian Andes since the mid-1990s. Echoing the findings of earlier research on Indigenous language shift and revitalization in Latin America (notably Hill & Hill 1986) and beyond (e.g., Dorian 1994), she documents devaluation of the Kichwa variety spoken by community elders, which is referred to as "authentic Kichwa" despite its considerable influence from Spanish lexicon, phonology, syntax, and morphology. Certain well-educated members of the community have begun to advocate for the use of the new and more "modern" Unified Kichwa, which they see as a relatively "pure" variety by virtue of its exclusion of Spanish loans.

Since the introduction of Unified Kichwa into BIE in Napo the mid-1990s, at least one generation of students has grown up with language standardization, while their parents and grandparents have also learned to recognize, categorize, and objectify aspects of its distinctive features. Metalinguistic discourses of purity and power have developed to such an extent that even nonspeakers of Unified Kichwa, like Santiago, now have access to its emblematic linguistic forms and speaker stereotypes, which they can appropriate in discourse for political commentary. Meanwhile, Tena Kichwa dialect has continued to solidify in linguistic consciousness as a distinctly local, proprietary variety. Its semiotic differentiation (Irvine & Gal 2000; Gal & Irvine 2019) from Unified Kichwa is achieved through the ongoing enregisterment of its distinctive features through frequent metalinguistic comparisons made by dialect speakers. By *enregisterment*, following Agha (2005b, 2007), I mean the processes through which language features become linked with differently valued types of speakers and ways of speaking. In what follows, I explore how Tena Kichwas use discourses about these distinct, enregistered ways of speaking to offer competing visions of Indigeneity.

The Linguistic Context

Designating Tena Kichwa dialect as the linguistic icon of a localized Napo Runa identity depends on its continuous objectification as a distinctly Amazonian variety in folk language taxonomies. As illustrated in Figure 6, linguists have long divided the Napo River region into upper and lower Napo dialect areas, with an *isogloss*, or dialect boundary line, located somewhere in the vicinity of the Napo River port of Francisco de Orellana (also known as Coca) (Lewis 2009; Orr & Wrisely 1965). The Tena Kichwa dialect, sometimes also referred to as the Upper Napo Kichwa dialect, has its historical center in the region containing the city of Tena and the Indigenous communities of Shandia, Arajuno, and Ahuano (Orr & Wrisely 1965).

For Tena Kichwas, there is an even more important Andean-Amazonian dialect boundary which corresponds to an important ideological divide in popular categories of Ecuadorian Kichwa identity. The Andean highland region, or *sierra* in Spanish, is usually conceptualized in Ecuadorian nationalist discourses as the historical center of Kichwa culture, where intellectual, artistic, and economic activities are concentrated. In Ecuador, the linking of Kichwa ethnicity and Andean origins is reinforced by nationalist narratives that portray Kichwa language and culture as derivative of Inca patrimony,

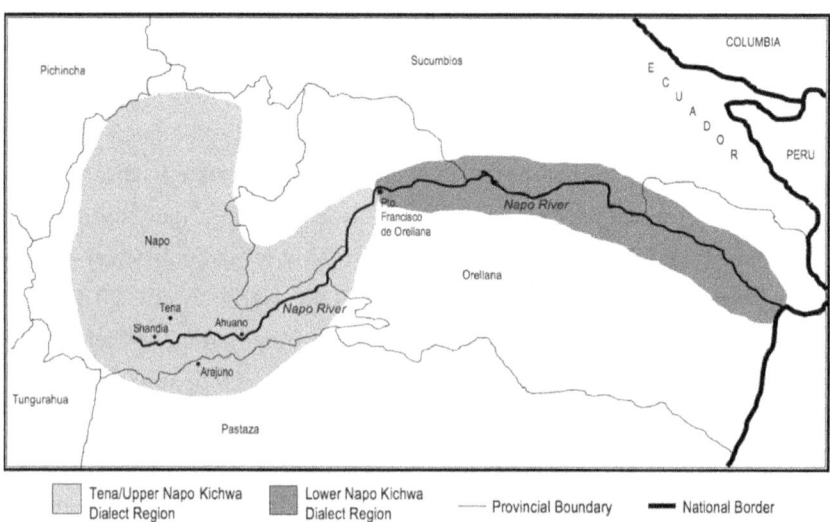

Figure 6 Map of Napo Kichwa dialect regions. Author's drawing.

and that identify the Andes as the historical site of Inca tradition (cf. Greene 2006 on Indigenous Peru). Consequently, Kichwa speakers of the Amazon region have been conceptualized by some Ecuadorian and foreign scholars and laypeople as "misplaced" migrants of a diasporic Andean Indigenous community (Whitten & Whitten 2008).

Adding to the pronouncement of this perceived divide is the conceptualization of the highlands by lowlanders as the fount of pan-indigenist politics and top-down Kichwa language planning. As a result, Kichwa ethnic unification and its corollary, Kichwa language standardization, tend to be viewed by lowlanders as "foreign" concepts, and Unified Kichwa, as Santiago put it, is seen as a "foreign" language variety. Although the expressed aim of Kichwa nation-building is the transcendence of such regional ethnic divisions, the political ideals of the highlands are seen by many lowland Kichwas as being decidedly un-Amazonian. Lowland opponents of Kichwa nation-building fear that regional unification, under the direction of highlanders and highland-orienting activists, will eventually replace local Indigenous language and culture with dominant Andean ones. These opponents further protest that the abstract goals of nation builders fail to address local cultural realities in the lowlands, particularly the immediate threats that urbanization, deforestation, migration, and language shift toward Spanish monolingualism pose to Amazonian Kichwa ethnic survival. As noted by Jackson (1991), a national pan-indigenist movement, "while trying to be a pluralist movement, still needs unifying symbols and ideology. Sometimes the symbols adopted are not, as thought, pan-Indian" (1991: 135–6). This point is being made exceptionally clear in Napo, where the ideology of unification actually fuels, rather than quells, Kichwa ethnic division. Linguistic unification has thus paradoxically become a catalyst for Napo Runa ethnic fission. Tena Kichwa dialect preservation is now equated with ethnic survival, and the objectification of dialect has become the operative tactic for enacting Tena Kichwa ethnogenesis.

The Proprietary Code and the Intercultural Code

Ideological opposition over the future of the Kichwa language in Napo is thus a driving force of Napo Runa ethnic reconfiguration. Although there is near-unanimous agreement that Kichwa language should be saved, sharp divisions have arisen over what "Kichwa language" means. Some support language revitalization through standardization, which involves active intervention and linguistic manipulation by language planners, while others stress the need for language maintenance, which enables the revitalization of the language through ongoing family socialization, community support, and, as Santiago put it, "respect" for linguistic diversity. Native Kichwa logics of recurrent destruction, transformation, and rebirth underpin ideology on both sides of the debate, simultaneously driving pan-indigenist revolutionary ideals and the preservationist goals of dialect defenders. In particular, the Indigenous Kichwa logic of **pachakutik**, the active, revolutionary returning of a more harmonious past into a planned future (Whitten 2003), clearly underlies the utopian visions of pan-indigenist activists, who hope to usher in a new era of postcolonial Indigenous autonomy and national legitimacy. In the introduction to its most recent Development Plan, DIPEIB-N writers assert, "We are the resistance to the **Wayra Apamushkas** ['Wind-Bearers'], who invaded our territories, destroyed our culture . . . and seeded injustice. . . . We have risen with the duty of reconstructing and strengthening our nationality" (DIPEIB-N 2009). Part of this revolutionary reconstruction involves making Kichwa language "purer," by purging Spanish loans and standardizing orthography, morphology, and syntax to counteract the effects of *linguistic drift*, or natural, unconscious, and ongoing processes of change that occur in all world languages. Linguistic manipulations meant to consciously redirect these changes, as one DIPEIB-N administrator explained to me, are necessary and normal. In order to correct, "We have to create. That is how the languages of the world formed," he explained, "so it's not anything strange."

In contrast to this progressive rhetoric of ethnic unification and language purification, rhetoric about dialect by Unified Kichwa opponents has taken on familiar defensive, traditionalist, and conservationist overtones often used by Amazonian activists and global supporters of language endangerment (see Hill 2002). Defenders of Tena Kichwa dialect liken it to a guarded "treasure," even an endangered native species that is threatened with extinction by the spread of pan-indigenism and the invasion of Unified Kichwa. Returning to a better time and place for these preservationists involves reinstituting the "respect" for dialect variation that existed before standardization and even before colonization, promoting a return to family language socialization practices, and allowing Tena Kichwa to evolve naturally in its geographic home. In his own critique of pan-indigenism during our interview, Santiago countered:

> In every region, every grouping, we should be Kichwas, Amazonians as much as highlanders. But in every region there is linguistic variation and this linguistic variation has to be respected, because it is the identity of a people. That is where differentiation between cultures is ... We are born with a language and we go on evolving. But evolving does not mean unifying all the languages in the universe, because the identity of a people is in their own form and their own manifestation.

Since the introduction of Unified Kichwa, the meaning of *Kichwa* has therefore become complex and situational. In its most general sense, Kichwa is still interchangeable with **Runa Shimi** or "human language." But *Kichwa,* when used in Kichwa speech, is now also interchangeable with *Unificado,* the colloquial Spanish word for Unified Kichwa. When *Kichwa* is used in this way, dialect speakers distinguish the local variety from *Unificado* by means of monikers such as *dialecto* "dialect," *lo local* "that which is local," *lo nuestro* "that which is ours," and, as Sanitago called it, *lo propio,* "our own thing" or "that which is proper [to the region]." The very terms used to name Tena Kichwa dialect have thus become relational to Unified Kichwa and connote proximity to a core identity: Tena Kichwa is vernacular, local, organic, and proprietary, as opposed to orthodox, extraneous, imposed, and alien. Unified Kichwa, as most nonspeakers in the upper Napo profess, is most simply "different" from the Kichwa that they learned in the home and from the Kichwa that they teach their children to speak. "It is altered," explained Carlos, a 53-year-old Kichwa grandfather,

> It is difficult to learn ... and we don't want it. What we want is our language, that of our ancestors. That is what we want to go on. Because that ((Unified Kichwa)) they are using, they invent it ... It is not what we were born speaking.

Echoing this statement, many learners and nonspeakers of Unified Kichwa have repeatedly complained to me that it is "strange," "confusing," "like a foreign language," and "unintelligible." Tena Kichwas like Santiago, who openly oppose the use of Unified Kichwa, often point out its foreignness and unintelligibility (cf. King 2001; Rindstet & Aronsson 2002). Unified Kichwa continues to be a learned written variety with no true "native speakers." Yet some Unified Kichwa words, as well as pronunciations suggested by its standard orthography, have increasingly entered into the speech of "educated" Kichwas, including leaders of Indigenous organizations, bilingual educators and their students, and select local celebrities. This spoken version of Unified Kichwa, which I refer to as the *intercultural code* (Wroblewski 2014), has become a normative variety in the classroom, in formal public meetings, and in urban cultural performances.

As a result, certain emblematic Unified Kichwa sounds, words, phrases, and stereotypical speaker types have begun to circulate in discourses about language revitalization, where they are used as counterexamples to dialect forms and speaker types. In this way, the two language varieties are juxtaposed as ideologies made manifest. While Kichwa-language planners regard local dialect forms as "deviations" from precolonial Kichwa, dialect defenders view these same features, even the ones derived from Spanish borrowings, as organic innovations that uniquely define a local Indigenous identity. From the point of view of dialect defenders, to speak dialect is thus to be Indigenous in the sense of being unselfconsciously Runa. To use Unified Kichwa, by comparison, is to show off one's education and status. To use "invented" words is to deliberately obstruct the natural processes of language variation and change. To speak in the elevated register of formal education implies accepting dominant institutions and ethnic hierarchies, as well as the dominance of Spanish, on which Unified Kichwa is modeled. For its opponents, using Unified Kichwa essentially implies denying one's community, territorial roots, and ancestral Indigenous identity.

In order to objectify Tena Kichwa dialect as "the" language of the Napo Runa, people like Santiago must paradoxically adopt the same linguistic self-consciousness as their purported adversaries. They deliberately equate speaking Tena Kichwa dialect with cultural maintenance and natural processes of cultural evolution. Saving dialect and local identity thus implies recognizing that both dialect and identity are under threat. What is dismissed by DIPEIB-N language planners as linguistic degeneration (e.g., Spanish borrowings and linguistic drift) must actively be shown to be the cultural core of the very Indigeneity that Kichwa nation builders claim to be "rescuing" and "revaluing." Napo Runa ethnogenesis thus requires active and ongoing *essentializing*, or identifying imagined essences, of language and culture. Through such continued objectification and local politicking, everyday language choice among Tena Kichwas has become increasingly divisive.

Iconic Sounds

Tena Kichwa dialect *phonology*, or sounds and pronunciation, tends to be the most apparent source of distinction in defining Tena Kichwa as the representative Napo Runa way of speaking. For example, when I asked her opinion on BIE and Kichwa-language planning, Luisa, a 38-year-old Kichwa told me,

> I reject what they have done. We don't want that language that spreads the *ta-ta-ta*, the, the *ma-ka-ta-ka*, I don't know what! … ((In)) the Indigenous beauty pageants they speak that language … By force they have to learn to speak it.

Professed aversion to Unified Kichwa and its "forced," harsh, staccato phonology was common in metalinguistic interviews, where it was sometimes summed up by exclamations of "¡*Qué raro!*" ("How strange!") and "¡*Qué feo!*" ("How ugly!"). Tena Kichwa dialect was regarded as contrastingly familiar and pleasing to the ear.

Much of the outcry over linguists' proposed changes to spoken Kichwa phonology is actually misplaced, as Unified Kichwa was originally intended to be a written variety only, and Unified Kichwa comes with no officially prescribed rules for pronunciation. Nevertheless, educational policies are currently inconsistent on clarifying this point, and students, teachers, and orators frequently transfer written norms, like the orthographic reconstructions in Table 3 into speech, enregistering the intercultural code and its mixture of dialect and Unified Kichwa as a new formal way of speaking.

Table 3 Examples of Phonological Differences between Tena Kichwa Dialect and Unified Kichwa

Tena Dialect Pronunciation	Unified Kichwa Orthography	English Gloss
wagra [**wagɾa**]	*Wakra*	cow
shu [**ʃu**]	*Shuk*	one
chi [**tʃi**]	*Chay*	that
rana [**rana**]	*Rurana*	to do
uktu [**uktu**]	*hutku*	hole

As one bilingual education administrator explained, the ideal of writing in Unified Kichwa while maintaining a distinct spoken dialect is central to language planning in Napo, but it is a plan that has so far been difficult to institute:

> At the level of unified writing, we are using ((Kichwa)) poorly ... Some people are writing in Unified Kichwa and pronouncing just as it is written. There is the problem. We ((educators)), on the other hand, are sending the message that we will command dialect ... and equally, we will know Unified Kichwa ... In writing we will unify, but at the spoken level, we will maintain our dialect.

As this objective of Kichwa education is repeatedly ignored, and Unified Kichwa orthographic forms enter into speech through the intercultural code, critics protest that spoken Kichwa in classrooms and public performances turns into discordant mixture of opposing dialect and Unified Kichwa phonetic systems, which should be kept separate. Patricia, a 23-year-old Kichwa enrolled in an adult Unified Kichwa literacy course, explained that her grandparents become angry when they see her writing in Unified Kichwa on homework assignments for class:

> They say ((language planners)) are changing their customs ... unifying that of the highlands with that of the Amazon region, where we speak differently. And they say "Why can't they leave them there and us here, leave each one alone?!" ... ((They say)) that ((language planners)) invent Unified Kichwa *de ganas* (('for fun')).

The categorical devoicing of obstruent phonemes /p/, /t/, and /k/ in Unified Kichwa is a particular source of contention. Under the old, informal orthographic rules, which are based on Spanish writing, *voiced allophones* (or variable pronunciations of these sounds using vibration of the vocal cords) are represented with graphemes *b*, *d*, and *g*. The Kichwa word for *toucan*, for example, which is pronounced [dumbigi] and commonly spelled **dumbigui** by Tena Kichwas, is now correctly spelled **tumpiki**, according to Indigenous linguists responsible for codifying Unified Kichwa orthographic rules. Linguists' reduction of voiced and *voiceless* allophones (pronounced without vibration of the vocal cords) to single graphemes *p*, *t*, and *k* leads learners of Unified Kichwa to read the voiceless phonemes as the prescribed ones for spoken pronunciation. Many Tena-dialect speakers see this devoicing as a growing, objectionable sound change that typifies the stiff staccato of Unified

Kichwa and as iconic of its perceived preference for devoiced "highland" Kichwa phonology. Consonant devoicing is seen to resemble a stereotyped, close-mouthed curtness and coldness that is associated with both Unified Kichwa and "highland" Kichwa speakers. It is antithetical to a professed Amazonian warmth and informality, typified by "clear" fluid speech, as described by Sofia, Sara, and Patricia (ages thirty-four, twenty-four and twenty-three, respectively), in the following:

Sofia: Unified- in the highlands they speak … very closed.
Sara: And very quickly.
Sofia: And they speak *pshpshpshpsh*. I don't know, ((everything)) ends with an *s*. On the contrary ours is clearer.
Patricia: More understandable.

The characterization of highland Kichwas as cold and relatively close-mouthed mirrors common lowland imagery of highland Spanish speakers in Ecuador, who are similarly described as relatively close-mouthed as a result of their tendency to reduce and delete unstressed Spanish vowels (see Lipski 1994). Lowland Spanish speakers are contrastively described as being relatively socially "warm" and exhibiting a relaxed attitude, as evidenced by their tendency to reduce their consonants and speak with more open mouths. These Tena Kichwas similarly point to their own "clearer" variety of Kichwa as evidence of their more hospitable and friendly style, in comparison to stereotyped close-mouthed and reserved highland Kichwas.[1]

In other words, Tena Kichwas recognize a first-order indexical relationship between consonant devoicing and the perceived highland origins of Unified Kichwa orthography. An overlapping second-order indexical relationship is taking shape between consonant devoicing and disfavored stereotypical highland practices, such as stilted, close-mouthed speech, and coldness, tight-lipped demeanor, and a perceived attitude of superiority. Apparent consonant devoicing in an inappropriate social context (i.e., outside of the classroom or a formal gathering) is thus policed by Unified Kichwa critics, as it may be perceived as a signal of a speaker's immodest display of formal Kichwa education or assent to highland cultural dominance. The dual indexical messages here are that (1) Tena Kichwa dialect is distinguished by the voicing of obstruent consonants and (2) Amazonian Kichwa-language identity is defined by informality, warmth, and humility.

The pronunciation of the phoneme /t/ in the accusative case marking suffix *-ta* (meaning the suffix that marks Kichwa nouns as objects) to -[ɾa] after a vowel is similarly cited by dialect speakers as representative of its distinctly "fluid" sound pattern. *-ta* is a high-frequency morpheme in Kichwa, so -[ɾa] is a frequently occurring sound combination in Tena Kichwa dialect. According to the new orthographic rules of Unified Kichwa, the -[ɾa] morpheme in a word like **tandara** "bread as an object," as in the spoken phrase **tandara mikuni** "I eat bread," is written as *-ta*, resulting in the written phrase **tantata mikuni**. When speaking the intercultural code, this phrase may be pronounced [tantata mikuni]. According to dialect defenders, the unvoiced /t/ in this phonetic environment sounds unpleasantly stilted and staccato, as expressed by Luisa earlier in her imitation of "*ta-ta-ta, ma-ka-ta-ka*" language.

Other idiosyncratic pronunciations in Tena Kichwa dialect are sometimes used as examples of lowland informality and unpretentiousness, as opposed to the pretentious formality of those educated in Unified Kichwa. Unified Kichwa's critics often deride linguists reconstructed sounds as foreign, superfluous "inventions." The introduction of the phoneme /k/ to the common Tena Kichwa verb **ana** "to be," forming the new word **kana** in Unified Kichwa, has been a notable focal point of protest in my metalinguistic interviews. Many dialect speakers reference it as an example of Unified Kichwa planners' penchant for needlessly adding *k*s (which are not part of local Spanish-based orthographies) to various words, and of their tendency to invent language simply "*de ganas*," "for fun." Similarly, Unified Kichwa's insistence on the inclusion of word-final nasals and word-final /k/, which are categorically deleted in Tena dialect (e.g., Unified Kichwa **kayakaman**, "until tomorrow," vs. dialect **kayagama** and Unified Kichwa **shuk**, "one," vs. dialect **shu**) are regarded as unnecessary phonological excesses. Dialect, by contrast, is talked about as an "economical" language variety. By way of second-order indexicality, such extra sounds are pointed to as exemplary of the contrived, unnatural feel of Unified Kichwa and the perceived phoniness of those who write and speak it.

Indexical Words

Like phonology, many of my informants had strong opinions on differences between Tena Kichwa dialect and Unified Kichwa *lexicon*, or vocabulary.

Table 4 Examples of Lexical Differences between Tena Dialect and Unified Kichwa

English Gloss	Spanish Gloss	Tena Dialect	Unified Kichwa
party	*fiesta*	*ista*	*raymi*
hour, time	*hora*	*uras*	*pacha*
to dance	*bailar*	*bailana*	*tushuna*
to work	*trabajar*	*tarabana*	*llankana*
pair	*pareja*	*parihu*	*ishkantin*

Unified Kichwa *neologisms*, or created words that have been introduced for non-Native concepts or to replace Spanish borrowings tend to be the main focus of contention. Examples of these are provided in Table 4.

By far the most talked-about Unified Kichwa neologism in my ethnographic interviews is **mashi** meaning "friend" or "companion" (a word the reader may remember from Eladio's speech on **Rayu Shinalla** in Chapter 1). **Mashi** is used frequently by those who speak the intercultural code as a polite, gender-neutral form meaning "friend" or "colleague." **Mashi** replaces a whole class of gender-specific kin terms that are normally required for identifying close relationships. These include **wawki** and **turi**, meaning "brother," in male-male and female-male relationships, respectively, and **pani** and **ñaña**, meaning "sister" in male-female and female-female relationships, respectively. Opponents of Unified Kichwa consider the local kin terms to be more appropriate ways to refer to close companions who are not actually family members, much in the same way English speakers informally use *brother* or *sister* to refer to close friends. Santiago invoked a **mashi**/**wawki** distinction in his respective voicing of Unified Kichwa and dialect in lines 27–34 of Speech Sample 4. Elaborating on this important difference later in our interview, he argued that kin terms like **wawki** are more inclusive than **mashi**, despite their gender specificity. As he explained:

> For friend we say **wawki**. With **wawki** I am speaking to my own brother, I am speaking to my neighbor, I am speaking to my friend … With only one word, I give many, many definitions. But suddenly they say … "No, **mashi** is the correct word for saying friend." But this vocabulary … is a foreign vocabulary.

While the Unified Kichwa word **mashi** indexes a measure of social distance between speaker and addressee, terms like **wawki**, for Unified Kichwa critics, contrastingly convey informality and warmth. As evidence of this point,

I often found that BIE administrators would refer to me as **mashi** when in a professional setting and **wawki** in their homes. **Mashi** has become such a deeply ideologized word, in fact, that it is even sometimes used as a mock metonym for BIE administrators, whom I have heard referred to in Spanish as "*los **mashis**.*"

Pagarachu (literally, "much payment"), is another high-frequency dialect word meaning "thank you" that is actually a Kichwa-fied Spanish borrowing (Spanish *pagar*, "to pay" + Kichwa -*chu*, "much") and that is being replaced by the Unified Kichwa neologism **yupaychani** (literally "I am grateful") in contexts of formal speech where the intercultural code is used, such as the closings of speeches. Like **mashi**, **yupaychani** is often referenced by my informants as indexical of the contrived, ceremoniousness of Unified Kichwa and the pretentiousness of its speakers. As Natalia, a 34-year-old Kichwa complained:

> Now they say **yupaychani.** I don't know what it means ... What is the other one? ... **mashi**. I don't know what that is. ((They are)) strange words that no one understands. I don't know where they got them from. These things, they confuse people ... It would be better like it was before, when *la gente* (('the people')) maintained the language.

While some critics dismiss Unified Kichwa neologisms as silly and meaningless inventions, others express outright panic that their language is being displaced by the larkish pursuits of highland-orienting language planners. If left unchecked, they believe, such language tinkering could potentially wipe out entire inventories of local terminology and linked ancestral knowledge. As examples, they often point to Tena dialect's rich and irreplaceable ecological, mythical, and cosmological vocabulary. DIPEIB-N administrators I have talked to about language change over the years often express a shared discomfort about the potential loss of local lexicon, despite their steadfast support for Unified Kichwa. As they are almost exclusively Kichwas from local communities, they recognize the need for parallel preservation of local vocabulary, as one administrator explained:

> The linguists who have written the materials, books, pamphlets, they have spoken for purely linguistic reasons, without considering the sociological part, the cultural part, the historical part, or the geographical part ... Well, we are going to lose a mountain of wealth, of ecology, of nature, meanings that we live by. So, in the field of ecology, of nature, we are going to maintain dialect, as much in the oral part as in the written.

While language revitalization in Napo has historically been directed by organized planning bodies—formerly DIPEIB-N and now the Ecuadorian Ministry of Education—there is no parallel institution for the preservation of Tena Kichwa dialect. In large part, this is due to the ideology espoused by dialect defenders, summarized by Santiago's statement that linguistic practice must be "respected," rather than engineered. Dialect maintenance, like the maintenance of a Runa identity, depends on a vibrant community of speakers and active family socialization processes that are impossible to recreate through top-down language planning tools such as dictionaries, grammars, and classroom-based literacy education. While literacy is valued as a means of empowerment by both language planners and their opponents, Tena Kichwas like Santiago believe that literacy planning should conform to the reality of linguistic diversity rather than attempt to institute linguistic norms that erase it. To their opponents, Unified Kichwa dictionaries, grammars, and the "foreign" words they introduce are menaces to Napo Runa ethnicity, knowledge, and a way of life that is in need of protection and redefinition.

Symbolic Morphemes

Standardized *morphemes*, or units of words, like the examples in Table 5, are a constant source of confusion for Unified Kichwa learners and uneducated audiences. While maintenance of regional diversity in spoken pronunciation is supported under the rubric of Unified Kichwa (ideally at least, if not in actual practice), standardized morphemes are actually designed to replace regional ones. While they are often regarded as stylistically alien and indexical of devalued cultural stereotypes, Unified Kichwa morphemes are also singled out as a particular source of confusion and communication breakdown. For many Tena Kichwas who are nonliterate in Unified Kichwa, these new morphemes are meaningless symbols of a "foreign" language that Tena Kichwa dialect speakers "do not understand."

In a pointed critique of Unified Kichwa morphology, a rare occurrence in my metalinguistic interviews, Patricia, quoted earlier, complained:

> We don't want that ... u::::h ***rikushpa***, I don't know, ***kishpa***. I don't say ***rikushpa***, I say ***rikuwka*** ... Sometimes it is unintelligible what they are speaking.

Table 5 Examples of Morphological Differences between Tena Kichwa Dialect and Unified Kichwa

Tena Kichwa Dialect Morpheme	Unified Kichwa Morpheme	Ex: Tena Dialect	Ex: Unified Kichwa	English Gloss
-S (unifying suffix)	*-PASH*	*ñukas*	*ñukapash*	I, also
-W- (progressive infix)	*-KU-*	*kallpawni*	*kallpakuni*	I am running
-NU- (third-person plural infix)	*-KUNA*	*rinun*	*rinkuna*	they say
-NGAJ (projective suffix)	*-NKAPAK*	*yachankak*	*yachankapak*	learn
-Y (locative suffix)	*-PI*	*wasiy*	*wasipi*	at home

In calling attention to the Unified Kichwa gerund morpheme *-shpa* in ***rikushpa*** "seeing" and the Tena dialect progressive infix *-w-* in ***rikuwka*** "was seeing," Patricia is actually conflating two related but distinct types of tense/aspect marking. Nevertheless, in her protest of this foreign introduction, she echoes a common aversion expressed among Unified Kichwa critics to its "unintelligible" morphemes.

As seen in the examples in Table 5, Unified Kichwa does in fact contain a number of prescribed morphemes that are distinct from those of spoken Tena dialect. While some of the standardized morphemes are entirely distinct from those of dialect, many include simple sound changes to morphemes that exist in both varieties. Most Tena Kichwas have not been educated in the grammar of Unified Kichwa, though, and are not always aware of the specific morpheme prescriptions that it proposes. The presence of unfamiliar morphemes in the intercultural code of education and media therefore results in protests of spoken Unified Kichwa's perceived "unintelligibility." The few examples I have of interviewees recalling specific morpheme differences, as in Particia's complaint about aforementioned *-shpa-*, were offered by former BIE students. For most dialect speakers, morpheme changes are noticeable in Unified Kichwa writing and speech, even though they could not easily talk about these differences abstractly (cf. Mithun 1979). As a result, unfamiliar Unified Kichwa morphemes were often talked about in analogous ways to Unified Kichwa neologisms, that is, as sounding "like a foreign language." Each time an encounter with a Unified Kichwa morpheme causes misunderstanding and communication breakdown, perceptions of Unified

Kichwa as a foreign, unintelligible language variety become reinforced. The opacity of Unified Kichwa morphemes reinforces the second-order indexical link between Unified Kichwa and pretentious, nonlocal, non-Indigenous qualities. Linguistic differentiation from Unified Kichwa through the use of Tena dialect morphology, as for pronunciation and word choice, thus comes to signal loyalty to a local identity that is expressly unrefined, unadulterated, homegrown, and meaningful.

A New Ethnolinguistic Identity

In sum, pan-indigenist language planners' use of Unified Kichwa as the language of an imagined Kichwa nation has spurred a counterclaim by critics, like Santiago, of Tena Kichwa dialect as the language of a real, territorial ethnic group. Top-down language revitalization, in other words, has become an impetus for bottom-up language preservation and maintenance. In response to language standardization, the boundaries of Napo Runa ethnolinguistic identity have come under revision, and the exclusion of identities that do not fit with the core has become part of this process.

More specifically, Napo Runa ethnic reconfiguration involves four important points of clarification. First, there is a re-emphasis on Amazonian territoriality. Once taken for granted, but now constantly asserted by critics of Unified Kichwa, is the principle that territory is an indispensable criterion of Indigenous identity. Dialect defenders see Unified Kichwa as "foreign," having been selected by linguists from "other" Kichwa varieties and locales. Their occurrence in local speech creates a glaring linguistic disorder, as multiple geographically linked codes (both local and extra-local) are being spliced together in seemingly arbitrary ways. Meanwhile, "the highlands" are invoked as a focal point for negative evaluation of Unified Kichwa-language style, as a rejection of second-order indexical stereotypes of un-Amazonian characteristics. The coldness, detachedness, social superiority, and orientation toward alien political ideologies associated with stereotypical highlanders overlap with stereotypes of elitist Unified Kichwa speakers and their unintelligible dictionary language that is devoid of local meaning. Following this view, haphazard mixing of "invented" Unified Kichwa words into the intercultural code threatens to contaminate all local language with linguistic icons of alien and objectionable social traits. For them, using Unified Kichwa means showing disdain for one's regional identity and deliberately deferring to an elevated social status as a more important source of identity. To do this is decidedly un-Indigenous, they suggest.

Second, this essentialized Napo Runa identity has no room for spurious culture. Tena Kichwa dialect, the argument goes, has grown out of a unique social and ecological history that includes ongoing contact with Spanish. The dialect that Napo Runa claim to be "born" speaking is a historical link between generations of speakers. While, for language planners, dialect has been adulterated by drift and mixing with Spanish, for dialect defenders, Tena Kichwa is local ethnic and interethnic history incarnate. To speak a synthesized Unified Kichwa is to go against nature, to ignore the realities of linguistic evolution and diversity, and to threaten the existence of a local language identity. To speak dialect, by contrast, is to ensure cultural and ethnic survival. In sum, Unified Kichwa is invented. Tena Kichwa dialect is real.

Third, redefined Napo Runa identity is largely a class-based identity and Tena Kichwa dialect is a class-marked variety (cf. Armstrong-Fumero 2009). For those who oppose it, using Unified Kichwa signals a tacit allegiance to an elitist political ideology and flaunts one's formal education. Unified Kichwa is seen as the dressed-up language of high culture, to which very few Napo Runa have access. Napo Runa should not betray their upbringing, they explain, by speaking like "**mashis**" to their *machetero* elders. Rather, they should speak in the clear, understandable, and unadorned language of egalitarian community life.

Finally, dialect defenders believe that Napo Runa identity is transmitted through the natural processes of cultural reproduction and family socialization, not formal education. It rests on collective memory, not invented "tradition." To speak Tena Kichwa dialect, particularly to one's children, is thus to engage in cultural transmission and the unimpeded reproduction of "national patrimony." Kichwa language and social practice are not to be imposed in some alien form in the classroom or in national policy, these traditionalists claim; rather, local cultural and linguistic heterogeneity are to be "respected," as Santiago puts it, and stimulated at the community level.

The Final Word

While I have tried to give a comprehensive picture of both sides of the debate over Kichwa-language revitalization, I would like to end by giving Santiago the last word, since his position as a dialect defender is so eloquently and artfully articulated. Returning to Speech Sample 4, we see Santiago making calculated semiotic choices in his performance of linguistic differentiation and conflict. In his play with voices in lines 26–34, Santiago aligns himself with the speech of a typical Tena Kichwa dialect speaker, using dialect words like ***riki***, "hey," and ***wawki***, "brother," dialect pronunciations like [kanda], with a voiced obstruent [d], and a Kichwa-fied Spanish borrowing ***salurani***, meaning "I greet," from Spanish *saludar*-"to greet" + Kichwa verbal suffix -***ni***. When voicing a speaker of the "other code," the one that "no one understands," he omits the ***riki*** and replaces ***wawki*** with the Unified Kichwa neologism ***mashi*** ("friend"). He also changes his pronunciation of [kanda], to a word that sounds more like ***kanta***, the way it is spelled in Unified Kichwa. And he replaces ***salurani*** with ***mushkun***, which, to the best of my knowledge, is a made-up word. Unified Kichwa is, of course, known by its critics for its "invented" vocabulary that "no one understands." Since he has never studied Unified Kichwa formally, knows few of its bona fide neologisms, and expressed refusal to learn them in our interview, Santiago fittingly makes up his own.

In this brief and improvised performance, Santiago aptly summarizes the current state of sociolinguistic affairs in Napo, where Tena Kichwa, Unified Kichwa, and Spanish coexist in an uneasy relationship. Seemingly small linguistic differences, like the ones he voices in his performance, are consequential enough for Tena Kichwas like Santiago to create overwhelming confusion. Their jarring juxtapositions signal the "failure" of DIPEIB-N's language revitalization model. Confronting Unified Kichwa, in the voice of the uneducated novice Kichwa speaker, Santiago thus finds himself hopelessly lost, lamenting (in lines 51–53), "Jesus, I won't speak at all. I am better off learning Spanish." Here, he artfully presents the stance of a dialect defender, who concludes that without "respect" for Tena Kichwa the future of Indigenous ethnolinguistic identity looks bleak. Many Tena Kichwa speakers would agree on these points, that language revitalization sends contradictory messages and that Tena dialect will likely never contend with Unified

Kichwa as an institutionalized, planned language in Ecuador. The problem, as Santiago alludes to in his resolution to learn Spanish, is that while Tena Kichwa dialect is achieving recognition as a threatened language, dominant tactics like standardization and grammatical ordering will not help, since they are contradictory to what Tena Kichwa represents. Tena Kichwa is seen as a proprietary code that must be free to evolve through natural socialization processes, not ordered and constrained through dominant institutions. For Tena Kichwa's protectors, to impose order on spoken dialect is to break the organic bond between speaker and speech. Tools of the dominant national order such as dictionaries and grammars are seen by these dialect advocates as decidedly un-Indigenous.

In any case, Tena Kichwa dialect has emerged in linguistic consciousness as a proprietary code, an icon of Napo Runa identity that contends with the intercultural code as an emergent code of Indigenous status and power. Meanwhile, as the struggle over planning the future of Kichwa language in Napo goes on, as Santiago suggests, more and more Tena Kichwas are incorporating the power code of Spanish into their daily lives, where it occupies an insecure role in popular ideas about Indigenous bilingual identity. This linguistic insecurity will be the subject in Chapter 3.

3

Bilingualism, Racialization, and "Poorly Spoken Spanish"

Ecuador is commonly imagined as a nation with three geophysical and sociocultural parts: the western coastal lowlands (*costa*), Andean highlands (*sierra*), and eastern Amazonian lowlands (*Oriente*). Remarking on their striking geographic, cultural, and linguistic contrasts, and in "such a small country," no less, is a cliché that Ecuadorians take great pleasure in indulging. Conversations about regional Spanish accents are particularly spirited. That is to say, conversations about *costeño* versus *serrano* accents are spirited. Any question about a corresponding *Oriente* accent, I have found, receives puzzled looks. While the *costa* and *sierra* have developed clear linguistic identities, the *Oriente* tends to be dismissed by most Ecuadorians as a region without a representative "accent." Sociolinguists would seem to agree, as those who bother to consider the topic at all treat Lowland Eastern Ecuador as a Spanish-language frontier. Pointing out the relatively large population of Native Amerindian-language speakers and the relatively recent colonization of the region by Spanish-monolingual Whites and Mestizos, sociolinguists tend to regard the *Oriente* as a region unsuitable for the study of Spanish dialect variation.

A lack of a stable and well-defined Spanish dialect, though, does not mean the *Oriente* is unworthy of *any* Spanish sociolinguistic study. Local discourse among my Spanish-speaking informants in Napo reveals a very interesting sociolinguistic picture. On countless occasions I have heard *Napeños* (Napo residents) comment on the varied pronunciations of the Spanish word *pollo* ("chicken"):

En la sierra dicen [poʒo], *en la costa dicen* [pojo], *en el Oriente decimos* [poʎo].

> In the highlands they say 'pozho,' on the coast they say 'poyo,' in the *Oriente*, we say 'polyo'.

Apparently for *Napeños*, the *Oriente* does have at least one signature accent feature, the pronunciation of Spanish double-*ll* as palatal lateral approximant [ʎ]. This sound, unfamiliar to most English speakers, is made by raising the middle of the tongue to make contact with the middle of the hard palate while lowering the sides of the tongue to let the air flow over them. Palatal /ʎ/ was historically the prescribed pronunciation for Spanish orthographic *ll*, but it has mostly fallen out of use in contemporary Spanish-speaking Latin America, where it tends to be merged with the lateral approximant /j/, the sound normally represented in English (and sometimes in Spanish) as the letter *y*. In the few areas where /ʎ/ remains, it tends to be stigmatized as a sign of rural and rustic speech (Lipski 1994: 140).

When I first heard talk about this feature during my early fieldwork in Napo, I was eager to get impressions from Spanish-speaking Kichwas. But whenever I raised the subject of *Oriente* Spanish in otherwise informative discussions about Ecuadorian Spanish accents, Tena Kichwas always seemed to want to change the subject. And they always wanted to change it to the same topic: their own linguistic shortcomings in Spanish. In one of my earliest conversational interviews about Ecuadorian Spanish, Carmen, a 31-year-old Tena Kichwa office worker, began a lively discussion about Spanish "dialects," claiming that

> People from Cuenca speak in a sing-songy way. People from Puyo too. Coastal people ... they cut out certain syllables. And, I don't know ... I think that the Spanish language, I don't think it has dialect, but rather customs, forms, I don't know.

Careful to mirror her terminology, I asked her, "Do you think there are forms unique to Tena or Napo?" She paused for a moment and replied,

> I don't think so ... That would be ... better said, that would be *Castellano mal hablado* (('poorly spoken Spanish')). I mean, there are- one fails to correct oneself. I mean, it's more failure. We need to prepare ourselves better in the Spanish language to speak correctly. This would be a failure. These are not forms of dialect ... I mean, we speak poorly ... I don't think they are dialects or customs, I think it's poorly spoken. We speak Spanish poorly.

Having witnessed this puzzling shift from discussions of "accent" and "dialect" to Kichwas' linguistic deficiency several times, I started asking Tena Kichwas more direct questions about their perceptions of the Spanish of Kichwa bilinguals. These conversations usually went like the one in the following, with Galo, a 41-year-old Tena Kichwa ecotourism guide:

MW: I am interested in the Spanish of Kichwa speakers. Some people tell me that they have their own style of speaking-
Galo: ((clears throat)), *Castellano mal hablado* ((''poorly spoken Spanish'')).
MW: Not poorly spoken, but rather a style of speaking. Do you think that-
Galo: Because normally the Kichwa people don't speak correct Spanish. We speak a bit, like, for example, like as in Kichwa. Like, some, it isn't poorly spoken but rather it is ... direct, you know? We don't speak like, like people from the *sierra* or the coast. They have a different accent of Spanish.
MW: Right. That's why I am asking, because some people believe that here in Napo there is no Spanish dialect-
Galo: The term that we use is *Castellano mal hablado* ... the people that come from other places, they say "Oh, you don't speak very well, you don't pronounce the *r* well" or "You don't pronounce some words correctly." But it's- that is how we have learned.

Despite my best efforts to use neutral descriptors like "styles," "ways," and "forms" to ask questions about both *Oriente* Spanish and the Spanish of Kichwa bilinguals, these conversations nearly always turned into disparaging discussions about Kichwas' deficient and incomplete acquisition of Spanish. And my informants all used the same phrase to name this linguistic disorder: *Castellano mal hablado*, or "poorly spoken Spanish."

What surprised me most about this discovery was my informants' near-unanimous references to pronunciation, as opposed to "bad" grammar or language mixing, as the telltale sign of this *Castellano mal hablado*. Like Galo in the aforementioned quote, they all seemed to single out Kichwas' "mispronunciation" of one particular sound: Spanish *rr*. In mainstream Latin American Spanish, the prescribed pronunciation of double *rr*, as in the word *carro* ("car") is an alveolar trill, a sound made by making multiple, quick taps with the tip of the tongue against the alveolar ridge (the bony protuberance just behind the teeth) in rapid succession. This is also the prescribed pronunciation for mainstream Latin American Spanish *r* in word-initial contexts, like *rico* ("rich"), and also somewhat variably when *r* comes after an *l*, *n*, or *s*.[1] Since my

Spanish-speaking informants referred to all expected trilled *r* environments as examples of "*la erre*" or "*la doble erre*" ("the double r"), I will henceforth refer to both orthographic *rr* and word-initial *r* collectively as Spanish *rr*. According to my informants, one can tell very easily if a Spanish speaker is "Indigenous" or "bilingual" just by listening to their pronunciation of "*la erre.*" Whenever I asked for examples of *Castellano mal hablado*, they almost always began with this same feature, as in the following cases:

> Javier: For me it is very easy to realize that one is a Kichwa speaker when they speak Spanish. For example, the *r*.
>
> Jazmín: For example, there are people who say '*caro*' [kaɾo]. They do not say, it isn't '*carro*' [karo], '*carro*' [karo] with the two *r*s. They say '*caro*' [kaɾo].
>
> Luna: They often get confused when they begin to speak Spanish. Instead of '*carro*' [karo] they say '*caro*' [kaɾo].
>
> Natali: The young people who know Kichwa and Spanish don't use the double-r well.

The "mistake" my informants all kept coming back to was the pronunciation of Spanish *rr* not as a trill (represented in the International Phonetic Alphabet (IPA) as [r]), or multiple taps, but as a single tap ([ɾ] in IPA). When pressed, they could often also reproduce a host of linguistic "errors" allegedly committed by their peers (e.g., mixing up Kichwa and Spanish vowels, using Kichwa words when they forgot the Spanish ones, saying Spanish words in the wrong order). But the "mispronounced" tap [ɾ] was consistently offered as the first, most recognizable feature of *Castellano mal hablado*.

So, while the pronunciation of *ll* in *pollo* as a palatal lateral approximant [ʎ] is iconic of *Oriente* Spanish, tap [ɾ] is iconic of *Castellano mal hablado*. Whereas using [ʎ] signals that one has an *Oriente* "accent," using a tap [ɾ] in place of a trill signals that one is Indigenous and lacks mastery of the language. It is worth noting here that the palatal lateral approximant phoneme /ʎ/ is also a distinguishing native feature of Tena Kichwa. As a result, Tena Kichwa bilinguals pronounce this sound habitually in their Kichwa and their Spanish. And yet, while all Spanish-speaking Napo residents reportedly say [poʎo], Kichwas tend to exclude themselves from this emergent *Oriente*-speaking identity. Only Kichwas "confuse" their tap [ɾ]s and trill [r]s, saying "*caro* [kaɾo] instead of *carro* [karo]." And even this small phonological transgression can signal an inability to speak any kind of Spanish properly, thereby overriding any possible self-identification as legitimate *Oriente* Spanish speakers.

But why is one phonological feature talked about as an example of an "accent" while the other is not? Why is [ʎ] celebrated as local while [ɾ] is lamented as incorrect? And how could a simple pronunciation "error" preclude identification as a legitimate Spanish speaker? Answering these questions requires investigating both Kichwas' Spanish-language practices and discourses surrounding these practices. It requires a multiscaled and multidisciplinary approach that goes beyond dismissive, prescriptivist characterizations of the *Oriente* as a Spanish-language frontier. In this chapter, I suggest a descriptivist ethnographic approach to Spanish in Napo from a Kichwa point of view, one that treats both [ʎ] and [ɾ] as significant *sociolinguistic variants*, or alternative ways of saying Spanish *ll* and *rr*, that have important social significance (Fasold 1990). In this chapter I explore Tena Kichwas' conflicting experiences of speaking Spanish as both a familiar code of Indigenous identity and an unmastered "non-Indigenous" language.

Following calls for the rapprochement of sociolinguistics and linguistic anthropology (e.g., Bayley et al. 2013; Woolard 2008) and building on studies that combine semiotic analysis and ethnographic sociolinguistics (e.g., Bucholtz 2010; Eckert 2012; Kiesling 2001; Mendoza-Denton 2008; Zhang 2008), I combine a quantitative study of Spanish *ll* and *rr* with an ethnographic description of surrounding *language ideologies* in discourse. By *language ideologies*, I mean pervasive sets of beliefs about language use that are treated as common sense, but that actually carry implicit moral and political evaluations that reproduce existing social hierarchies (Kroskrity 2000; Schieffelin et al. 1998; Silverstein 1979; Woolard & Schieffelin 1994). In so doing, I will try to answer two related research questions: (1) How do Tena Kichwas pronounce Spanish *ll* and *rr* in socially patterned ways? (2) How do ideologies about race, class, bilingualism, and Indigeneity affect Tena Kichwas' perceptions of their Spanish? In my sociolinguistic analysis, I will show how use of [ʎ] and [ɾ] by Kichwa-Spanish bilinguals patterns with ethnographically important social variables including age, gender, education level, and residence history. Like many linguistic anthropologists and ethnographically oriented sociolinguists, however, I argue that simple correlations between variables alone cannot fully explain the meanings of these language forms or their effects on actual language use. In order to do this, I centralize Tena Kichwa discourse, namely conspicuous ideological discourses that mark [ʎ] as "*Oriente*" Spanish and racialize [ɾ] as "poorly spoken Spanish." These discourses, I argue, exert powerful pressures on ongoing language use and the development, or lack thereof, of stable linguistic identities.

Racializing Discourses

While Tena Kichwa discourse about Kichwa varieties reveals competing ideologies of Indigenous ethnic identity, as we saw in Chapter 2, discussions of Spanish and *Castellano mal hablado* are fundamentally discussions about race. While ethnicity links groups of people based on shared geographic origin and sets practices, norms, and values, race is a social construct that links people together based on perceived biological similarities like physical appearance and other attributes assumed to be "natural" and inborn. Reflecting on linked discourses of ethnicity, race, and language in the US context, linguistic anthropologist Bonnie Urciuoli (1996) theorizes how languages and language varieties associated with social groups can become contrastingly *ethnicized* or *racialized* (see also Chun & Lo 2016; Dick & Wirtz 2011). When linguistic practices are ethnicized, they, like the ethnic groups with which they are linked, are presented as safe, ordered, and valuable contributions to a nation-state. Such differences are seen as evidence of a legitimate national or cultural origin and welcomed as signs of diversity. In countries like the United States, ethnicized foreign words and accents may be celebrated as cultural authenticity, especially in select spaces of ethnic "performance," where they do not present any real challenge to nationalist ideologies of monolingualism (see also Silverstein 1996). Contrastingly, when groups of people are seen in racial terms, their language forms become ideologically problematic. In racializing discourses, Urciuoli explains that racialized people are seen as "matter out of place," as disordered and dangerous. Their disorderly language practices are correspondingly seen as impediments to social mobility, as problems in need of fixing. In discourses about racialized people and language, emphasis is thus placed on "natural attributes that hierarchize them and, if they are not White, make their place in the nation provisional at best" (1996: 15).

Despite an abundance of linguistic studies demonstrating the inherent artfulness, systematicity, and legitimacy of racialized languages and varieties that spans several decades, ideologies of linguistic deficiency maintain powerful holds on popular perceptions of them (Rosa 2016). As a result, recent studies in *raciolinguistics* (Alim et al. 2016; Flores & Rosa 2015; Rosa 2016, 2018; Rosa & Flores 2017) have renewed critical attention to discourses that present connections between language, racialized speakers, and disorder as natural and self-evident. Rosa and Flores (2017) argue that such stigmatizing practices have deep historical and structural roots, in which hierarchies of racial and linguistic legitimacy are central to processes of "modern subject formation" (622). Contributors to the growing body of study on language and race have sought to expose and critique racializing discourses in policy, education, mass media, and everyday language. Many of these studies have been concentrated in the United States (e.g., Alim & Smitherman 2012; Bonfiglio 2002; Fought 2003; Hill 2008; Lippi-Green 1997; Meek 2006; Urciuoli 1996; Zentella 2014), though research has recently expanded to include focus on the systematic stigmatization of racialized groups and their language practices in global, transnational, and colonial contexts (e.g., Collins 2017; Kubota 2014; Lemon 2002; Roth-Gordon 2016; Veronelli 2015; Vigoroux 2017).

A central theme within racializing discourses is the widespread assumption of linguistic deficiency of racialized speakers vis-à-vis standard languages and varieties, an assumption that is shared by members of dominant and subordinate groups. This ideology of deficiency has been revealed in a wide range of racializing discourses, from academic discussions about "language gaps" (Johnson & Zentella 2017) and the linguistic "handicaps" of bilinguals (Zentella 2007; Rosa 2016), to media musings about the unexpected articulateness of a Black US president (Alim & Smitherman 2012), everyday discourses about the ungrammaticality of American Spanish (Hill 2008), African American English (Jacobs-Huey 2006; Rickford 1999; Wolfram 1969), Chicano English (Fought 2003), and the English of Native Americans (Meek 2006). Despite their demonstrated skills in negotiating multiple varieties and languages, this persistent ideology of deficiency excludes racialized speakers from participation in "legitimate" identities, communities, and polities. Rosa (2016, 2018) further identifies related ideologies of *languagelessness*, which call into question the overall competence and legitimacy of entire racialized groups in any language, even their home varieties. Multilingualism, as Rosa points out, is often touted in nationalist discourses, educational contexts, and neoliberal imaginaries as a valuable multicultural and economic resource (see also Duchene & Heller 2012). For racialized speakers, however, the promotion of foreign-language acquisition and multilingualism can deceptively reproduce stigmatization (Rosa 2016) as multilingualism is cast as an impairment or sign of failure, rather than as a skill (Meek 2011; Zentella 2007).

For Indigenous Peoples, the learning of dominant national languages can open up economic opportunities and allow for social mobility. Many of my Tena Kichwa informants, as I have already noted, cite access to superior urban schools and jobs as primary reasons for why their parents pushed them to learn Spanish as children, often at the "expense" of learning Kichwa. Marr (2011) has even shown how Quechua speakers in Peru, reflecting on their shifts toward Spanish monolingualism, deliberately avoid notions of language "loss." Instead, they tout Spanish acquisition as a step toward modernization and self-empowerment. While self-denigration of Indigenous languages in the pursuit of dominant-language fluency has a long history in Latin America, the rise of constitutionally mandated multiculturalisms have shifted popular attitudes. The maintenance of Indigenous languages, alongside dominant languages like Spanish and Portuguese, is now commonly promoted in policy and nationalist rhetoric, as Indigenous languages are evidence of celebrated multicultural patrimony. Officially sanctioned bilingual education programs, like Ecuador's BIE, are similarly promoted by Latin American governments for fostering Indigenous bilingualism and successful integration into the nation-state.

These global ideologies of multiculturalism are echoed in local discourse among *Napeños*. Kichwa language and culture revitalization are openly supported by Napo provincial government bodies, which draw on Kichwa cultural identity to promote the region as an international, multicultural travel destination. As Kichwas are touted as models of ancient heritage and sustainable forest living, cultural and ecotourism projects become especially vital sources of income for local governments and rural Kichwa communities seeking economic alternatives to destructive natural resource extraction that is common in other Amazonian locales. Napo's much-hoped-for future as an international tourist destination thus rests on the continued presence of a viable Indigenous community and its bilingual Indigenous liaisons.

Everyday discourse among Tena Kichwas, however, reveals that while bilingualism is valued in the abstract, the racialization of *Castellano mal hablado* continues to reproduce ideologies of Indigenous languagelessness.

Despite obvious signs of mastery of Spanish by bilinguals occupying a range of social strata, Tena Kichwas still see even subtle shifts into Kichwa-inflected pronunciation as evidence of categorical linguistic deficiency. Vigoroux (2017) offers a poignant example of how select linguistic features can become emblematic of stereotypical linguistic deficiency in this way, through their repeated reference in racializing discourses. She traces the enregisterment of grammatical features in the French of speakers of sub-Saharan African origin as indexes of Africans' alleged incapability of speaking French competently. Just as French is ideologized as an "exceptional language" and Africans' approximations of it as "rudimentary" (Vigoroux 2017: 6), Spanish has become ideologized as a "foreign" language for Kichwas, who can never seem to get it right. The pronunciation of Spanish *rr* as tap [ɾ] has come to signify this incomplete acquisition, and Indigenous linguistic incompetency and racial disorder more generally. *Castellano mal hablado*, exemplified by this one, highly marked "mispronunciation," is the racialized language of Tena Kichwa bilinguals.

Castellano mal hablado is always evaluated within an "ideology of correctness" (Urciuoli 1996) that does not apply to the emergent, racially neutral, *Oriente* accent. The responsibility to correct one's speech according to dominant norms, Urciuoli reminds us, is ideologically given to individual speakers. People who do not correct their language, like Kichwas who "improperly" pronounce *carro* as "*caro*," cannot control the influences of their native tongue on their secondary one. They therefore cannot disconnect race from class and thus "abdicate any hope of metacommunicative control" (126). Despite a widespread revaluing of Kichwa culture and bilingualism, these concerns over correctness and purity outweigh allowances for potential ethnicization of Indigenous Spanish. In other words, while palatal lateral [ʎ] may be emblematic of an emerging regional "accent," the racialization of Indigenous Kichwas and their language precludes any potential recognition of tap [ɾ] as either a feature of a regional or foreign "accent." Its presence in Indigenous Spanish-language speech is always read as incorrectness and bilingual interference, or as "poorly spoken Spanish." Despite apparent signs of upward mobility among Kichwas in Napo, the racialized stereotype of the uneducated, disorderly, language-mixing Kichwa prevails. Whenever language indexes Indigenous identity, or whenever Napo residents hear race in the speech of Indigenous bilinguals, they also hear linguistic disorder and subordinate status. These are powerful impediments to Kichwas' ability to achieve a respected and valued Oriente, bilingual, or Hispanophone identity.

Prescriptivist Discourses

Linguistic prescriptivism among sociolinguists further adds to this ideology of Indigenous linguistic deficiency and, relatedly, to the *Oriente*'s unworthiness as a site of sociolinguistic study. Toscano Mateus's (1953) foundational survey of Ecuadorian Spanish overlooks the *Oriente* entirely, dividing Ecuadorian Spanish into two classes of highland and coastal dialects. Four decades later, Lipski (1994) declared in his comprehensive study of Latin American Spanish varieties that it is still "too early for any 'Amazonian' dialect of Ecuadorian Spanish to have formed." And, at the turn of the twenty-first century, Aguirre (2000) reports no change, labeling the *Oriente* as a region that "do[es] not present dialectal variants worthy of consideration" (7). According to these characterizations, it seems, if there is no stable or easily recognizable dialect, detailed sociolinguistic study of the region is pointless.

In their dismissal of the *Oriente* as a Spanish dialect void, sociolinguists tend to point out the relatively high percentage of Indigenous inhabitants and the relatively recent colonization of the region by monolingual Spanish-speaking Whites and Mestizos. As Lipski (1994: 249) summarizes,

> Native Americans living in this region continue to speak Spanish precariously, with heavy influence from their native language, while immigrants from Spanish-speaking regions continue to speak their respective regional varieties of Spanish. In time, if the Hispanophone population stabilizes, a representative Amazonian dialect will emerge, but, at present, Spanish continues to be an immigrant language in this region.

It is in fact true that large-scale, permanent colonization of Napo by Spanish-speaking *Colonos* (Whites and Mestizos) has been a relatively recent phenomenon. While the Napo Runa have had sustained contact with Spanish speakers from the highlands since the mid-sixteenth century, it was not until the early twentieth century that Napo Runa began to see the gradual loss of their community lands to White and Mestizo immigrants, which intensified during the development of the first official settlements, haciendas, and "white towns" in the 1920s (Muratorio 1991), and has continued through the ongoing economic development of the region. Despite frequent protests by Napo Runa inhabitants, who have lived in the area since "time immemorial," the occupation of Napo has long been promoted by the Ecuadorian state, which has hoped to create a stable, populated frontier area with neighboring Peru.

While sociolinguists' characterizations of the *Oriente*'s recent history of immigration may be accurate, labeling Spanish as an "immigrant" language in Napo is an oversimplification. The idea of Napo as a Spanish-language (which is also code for "White") frontier overlooks the intercultural and multilingual processes that have come to define contemporary Napo Runa identities. While Napo Runa have had little control over the colonization of their lands, missionization, urban development, and the expansion of the international labor market, Muratorio (1991) reminds us that such processes nevertheless "gave rise to the structures, opportunities, pressures, and oppressions that shaped the life experiences of several Napo Runa generations and are an integral part of their cultural history" (13). Not all Napo Runa see themselves as living in a disappearing Native hinterland. Many, instead, view contemporary life in the province, particularly around its urban centers, as defined by interculturality and the adaptive blending of Native and non-Native practices, including linguistic ones.

The establishment of state schools in Napo in the early twentieth century played an especially important role in shaping a contemporary Napo Runa cultural and linguistic identity, as these schools continue to be sites where many Indigenous youth learn to read and write in Spanish to prepare them for participation in local, national, and international labor markets. Until only recently, learning Spanish in state-run schools involved forced abandonment of Kichwa. Decades of state-endorsed colonization and cultural assimilation led to a deep internalizing of subordination by Kichwas of their traditional language and culture, fueling the ongoing generational language shift from Kichwa monolingualism among seniors to Spanish monolingualism among youth. Bridging the communicative gap between the grandparent and youth generations, however, is a large population of Kichwa-Spanish bilingual adults. Many of these Indigenous bilinguals were raised in rural Kichwa-speaking homes and educated in urban Spanish-speaking schools. Many of them see Spanish fluency as a defining element of their intercultural identity and composite urban-rural lives in which they move constantly between ancestral Kichwa-dominant family landscapes and the Spanish-dominant urban centers of political and economic power.

Highland-focused sociolinguistic studies tend to overlook the contributions of this large portion of the "Hispanophone" population, and consider only recognizable Spanish dialects as worthy of study. To them, the *Oriente* continues to be a marginal zone of ongoing colonization and resulting "interlingual" Spanish (Selinker 1972). Lipski (1994) describes it as a region where Native Americans use Spanish only occasionally and tend to speak an *interlanguage*, or way of speaking unique to foreign-language learners who retain aspects of their first language in their production of a second one. But the description of Indigenous Spanish as "interlanguage" can be misleading, for two reasons. First, in the case of Tena Kichwa bilinguals, the concept of "interlanguage" may be an oversimplification. As Hamilton (2001) explains, an interlanguage requires permanent fossilization of errors and stability, otherwise "there is no need for an interlanguage theory" (80). While *Castellano mal hablado* is marked by recurrent "errors," such as tap [ɾ] transference into trill environments, the use of this feature is widely graded among speakers and appears to be in transition across generations, as I will show later in the chapter.

Second, and more important, labeling Indigenous innovations in Spanish that have not influenced non-Indigenous Spanish varieties as "transitional" or "incomplete" is dismissive and potentially destructive. Considering only completed change, that is, the presence of a clearly distinctive "dialect," as worthy of study means neglecting the important, gradual processes by which new language systems and varieties are formed. Such an approach also undermines the complex, variable, and innovative ways of speaking recognized by local people but not yet named and classified by linguists. Hill and Hill (1986) characterize prescriptivist views of language contact, like that between Spanish and Kichwa, as basic to Western linguistic tradition. Though linguists may claim to have abandoned this heritage, such ideas about linguistic purism and degeneration have nevertheless continued their hold on popular language ideologies, where they can have disastrous consequences for speakers of nonstandard languages and varieties. This is certainly the case in Napo, where Kichwa-influenced pronunciations like tap [ɾ] invariably mark Indigenous speakers as a degenerate, racialized population that has not yet fully acquired Spanish, rather than as a bilingual population that has imposed its own ethnic style on local Spanish speech. As long as the *Oriente* continues to be characterized as a Spanish frontier by academics and everyday Ecuadorians, it is unlikely that even clearly enregistered sociolinguistic features will ever be accepted as evidence of anything more than "accent," in the case of [ʎ], and as an "interlingual" Spanish or *Castellano mal hablado,* in the case of [ɾ].

In keeping with a central tenet of linguistic anthropology, however, I offer in this chapter a *descriptivist,* as opposed to prescriptivist, approach to language change that rejects characterizing change in terms of correctness, stability, and completeness. Instead, I offer a sociolinguistic picture of Tena Kichwa-Spanish that is drawn from long-term ethnographic experience of people talking about their own language use. Following Hill and Hill (1986), I approach Spanish [ʎ] and [ɾ] as examples of culturally meaningful linguistic difference. Central to this attitude toward analyzing language contact and Indigenous bilingualism is a notion of a "continuum of ways of speaking" (see also Hymes 1974). This means analyzing language practices that are recognized and meaningful to speakers themselves, as seen in their own categorizations of linguistic differentiation and in their uses of these in real instances of socially occurring speech. In a similar vein, Woolard (2008) stresses a need for linguists to increase their focus on ongoing processes of ideologization of language use in studies of language change. In doing so, she argues, we may begin to account for how particular linguistic elements "get picked out, ideologized, mobilized, and iconized for social purposes by specific speakers, and for how these elements become not just socially productive but linguistically (re)productive" (447). In the case of Napo, applying these insights means recognizing Spanish [ʎ] and [ɾ] as socially salient and culturally meaningful language innovations, rather than as unclassifiable aberrations from recognized language varieties. It also means recognizing that talk about talk contributes to the enregisterment, or fixedness, of Spanish [ʎ] and [ɾ] as markers of locality, ethnicity, race, and class.

Furthermore, such renewed approaches to understanding the "continuum of ways of speaking," of language change in progress, must involve multiple forms and levels of analysis. As demonstrated throughout this book, this means combining a detailed account of the structure of a given speech community, its sociolinguistic environment, and the discourses that shape them. This also means paying attention to linguistic forms that, while prominent in popular discourse, may not yet have made it into the prevailing dialectological catalog. So, in the brief sociolinguistic analysis that follows, I take a descriptivist approach to Spanish-language variation in Napo, treating [ʎ] and [ɾ] as equally salient, yet ideologically different, emblems of local linguistic identity. In so doing, I present Tena Kichwas not as foreign-language learners, but as Spanish speakers and linguistic innovators.

The Social Stratification of [ʎ] and [r]

If [ʎ] and [r] are so important to *Napeños*, how often do they actually show up in the Spanish of Tena Kichwas? Who tends to use them? And how are their usage patterns similar or different? As I will show later in the chapter, usage of each of these variants by Indigenous bilinguals is frequent and patterned according to social variables such as age, education level, residence history, and gender. While they may not be "dialect" variants, strictly defined, [ʎ] and [r] are thus important markers of linguistic identity and indicators of ongoing Spanish-language variation. In order to document their presence in Indigenous Spanish, I draw primarily from data in recorded conversational interviews conducted between 2008 and 2009 among twenty-four Tena Kichwas, which I compare with data from similar recorded interviews among *Colonos*. This Tena Kichwa speaker population includes males and females of varying ages, education levels, and occupations, whose command of Spanish ranged from Spanish-dominant to fully bilingual in both Spanish and Kichwa.[2] The interviews ranged from thirty minutes to one hour and were selected for analysis because of their relatively good sound quality and the presence of a sufficient number of tokens (at least ten) of each sociolinguistic variable, Spanish *ll* and *rr*.

Oriente [ʎ]

The pronunciation of Spanish *ll* as palatal lateral [ʎ] happens frequently in the Spanish of both Kichwa and *Colono* residents of Napo. Its mere presence in Napo Spanish is notable, given that this feature is somewhat rare in Spanish-speaking Latin America, the fact that it has become an explicitly valued feature of "*Oriente*" Spanish is especially surprising. Lipski (1994) reports that in most countries where the phoneme /ʎ/ is still found, neutralization with /j/ (or the pronunciation of *pollo* as "*poyo*" [pojo]), "has spread rapidly in the last century, and /ʎ/ has been relegated to rural regions, where it is associated with rustic speech" (140). Furthermore, he claims, even in those regions where virtually all speakers retain /ʎ/, "little positive value is attached to this sound." Though there does seem to be some indication that *yeísmo*, or neutralization of /j/ and /ʎ/, is very recently spreading among youth in Napo, this appears to be an exceptional region where residents positively value [ʎ] as an index of local Spanish-speaking identity. That they do so may be further evidence of a renewed interest in local ethnic and linguistic idiosyncrasies as part of the rise of Napo as a cultural and ecotourism hotspot. Here, rurality becomes a positive attribute as it is thought to promote the maintenance of nonmainstream ethnic traditions and sustainable biodiversity. The explicit retention of a rural-sounding [ʎ] may thus be explicable, at least in part, to marking as a signifier of regional ethnolinguistic flavor.

While Napo residents have come to recognize this feature as distinctive of local speech, *folk*, that is, nonacademic, explanations for the possible source of /ʎ/ retention seem to be absent. This is also notable, given that this phoneme is a defining feature of Lowland Kichwa, which has been in contact with Napo Spanish since the early conquest of Ecuador. And yet, unlike tap [ɾ], which has become iconic of "incomplete" bilingualism, or "interference" of Kichwa into Indigenous Spanish, I never heard Napo residents point to Indigenous bilinguals' pronunciation of *ll* as [ʎ] as a sign of bilingualism or even reference its presence in Lowland Kichwa.

The existence of the palatal lateral /ʎ/ phoneme in Napo Spanish may in fact be attributable to a complex of multiple historical processes. Many classic linguistic explanations for the retention of /ʎ/ in pockets of Latin America rest on the notion that these areas were relatively socially or geographically isolated from linguistic changes in peninsular Spanish during the colonial period (e.g., Canfield 1979; Lloyd 1987).[3] Lipski (1994: 43), however, offers several notable exceptions to this model, explaining that /ʎ/ has been maintained in a number of regions that have exhibited highly variable degrees of historical contact with colonial metropoles. Additionally, he highlights the important presence of /ʎ/ in Indigenous *substrate languages*, or languages with lower relative prestige. Andean Spanish dialects from southern Colombia to Northern Chile tend to display phonetic influence from Quechua and Aymara, including the retention of some form of /ʎ/ and the widespread presence of fricative *rr*, pronounced as [ʒ] (Lipski 1994: 81).

Complicating the possible transference of /ʎ/ from Indigenous languages is the fact that the imposition of Quechua as a lingua franca by colonial

Spanish clerics into areas where it was not necessarily Indigenous also led to the absorption of "Hispanisms" into local Quechua varieties. Lipski (1994) specifically mentions that there is "some indication" that Ecuadorian Kichwa dialects containing the palatal lateral /ʎ/ (such as Tena Kichwa) actually acquired it from Spanish, rather than the other way around. When considering the colonial and postcolonial history of the Upper Napo, the origins of /ʎ/ become even murkier, as the region has been marked by several periods of colonization, abandonment, and recolonization, and it continues to be characterized by a high degree of Kichwa-Spanish bilingualism and language contact. In other words, the presence of /ʎ/ in contemporary Napo Spanish can be potentially attributable to (1) its spread from the Spanish of early (sixteenth century) or late (twentieth century) highland migrants to the region into the Spanish of Napo Runa, (2) a more recent spread from Lowland Kichwa into Spanish, or (3) *back* into Spanish, since Kichwa speakers may have originally acquired /ʎ/ through contact with the first wave of Spanish colonizers. Though the exact origins of /ʎ/ in Napo Spanish are uncertain, historical Kichwa-Spanish language contact clearly played a part in its retention and ongoing language contact undoubtedly reinforces its continued maintenance.

In order to examine the distribution of palatal lateral [ʎ] in the speech of Kichwa-Spanish bilinguals, I coded all tokens of Spanish orthographic *ll* in twenty-four conversational interviews using Praat phonetic analysis software. Each word-initial and *intervocalic* (or between-vowel) *ll* was coded based on my own impression as one of four possible allophones: palatal approximant [j] (which sounds like English *y*), palatalalveolar fricative [ʒ] (which sounds like the *s* in the English word "pleasure"), palatal lateral approximant [ʎ], and "other."[4] Statistical analysis of *ll* allophone frequencies, along with independent social and linguistic variables, was conducted using GoldVarb software. The frequencies of use of word-initial and intervocalic *ll* allophones, according to locally important sociocultural and socioeconomic factors, can be seen in Figures 7–9.

As Figure 7 illustrates, Spanish *ll* allophone frequency varies significantly according to generation, as [ʎ] frequency drops from a rate of 77 percent among middle-aged speakers and 76 percent among young adults to 46 percent among youth. For youth (born 1985–91, or aged eighteen to twenty-four in 2008–9), Latin American standard [j] appears to be replacing local [ʎ] to some degree, despite the recent popularizing of [ʎ] as an index of *Oriente*-language

Bilingualism, Racialization, and "Poorly Spoken Spanish" 99

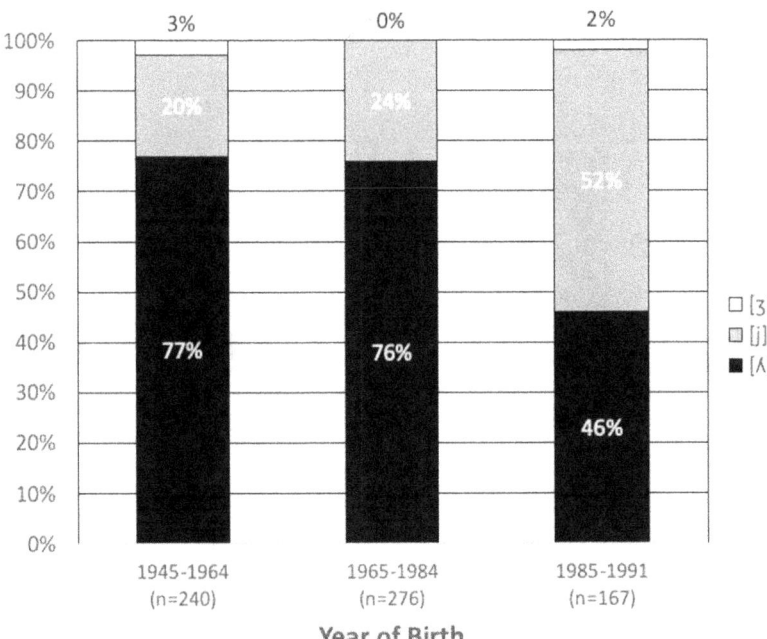

Figure 7 Spanish *ll* allophone frequency according to generation.

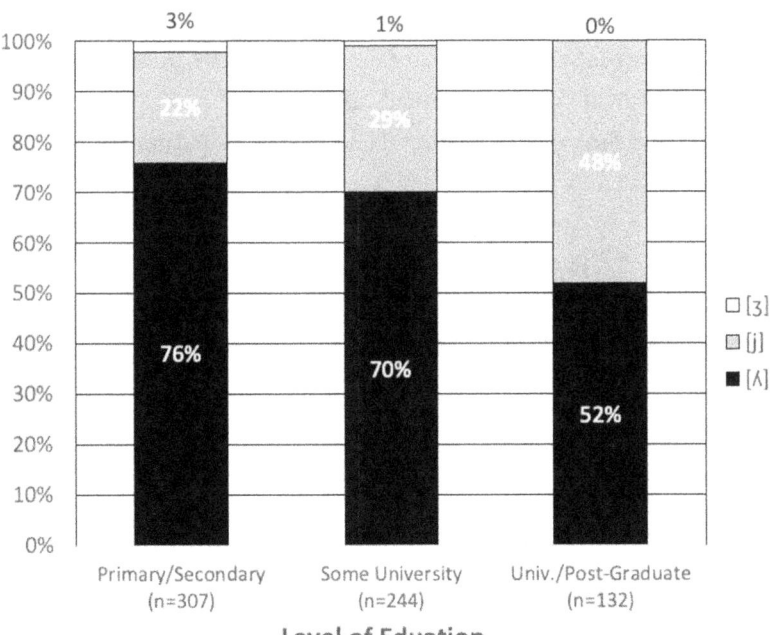

Figure 8 Spanish *ll* allophone frequency according to level of education.

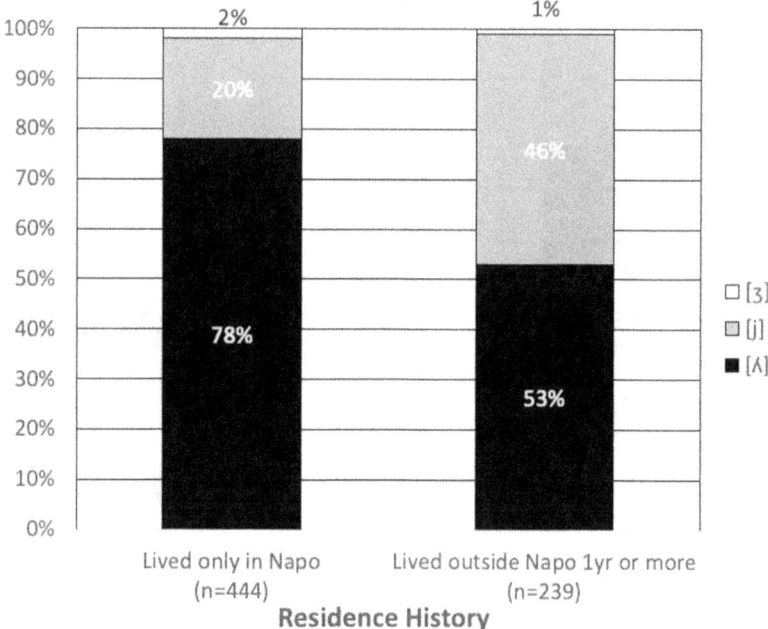

Figure 9 Spanish *ll* allophone frequency according to residence history.

identity. This apparent discrepancy could be explained by the high influence of nonlocal Spanish-language media in everyday social life among youth, where *yeísmo* is widespread and [ʎ] is virtually absent.

Figure 7 also shows, as do Figures 8 and 9, that the palatoalveolar fricative [ʒ] allophone is rarely used by any speaker for Spanish *ll*. This trend was also evident in the speech of several *Colono* interviewees, who have similarly low rates of fricative [ʒ] in their pronunciations of Spanish *ll*.[5] Fricative [ʒ] appears to be part of an Andean-influenced [j] / [ʒ] distinction, a previously prestigious mark of the Quito/highland standard, that has quickly fallen out of use among Napo residents. The oldest Napo-born *Colono* speaker I have interviewed (male, aged eighty-four), for example, has a [ʒ] frequency of 68 percent and no [ʎ] tokens, while all but one middle-aged speaker had [ʒ] frequencies below 10 percent.

Taking language ideologies into account, the very low rates of [ʒ] and continued high rates of [ʎ] are not surprising, since [ʒ] has become widely recognized as a distinctly central Andean Spanish feature that is not part of an emerging *Oriente*-language identity, which is reproduced in the often-repeated assertion that "In the highlands they say [poʒo] . . . in the Oriente we say [poʎo]." Though *yeísmo* appears to be gaining ground among Napo Kichwa youth, the overall maintenance of the /j/—/ʎ/ phoneme distinction and, more specifically, a high rate of palatal lateral [ʎ], points to the importance of continued language contact between Spanish and Lowland Kichwa in this bilingual context.

The related effects of higher education and residence patterns are made evident in Figures 8 and 9, as [ʎ] frequency drops from 70 percent for those speakers with some post-secondary education to 52 percent for those with university and postgraduate degrees. A similar trend is evident in comparative [ʎ] frequencies among those speakers who have never lived outside Napo (78 percent) and those who have lived outside Napo for one year or more (53 percent). In fact, extra-local residence was the strongest determining factor disfavoring [ʎ] use. Again, the /j/—/ʎ/ distinction appears to be giving way to *yeísmo* somewhat here, probably through direct exposure to Latin American standard Spanish among academic peer groups. Nevertheless, [ʎ] continues to be realized in a majority of overall tokens among even the most educated, widely traveled speakers in this study. This appears to be true for *Colonos* as well as Kichwas, based on the relatively small pool of evidence collected in my *Colono* interviews. For example, one sixty-year-old, Napo-born, university-educated *Colono* had a [ʎ] frequency of 91 percent.

Two other patterns are worth noting. First, gender was not a significant factor for [ʎ] frequency. Males and females use [ʎ] at similarly high frequencies (72 percent and 66 percent, respectively), which may be further evidence of its widespread acceptance as a regionally normative feature in Napo. Second, while this study focuses on patterning of [ʎ] across social variables, it should be noted that phonetic environment was found to be a significant factor affecting [ʎ] allophone frequency ($p < 0.01$), as word-initial position slightly disfavored production of [ʎ] (with a factor weight of 0.336).

To summarize, Napo residents use of [ʎ] appears to be a product of local historical Spanish-Kichwa-language contact that, despite its common stigmatization as "rustic speech" elsewhere in Latin America, has become positively valued as a defining feature of a racially unmarked *Oriente*-language identity. Though [ʎ] frequency may be giving way to *yeísmo* among Napo Kichwa youth, it is still clearly the dominant Spanish *ll* allophone for young adults and middle-aged speakers, and even for the most educated and widely traveled Napo Kichwas, a pattern that appears to be shared by *Colonos*. The central Andean fricative [ʒ] allophone of Spanish *ll* is rarely used by Napo residents born after 1945. I conclude that [ʎ] has quickly emerged as a widely recognized feature of *Oriente* Spanish that should be included in future sociolinguistic surveys of Ecuadorian Spanish varieties.

Indigenous [ɾ]

Pronunciation of Spanish *rr* has long been considered a primary classifier of Latin American Spanish dialects.[6] Toscano Mateus (1953), Lipski (1994) and Aguirre (2000) all list two major allophones of Spanish *rr* in Ecuador. The first is a multiple or trilled alveolar [r], which is common throughout the coastal region and the extreme north-central and extreme south provinces of Carchi and Loja, respectively. The second allophone is, again, the palatoalveolar fricative [ʒ], which is common throughout the central highlands, including the capital city of Quito, and is especially prominent in the south-central Andean provinces of Cañar and Azuay, including the urban area of Cuenca.

Based on its prevalence in the speech of Kichwa-Spanish bilinguals and as a racialized identity marker in discourse, I consider alveolar tap [ɾ] to be a highly salient third variant in the Ecuadorian *Oriente*. Alveolar tap [ɾ] is part of the native sound systems of both Spanish and Tena Kichwa (see O'Rourke & Swanson 2013). While tap [ɾ] is the exclusive realization of the /r/ phoneme in Lowland Ecuadorian Kichwa, it is not expected in Ecuadorian Spanish in word-initial *r* (e.g., *rico*) or intervocalic *rr* orthographic environments (e.g., *carro*). However, in the Spanish of Napo Kichwas, alveolar tap [ɾ] occurs frequently in both of these phonetic environments.

Though other researchers who work among Kichwa-Spanish bilinguals in Ecuador have noted discourses surrounding an "Indigenous-sounding *r*" in Spanish speech, there has been little sociolinguistic study of this variant—of its phonetic characteristics or its actual prevalence among speaker populations. Studies of influence of Kichwa on Ecuadorian Spanish, which have tended to focus on lexicon and syntax (e.g., Guevara 1972; Haboud 1998; Muysken 1979; Vásquez 1980) have largely ignored alveolar tap [ɾ], undoubtedly due to its invariable dismissal as a sign of phonetic interference of Kichwa into Spanish and as a degenerate form of Spanish *rr* that signals *interlanguage* and incomplete acquisition.

While alveolar trill [r] may be a target Latin American standard variant of *rr* in Spanish-language media and education, its actual presence in the everyday speech of native Spanish speakers is under debate. Hammond (1999), for example, argues that the trilled [r] prescribed by the *Real Academia Española* hardly exists in normal Spanish discourse of most native Spanish speakers. He claims, rather, that there is widespread neutralization of the tap/trill distinction in many Spanish dialects and that the trilled allophone occurs only in the speech of a small group of monolingual Spanish speakers, or otherwise only in "highly affected discourse" (1999: 136). Willis & Bradley (2008), meanwhile, reject this idea of neutralization based on evidence from Dominican Spanish. In essence, they conclude that Dominican Spanish speakers' double *rr*s sound different from their single *r*s, but double *rr*s are not always pronounced as trills.

Despite such evidence of variable realizations of *rr* even in Spanish monolinguals' speech, Napo residents always view Napo Kichwas' use of tap [ɾ] for Spanish *rr* as "incorrect." As a result, tap [ɾ] has become a prominent marker of Napo Runa Indigenous identity in discourse, and therefore important for this study of Indigenous language practices. In order to document the prevalence of tap [ɾ] among Kichwa-Spanish bilinguals in Napo, I coded all instances of Spanish *rr* in the recorded speech of twenty-two male and female Napo Kichwas.[7] Each token of *rr* was coded, based on my own impression, as one of four phonetic variants: trilled [r], fricative [ʒ], tap [ɾ], and "other."[8] Statistical analysis of Spanish *rr* allophone frequencies based on relevant social and linguistic factors was conducted using GoldVarb software. Usage frequencies of word-initial and intervocalic *rr* allophones, according to significant sociocultural and socioeconomic factors, can be seen in Figures 10–13.

Alveolar tap [ɾ] was produced in 36 percent of all Spanish *rr* tokens in the interviews. Though the usage rate of tap [ɾ] varied greatly among speakers (from 0 percent to 100 percent of tokens), this overall rate of tap [ɾ] suggests that tap [ɾ] is an important variant pronunciation of Spanish *rr* in Napo. For Tena Kichwas in this study, the position of *rr* (i.e., word-initial vs. intervocalic) was not a significant factor influencing frequency of tap [ɾ] ($p = 0.128$), though word-initial position very slightly favored its production (with a factor weight of 0.535). There are, however, several clear, socially determined trends regarding Spanish *rr* allophone frequency variation.

104   *Remaking Kichwa*

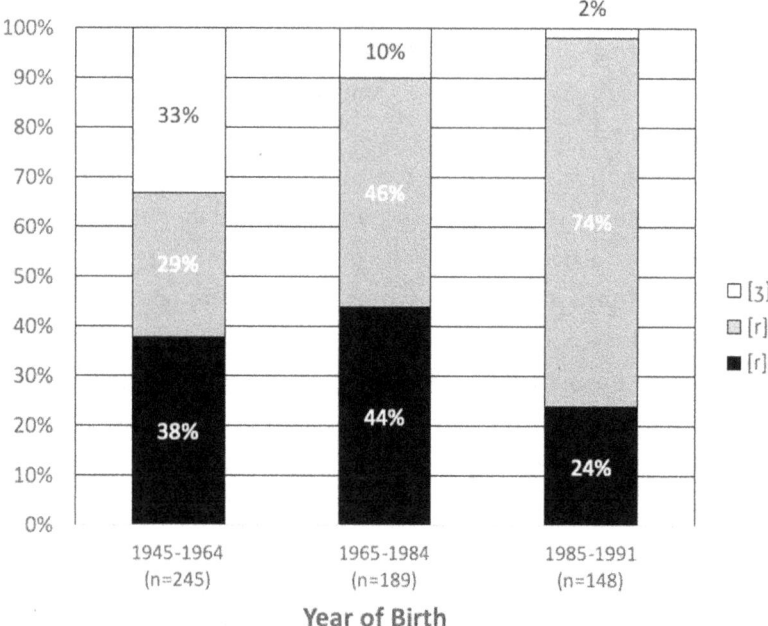

Figure 10 Spanish *rr* allophone frequency according to generation.

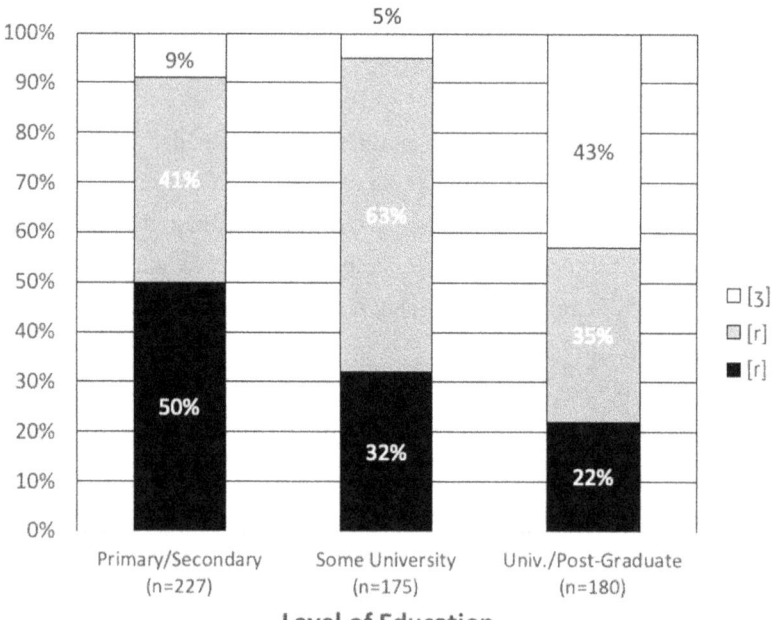

Figure 11 Spanish *rr* allophone frequency according to level of education.

Bilingualism, Racialization, and "Poorly Spoken Spanish" 105

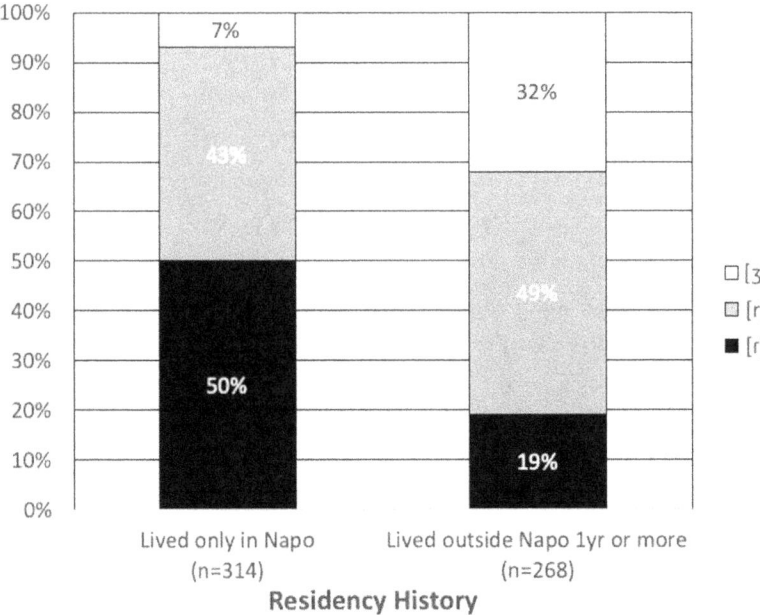

Figure 12 Spanish *rr* allophone frequency according to residence history.

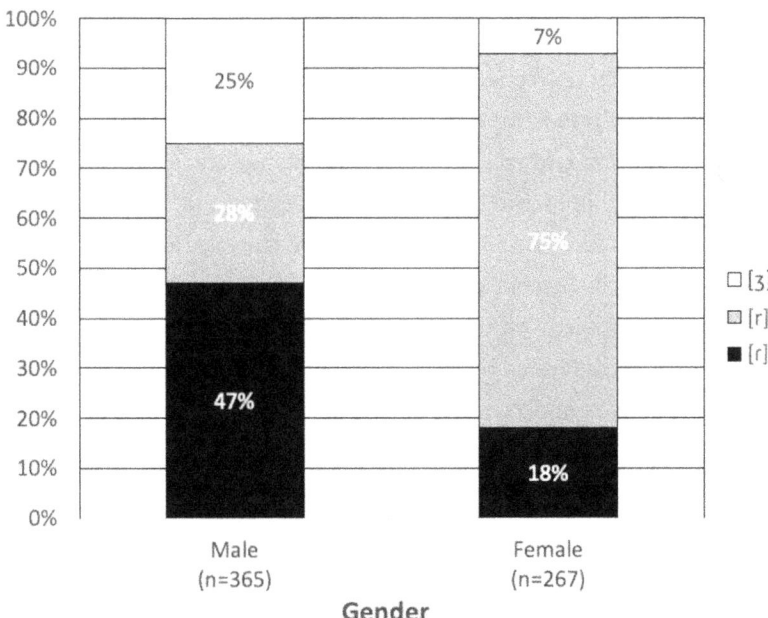

Figure 13 Spanish *rr* allophone frequency according to gender.

Figure 10 illustrates that *rr* allophone frequency varies significantly across generations of Napo Kichwas. Tap [ɾ] frequency is a bit higher (44 percent) among young adult Napo Kichwas (b. 1965–84) than it is (38 percent) among middle-aged Tena Kichwas (b. 1945–64), despite the fact that both groups of interviewees claimed to have similar rates of bilingualism. This decreased rate of tap [ɾ] among middle-aged interviewees can potentially be explained by their comparatively higher level of education, and accordingly, their exposure to highland Ecuadorian Spanish prestige dialects through national university education, which was not offered in Napo at the time of this study. Young Tena Kichwa interviewees have the lowest frequency of tap [ɾ] (24 percent), which is likely due to the fact that they are the generation with the lowest degree of native Kichwa fluency and the group of interviewees for whom foreign Spanish-language broadcast media and music (where trill [r] is dominant) was reported to be most prevalent in daily social life.

The influence of age-grading, extra-local education, residence patterns and the potential effects of Spanish-language media exposure are also clear in the frequency of fricative [ʒ] (which is largely the highland Ecuadorian/Quito standard allophone) across interviewee generations. The oldest speakers realize Spanish *rr* as [ʒ] most frequently (33 percent), while in younger generations, with comparative [ʒ] frequencies of 10 percent and 2 percent for young adults and youth, respectively, [ʒ] appears to be dying out and replaced by Latin American standard trill [r]. These generational trends for *rr* allophones are simultaneously influenced by local language attitudes, in which tap [ɾ] is racialized and devalued and an emerging *Oriente*-language identity is becoming increasingly valued. In contemporary Napo, [ʒ] is an allophone associated with older generations who orient toward a highland/Quito prestige variety and who were also educated by Spanish-monolingual migrants from highland cities. Similar trends of decreasing rates of [ʒ] and increasing rates of the trill [r] allophone were observed across generations of several *Colono* speakers, who were also coded for Spanish *rr* allophones, suggesting that the influence of pan-Latin American Spanish on local speech is not limited to young Kichwas. While most young *Colonos* displayed no [ʒ] allophones in their productions of Spanish *rr*, the oldest Napo-born *Colono* speaker in this study, male, aged eighty-four, pronounced *rr* as [ʒ] in 85 percent of tokens, the highest for any speaker.

It is clear in Figures 11 and 12 that education and residence patterns have similar effects on Spanish *rr* pronunciation, which is unsurprising, as education and residence are fundamentally linked for Tena Kichwas. Frequency of tap [ɾ] steadily decreases with increasing levels of education, from 50 percent among speakers who had received only primary (*escuela*) or secondary (*colegio*) education, to 32 percent among those who reported receiving some "university" education (including local community college, professional degree-seeking, and extra-local university programs), to 22 percent among those who achieved university and postgraduate degrees. Similarly, the comparative frequencies of tap [ɾ] for Tena Kichwas who had never lived outside Napo Province and those who had lived outside Napo for one year or more are 50 percent and 19 percent, respectively.

The popular idea that tap [ɾ] is an index of poor Spanish-language education alone is thus not entirely accurate. Napo Runa who seek higher degrees are forced to move out of rural-speaking Napo communities (where the majority of education reaches only the primary level) and relocate to urban areas like Tena for secondary education, and then out of Napo entirely for university education, which is typically sought in nearby central Andean cities like Quito, Riobamaba, and Cuenca. Not only do migrating university students learn standard academic pronunciations, but they also are exposed to Andean Spanish varieties, hence the comparatively high rates of [ʒ] allophone frequency among the most educated speakers (43 percent) and those who have lived outside Napo Province (32 percent).

Finally, as seen in Figure 13, Spanish *rr* allophone frequency also varies significantly according to gender. Male interviewees have a much higher rate of tap [ɾ] (47 percent) than females (18 percent), as well as a much higher rate of [ʒ] (25 percent) than females (7 percent). In other words, female Tena Kichwas in this study were much more likely to pronounce the Latin American standard trill [r] allophone of *rr* versus other, nonstandard, variants than their male counterparts. Comparative trill [r] frequencies were 75 percent and 28 percent for females and males, respectively. It may seem tempting to explain these data according to classic sociolinguistic theories of gendered variation according to which female speakers are believed to adhere most strictly to prescribed pronunciations (e.g., Labov 1990). Ethnographers working in Indigenous communities, however, have shown a much more complicated picture regarding men's and women's comparative exposures to and adoption of change toward dominant norms (e.g., Leonard 2012; Meek 2014; Trechter 1999, 2003). Hill (1987) cautions linguists against overgeneralizing gendered linguistic change. Especially problematic, she explains, is the commonly held sociolinguistic idea that women move toward elite language forms as a result of their "natural sensitivity" to such norms (158). In her own work on Mexicano, Hill finds that Mexicano-Spanish bilingual women are apparently sensitive to stigmatization from both a "power code" and a "solidarity code," making their usage a "tangle of contradictory tendencies" (151). Thus, it is important to consider both Tena Kichwa women's increasing access to prestige Spanish norms through education and employment and their continued sensitivity to stigmatization of "poorly spoken Spanish." Their higher rates of standard Spanish *rr* usage compared to men, however, does not suggest that their Spanish use is more standard across the board, or that their use of the standard *rr* is necessarily valued by others.

In sum, evidence from ethnographic research among Napo Kichwa speakers suggests that along with alveolar trill [r] and fricative [ʒ], tap [ɾ] is a third, highly salient variant of Spanish *rr* in Napo, where Kichwas represent an ethnic majority and Kichwa-Spanish bilingualism is prevalent. Frequencies of Spanish *rr* allophones in Napo vary significantly according to age, level of education, local residence patterns and gender. These social variables further interact with local language ideologies in which the tap [ɾ] variant is widely devalued as an index of a lack of education, trill [r] is becoming increasingly valued through both education and exposure to extra-local Spanish-language media, and fricative [ʒ] is falling out of use as a feature of an outdated, Andean prestige variety that no longer fits with an emerging local language identity. Finally, tap [ɾ] continues to be a devalued index of Lowland Kichwa racial identity, even though it persists even among highly educated, well-traveled speakers. The question of whether these trends—the decreasing use of [ɾ] and its racialization as a degenerate allophone of *rr*—will continue is a potential subject of future sociolinguistic study.

The Power of Ideology

The prevalence and patterned usage of [ʎ] and [ɾ] among Indigenous bilinguals demonstrate that these features are significant, systematic innovations-in-progress in Napo Spanish that have arisen through prolonged Spanish-Kichwa-language contact. As explained earlier, language ideologies must be taken into account in explaining the comparative rates of these two features. First, a complete sociolinguistic picture of [ʎ] and [ɾ] in Napo must recognize the ideological discourses that extol *Oriente* [ʎ] and disparage Indigenous [ɾ], leading to clear divergence in their ongoing use. Second, the continued dismissal of [ʎ] as locally idiosyncratic "accent," but not quite "dialect," and the racializing of [ɾ] as *Castellano mal hablado,* or "poorly spoken Spanish," have undoubtedly been influenced by a persistent academic language ideology that recognizes only "completed" linguistic change as worthy of attention.

While [ʎ] and [ɾ] are clearly linked to social categories in Napo, ethnographic attention to local metalinguistic discourses reveals how language ideologies continue to strengthen these links, exerting powerful effects on ongoing language change. More specifically, these discourses demonstrate the ongoing process of iconization of [ʎ] and [ɾ] as linguistic representations that have come to stand in for two different social groups and their linked social qualities. Notably, the phoneme /ʎ/ and the exclusive use of tap [ɾ] in /r/ environments are defining features of Lowland Ecuadorian Kichwa. The pervasiveness of both of these features in the Spanish of Indigenous bilinguals could thus be explained by influence from Kichwa. And yet, even though it is used frequently by Indigenous speakers, [ʎ] has become valued as marker of locality that does not include Kichwas, whose Spanish is racialized, first and foremost, as disordered *Castellano mal hablado.*

Conclusion

While it seems tempting to dismiss multilingual areas where Indigenous language speakers remain demographically prominent as "transitional" with respect to European language use, such transitional zones may, in fact, hold important keys to understanding (1) Indigenous ethnic and racial identity formation and (2) the sources of ongoing language variation. Ecuador's *Oriente* has long been depicted as a Spanish dialect void, but given the ethnolinguistic changes taking place here, it may more accurately be portrayed as a site of potential Spanish-language innovation.

Drawing on data from metalinguistic discourse, I have attempted to provide a descriptivist picture of Napo Spanish and subject it to a kind of sociolinguistic analysis that it has so far been denied as an "unstable" and "transitional" variety. We see clear divergence in both usage rates and ideological valuation of the racially unmarked and positively valued *Oriente* [ʎ] and devalued, racialized Indigenous [r]. As we have seen, analysis of the ongoing use of these variants must be historically contextualized. *Oriente* [ʎ] and Indigenous [r] are products of long-term Spanish-Kichwa-language contact and a rapidly transforming Ecuadorian *Oriente* sociocultural environment. An emergent *Oriente* identity is beginning to map onto Spanish variants. Meanwhile, Indigenous Kichwas are negotiating sociopolitical changes, including a revaluation of their contributions to local mainstream culture. Language ideologies play an important role in selecting for or against local linguistic idiosyncrasies, as attitudes toward Amazonian rurality become increasingly positive and attitudes toward bilingualism shift between competing narratives of hybrid cultural wealth and half-bred linguistic deficiency. *Oriente* [ʎ] and Indigenous [r] challenge the classic sociolinguistic picture of Amazonian Ecuador as a region with borrowed Spanish dialects and a disorderly Indigenous "interlanguage." Instead, these two forms represent contact-induced language innovations within a dynamic "continuum of ways of speaking." Like speaking Kichwa, Tena Kichwa ways of speaking Spanish draw from a complex, multilingual pool of resources and a complicated history of interethnic, intercultural exchange.

Tracing the processes through which single phonemes come to index multiple social categories and at the same time are affected by situated language ideologies demonstrates the importance of combining a sociolinguistic and linguistic anthropological approach to speech phenomena. It also demonstrates how each field of inquiry can be "nested within" and broadly overlap with the other (Woolard 2008). Traditional sociolinguistic approaches can illuminate the quantifiable effects of social variables on language change through language contact. However, ethnographic work is needed in order to explain how these social variables come into being, how they acquire complex local meanings, and by what semiotic processes these meanings are reproduced in discourse. In the next two chapters, I continue my ethnographic study of language choices by showing how both Kichwa *and* Spanish are key vehicles for communicating Tena Kichwa histories and intercultural identities.

4

Intercultural Memories

Ritual Activism in Discourses of the Past

While walking through the lively streets of central Tena on a bright and sizzling Saturday afternoon in 2015, I spotted my friend, Victor, out running errands. I had just seen him a few days earlier at a cocoa bean processing plant on the outskirts of town where he had recently started working. He offered to give me a tour of the facility and let me video record his step-by-step explanation of the local **chakra**-to-chocolate production process, which was peaking that spring along with the price of cocoa. As we walked around the plant, local Kichwa residents arrived in droves to offload bags of cocoa pods from chartered pickup trucks. When I last saw him that day, Victor was beaming with optimism about the future of his small, Indigenous-run company.

But on this subsequent Saturday afternoon in Tena, his mood had noticeably soured. After a brief exchange of small talk, I learned that his elderly parents, whose house in the rural community of Lumullakta I had visited many times, had been having health problems. Victor, a father of two in his mid-forties and a respected artisan of seed jewelry and wood carvings, moved his family from Lumullakta to a *barrio* in the hills above Tena to be closer to his day job in cocoa production and to Tena's tourist handicraft markets. In 2015, he began work on a simple, one-room shack on his parents' plot in Lumullakta, where he still spent most weekends. He was wondering if I would be interested in seeing how the construction was progressing. While we were in Lumullakta, he added, perhaps I could bring my video camera to make a recording of his parents telling stories. He was worried about how much time they had left and wanted to get at least one more memorial to preserve their legacy for his siblings and children.

This was a familiar request. On numerous occasions during my dissertation fieldwork, I was asked by younger Kichwa family members if I could lend my recording services to preserve the stories of their elders for posterity. Such requests are not uncommon among ethnographers working in Indigenous communities, and, given the wealth of knowledge we gain from our informants, I consider such small chances to reciprocate with my own resources to be a top priority. So, I agreed to ditch my plans for the day and fetch my camera while Victor finished up his tasks downtown. We met up again about an hour later at a corner grocery, where Victor was busy scooping up a bag full of live tilapia from a frenzied fish tank—his contribution to Saturday family dinner. We paid for the fish and quickly boarded a cramped bus for the bumpy forty-five-minute ride to Lumullakta.

As usual, Victor's parents' humble one-room house near the center of the village was brimming with activity. His brother sat at a table chatting in Kichwa with his parents while his two sisters moved industriously about the room, cleaning, organizing, and periodically tending to a cooking fire in the open firepit dug into the earthen floor. Victor's children and their cousins scurried intermittently in and out of the house, doing their best to weave around the scissoring legs of busy adults. After we greeted these three generations of his family and delivered his catch of the day for preparation, Victor explained to his parents the reason for my unexpected visit. They agreed that making a recording was a good idea. After some collaborative deliberation about how to get the best angle, I set my video camera on a short wooden stand in the center of the room. Victor's parents, Luis and Marta, took their positions on slightly taller, hand-carved wooden stools. From their elevated position relative to the camera, and backgrounded by the smoke of the firepit swirling behind them, these usually stooping elderly grandparents transformed into exalted orators. After a nod from Victor, I started the recording. He squatted down into the camera's frame next to his parents and asked them, in Kichwa, if they would tell "***shu ichilla*** *historia*," "a little history" of Lumullakta:

Speech Sample 5. Victor asks his parents to tell a story.

1 *Ña, ñawpa punta, papita, mamita,* **kankunara ashka llakishkawa ... kuna munawni**
2 **kankuna kawsaymanta, kankuna ashka watakunara apamushkankichi kay**
3 **Lumullaktara ñawpakma kay chisha. Chasnakllayra, ashka** misionerokuna

4 *paktamunawshka, patrón*kuna *paktamunawshka, y Lumullakta llakta rishka kuna*
5 *punchaypi. Chaymanta munawni kankunara shu ichilla* historia ... *kankuna*
6 *shamushka punchamanta kuna punchakama,* ## *imasnara rasha* misionerokuna
7 *kayma paktamushka ima, imara yanapanawka ... Chay kuintaira munawnchi*
8 *ishkintimanta* parihulla *kuintasha shu* historiara *llukshingak ... Munawni,* mamita
9 papito ... *kuintarasha ñawpa punta kankuna karan shutira, kuintaychi,*
10 *chymandawasha kallarinkichi. Ashka pagarachu.*

1 Okay, as before, mom and dad, with much love, today we want ((to know))
2 about your life, about how Lumullakta came to be over its many years. And about
3 the many missionaries who helped, the many patrons that helped to make
4 Lumullakta what it is today. And so, we would like you to tell a little story ... of its
5 becoming from then until now, ## of what did the missionaries did to help. That is
6 the story we would like you to tell, to tell your story together ... We would like you,
7 mom and dad, to first tell us your names, and then we will begin. Thank you very
8 much.

Victor's father, Luis, began in the time when he was a small child, when a Catholic missionary settled in Lumullakta and took on the role of his family's patron (*patrón*). For the next hour, while family meandered in and out of the camera's frame behind them, Luis and Marta recounted the story of their work with the missionaries to build Lumullakta from a scattered collection of Kichwa family homes in the forest to a prosperous community complete with a central square, a *cancha cubierta* ("covered ball court"), a church, and even a grass airstrip that the missionaries used to travel to more remote Kichwa and Waorani communities in the forest interior.

At the end of their story, Marta rose from her stool and, with tears in her eyes, took the hands of her children one by one to bless them and tell them how much she loved them. She then turned to me and thanked me for being there to record their story. After I turned off the camera, the adults settled together at the central table for steaming portions of grilled tilapia, boiled plantains, and manioc. Marta brought out old photos and letters sent by the missionaries years after their return to their homes abroad. Once everyone had a chance to rest and digest, Victor asked his mother if she would tell another story, this time "***shu ichilla leyendara***," "a short myth." By now the light inside the house had grown dim, the setting sun sliced into descending orange beams between the wooden slats of the house. Victor switched on a single bare lightbulb that dangled from the center of the open-air roof.

Under its bright artificial glow, with two of her young granddaughters by her side, Marta began an energetic account of the myth of **Amarunkachi**, the anaconda who owns the rivers and is the source of all animal life (see Uzendoski 2005: 127–8).

When Marta finished her narrative, Victor squatted again next to her, into the camera's frame. He said he wanted to end the recording with a "short message," which he delivered in Spanish (and which I have translated below into English):

Speech Sample 6. Victor's closing speech

1 I want to thank my mother and my father, who have given us this space to tell the
2 history, the past, stories and myths of how, many years ago, they knew how to
3 sacrifice and live in this marvelous land of Amazonian Ecuador. Our mothers, our
4 fathers, our ancestors have generated all of these teachings for our children, for the
5 future generations. Today, we, the young, want to rescue these ancestral values,
6 these cultural values. Because for us, these are the roots, the origins that day by day
7 we go on feeling in our lives in each of our families … This is a teaching, a
8 bibliography of how we live here in our communities, in our lands. As these
9 histories, legends, and stories are being lost … as a young person, I want to rescue
10 them for our sons and daughters, for them to persist. For us, this is an ancient
11 culture. The wealth of all of the peoples is here … Our Indigenous people in the
12 communities are submissive, are easy prey for intermediaries who have great
13 economic power and have not allowed us to control our own products … Today our
14 Indigenous people have many abilities. They are young people who are very
15 prepared. And today, as a young person, I want to fight for all of these communities
16 so that our products are valued … So, I leave this message to the youth, that if we
17 work together, we can be powerful … Thank you very much.

So, what began earlier that day as a spontaneous home video turned into a multigenerational, multi-act storytelling performance, framed by Victor as an act of political resistance. Except for the fact that it occurred in the middle of a private home, while family members went undisturbedly about their evening, the event had all the elements of the staged public oratory exhibitions I had seen on various stages in Tena during the time when DIPEIB-N was still operating as the "Council of the Kichwa Language" (see Wroblewski 2010, 2019b). Victor's parents' telling of **shu ichilla** *historiara* ("little history") and **shu ichilla** *leyendara* ("little myth"), that is to say, were entries into a long-standing tradition of Napo Runa oratory. In the era of language revitalization, when Native discourse traditions are being "rescued and revalued," the exhibition of Kichwa oratory can become recast as resistance to culture loss. On that day in Lumullakta, Luis and Marta's stories, reframed according to Victor's agenda of language reclamation and Indigenous empowerment, became an important display of what I have elsewhere referred to as *ritual activism* (Wroblewski 2019b). This kind of activity involves reframing and repurposing ritualistic discourse practices as forms of Indigenous political engagement. This sometimes requires deliberately moving forms of Native verbal art—for example, narrative, mythology, music, and shamanic ritual—to politically oriented, public contexts of performance. During its tenure in Napo, DIPEIB-N regularly showcased Kichwa verbal art and material culture in high-profile urban culture exhibitions, scholastic oratory contests, and televised Native beauty pageants. Following their lead, Tena Kichwas like Victor have brought ritual activism into low-profile private settings, where verbal, artistic practices are objectified and reframed as outward-oriented expressions of a threatened "ancient culture" (as Victor put it in lines 10–11 in Speech Sample 6). This kind of activism requires working outside of formal systems of public politicking, while still drawing on the rhetoric and conventions of publicly staged events. In both public and private forms of ritual activism, the use of Indigenous discourse becomes repurposed as a vehicle for self-conscious cultural transmission and political agency.

Oral Histories, Discourse-Centered Ethnography, and Interdiscursivity

As stated in the introduction to this book, I build on an established tradition in discourse-centered ethnography (Sherzer 1987) by offering *thick descriptions* (Geertz 1973) or contextualized ethnographic explanations, of Tena Kichwa discourse performances like these. In a recent reflection on this theoretical approach, Webster and Barrett (2019) and their co-contributors demonstrate the continued vitality of the discourse-centered approach, of investigating how languages and cultures "come into being through discourse," notably through forms of speech play and verbal art (147). Adding analyses of Tena Kichwa discourse to an already-rich body of discourse-centered literature on the languages and cultures of lowland South America (see the introduction to this book for example references), I hope to shed light on the pluralistic character of contemporary Indigenous discourse more generally, where distinct languages, voices, discourse types, and intellectual traditions are plainly juxtaposed in talk. This skilled blending of diverse ways of knowing, experiencing, and representing the world signifies a creative communicative adaptation to ongoing historical change.

Hill (2019) points out a critical theoretical development in discourse-centered research in Amazonia, from an original focus on "inward" expressions of culture through discourse to a later inclusion of outward-facing engagements with surrounding political contexts. Since the pioneering works of the 1980s, discourse-centered Amazonianist ethnography has come to combine its emphasis on "traditional" forms of discourse (Urban & Sherzer 1986) with focused attention to semiotically hybrid and self-consciously political Native performances, which have become oriented toward both local and global audiences (e.g., Ball 2018; Conklin 1997; Graham 2002, 2005; Graham & Penny 2014; High 2015; Oakdale 2005; Oakdale & Course 2014a). While emphasizing Native verbal artists' renowned skills in adapting discourse practices to ongoing ecological, social, and political transformations, discourse-centered ethnography continues to show its crucial applicability in documenting the nexus of language and culture in times of social change (Tetreault 2019). One pivotal development has been the critical attention to public "performances of Indigeneity" in contemporary global politics (Graham & Penny 2014). Indigenous citizens like Victor, Luis, and Marta must work constantly to remind the world, including members of their own communities, that their ancestral practices still exist and are worthy of recognition and value (cf. Ball 2018; Graham 2005).

In this chapter, I show pluralism as a defining feature of contemporary Indigenous discourse, by focusing on the intercultural, multilingual, and politically charged character of Tena Kichwas' stories of the past. Following Victor's prompting, Luis and Marta brought the past alive in double form, as "history," or a chronological account of events from **ñawpa**, the experiential past, and as "myth," which is set within **unay**, or deep ancestral space-time (see Uzendoski 2005). In his opening and closing addresses to their stories (in Speech Samples 5 and 6), Victor framed the recorded speech event as an act of "rescuing" Kichwa language and culture and as a step toward Indigenous empowerment. In his closing to the video in Speech Sample 6, he mirrors the formal, bilingual rhetoric of speechmaking that I have documented repeatedly in high-profile urban culture and language exhibitions in Tena, which are also explicitly designed to "rescue and revalue" Kichwa language and culture and decolonize the mainstream linguistic landscape (see Wroblewski 2014, 2019a, 2019b and Chapter 5 of this book for examples).

While myth telling, like Marta's story of **Amarunkachi**, reconnects living Kichwas with ancient culture and cosmology, "little histories" like Luis and Marta's story of development in Lumullakta, are also pluralistic performances of Indigeneity that connect living Kichwas with what Uzendoski and Calpucha-Tapuy (2012) refer to as an ancient "storytelling soul," in which the mythical and historical past are connected. Amazonian Kichwa oratory traditions have long been recognized by ethnographers as distinctive for their artful reanimations of direct experience through culturally patterned forms of gesture, imagery, bodily kinesthetics (Uzendoski & Calapucha-Tapuy 2012) and highly developed sound-iconic language, or ideophones (Kohn 2005; 2013; Nuckolls 1996, 2010). These modes of expression for recreating imagery, ethnographers have shown, are linked with a Native Amazonian cosmological view of "nature" as a social domain full of subjectivities (Uzendoski & Calapucha-Tapuy 2012; Wroblewski 2019b; see also Viveiros de Castro 1998) that is most accurately represented through mimesis and the performance of multiple speaker-subject perspectives in discourse. Such storytelling strategies derive, ethnographers have argued, from an Amazonian Kichwa inclination toward "earthy concreteness" (Nuckolls & Swanson 2014) and away from abstract generalizations of the world (Kohn 2005). Amazonian Kichwas, according to Uzendoski and Calapucha-Tapuy (2012), thus consider "artful expression a necessary ingredient for quality living" (2012: 3), and see storytelling as way to directly reconnect with ancestral ecologies and histories.

Meanwhile, artfully reanimating the past in the present also enables Amazonian Kichwas to create cultural and cosmological "communitas," as people reconnect mythological truths with community destiny (Uzendoski & Calapucha-Tapuy 2012). As stories link orators and audiences with their rightful ecological and historical places, simply telling a story in Tena Kichwa dialect further restores an ancestral connection to the threatened Indigenous proprietary code. As always, speaking in Tena Kichwa involves frequent codeswitches and codemixes with Spanish and multiple modes for representing experience. Tena Kichwa histories, even among the oldest living monolinguals, are always intercultural ones, as they reveal prolonged experiences of contact between Kichwas and non-Indigenous "others" that are integral to Napo Runa cultural identity (Muratorio 1991). In other words, Tena Kichwa storytelling practices are pluralistic on multiple levels, in that they reproduce ancestral aesthetic and cosmological values while also drawing on multiple aesthetic traditions and postcolonial political realities

In this chapter, I focus on two exemplary oral histories that reveal Tena Kichwas' intercultural social memory in both content and form. I begin with Luis's Kichwa-language autobiographical narrative about the development of Lumullakta, drawing from a version of this story that I recorded in 2009. I contrast this with a Spanish-language biographical narrative told by Martín, a middle-aged Tena Kichwa, about his father's role in the building of Tena into a modern intercultural city. Though these narratives are told from different experiential perspectives and in different languages, they show important parallels in theme and style.

In addition to invoking sound-iconic language and artful reanimations of direct experience through complex "image forms" (Uzendoski & Calapucha-Tapuy 2012), both stories in this chapter call on a central Tena Kichwa chronotope of life on the late colonial frontier. *Chronotopes*, according to literary theorist Mikhail Baktin (1981), are artistically rendered units of historical time-space. While Bakhtin originally developed this concept to analyze time-space construction in the modern novel, the chronotope has been widely extended in linguistic anthropology to refer more generally to fused objects of time-space that are configured through discourse. In reanimations of the past, they act as "invocable histories," or frames in which time, space, and social activities coincide, creating unified contexts of meaning that can be set off against other chronotopes (Blommaert 2015). The oral histories at the center of this chapter reanimate a chronotope of early to mid-twentieth-century colonization of Napo, a foundational period in the development of contemporary Tena Kichwa cultural identity. During this critical transition period, one among many in a series of waves of colonization of the region, social activity is typified by culture contact, economic development, interethnic conflict, and struggles for Indigenous agency. In the stories that follow, this struggle is made palpable through creatively rendered reproductions of direct experience.

As performances of ritual activism, both oral histories display an interdiscursive connection with other Tena Kichwa speech events. By describing them as *interdiscursive*, I draw on a concept that has become prominent in recent semiotic approaches in linguistic anthropology, that aims to show how texts "fold within them other texts, other utterances, and draw upon multiple discoursal contexts" (Bartesaghi and Noy 2015; see also Agha & Wortham 2005, Ball 2018; Cavanaugh 2012; Gal 2018; Harkness 2011; Silverstein 2005). Interdiscursive performances like Victor's speechmaking, and Luis, Marta, and Martín's stories, show revealing linkages across other performative events. These linkages are evident in signs that include emblematic words, languages, topics, ideas, material culture elements, and even previous utterances. As we will see in more detail in Chapter 5, such signs are repeatedly recirculated across performance contexts, thereby framing the performances as "the 'same thing, again,' or as yet another instantiation of a recognized type in some cultural framework" (Gal 2018: 2). All elements of the speech events at the center of this chapter are in dialogue with others that I investigate throughout this book, including wider discourses about Tena Kichwa history, culture change, language endangerment, loss, and revitalization. Victor's discourse in Speech Samples 5 and 6, as I have already pointed out, are in direct dialogue with urban bilingual activist speechmaking. Luis's and Maritín's oral history narratives, though "inward" oriented, are interdiscursive with "outward" discourses about Indigenous identity and agency in the postcolonial era.

Oral history narratives are especially rich examples of the language-culture nexus that is at the focus of discourse-centered ethnography. In my positioning of Tena Kichwa oral histories as ritual activism, I hope to add to a growing literature on lowland South American autobiographical and biographical narrative, which have, until only recently, been largely underrepresented topics in ethnographic research. In so doing, I follow the lead taken by Oakdale and Course (2014a) and their co-contributors, who have redirected attention to lowland South American narrators' skills at blending disparate generational experiences, modes of representation, and forms of historical consciousness. Expanding discourse-centered research on the intersections between Native discourse and global politics, these path-breaking authors highlight the especially complicated experiences of Indigenous narrators who simultaneously inhabit multiple social roles and identities in their forging of interethnic networks.

Life on the Late Colonial Frontier

As discussed in Chapter 3, social life in the Ecuadorian *Oriente* operated much like a frontier area well into the twentieth century (Muratorio 1991). White colonization of the area happened in several historical phases, starting with the first arrival of Spanish explorers in the mid-sixteenth century (see Hidrovo-Castellanos 2000; Muratorio 1991; Oberem 1980; Uzendoski 2004; and Wroblewski 2010 for detailed histories of early colonization). In the late 1800s, the upper Napo River region underwent a particularly transformative period of settlement by rubber tappers, farmers, hacienda builders, missionaries, and military officials who established new posts to govern the Amazonian territories. Tena, which had a population of less than 300 Spanish colonizers in the late 1880s (Hidrovo Castellanos 2000: 12), was quickly burgeoning into a populous Amazonian town. State-appointed political chiefs (*jefes políticos*) and political deputies (*tenientes políticos*) migrated to the area temporarily, usually returning to the highlands after their term in office. The few that resettled permanently aided in the establishment of semipermanent villages and agricultural colonies where they installed networks of exchange with the Napo Runa, beginning what Hidrovo Castellanos (2000) refers to as a process of physical and cultural *mestizaje*. "The Ecuadorian Amazon region did not have an efficient plan of colonization in order to permit harmonic development," one local Tena historian writes. "Amazonia was considered a place for the military sector and 'punished' policemen, as well as for adventurers and others who were fleeing from legal, social and domestic problems." "Nevertheless," he continues, "the Eden of Amazonia welcomed all of these people and families for the construction of a cultural mosaic" (Ramírez 2008: 5). Lucas, an 84-year-old *Colono* I interviewed in 2009, remembered Tena during early twentieth-century colonization not as an Amazonian Eden, but rather as a harsh and undeveloped jungle outpost. *Colonos*, as he saw it, brought modernity and progress to the Native people:

> In the beginning, living here was harsh. There was no business, there was nothing with which to survive. Cultivation was the only way to eat ... The Kichwa people, of course, had no education, they had a natural culture, you know ... from their ancestors. And we got along amicably with the Indigenous people. Later there began to be work for them too ... With the arrival of the *Colonos*, they began to build their farms and they needed

manual labor. So, they used the Indigenous people for the machete, to clear the forest and plant crops. And in that way, of course, the Indigenous people were also advancing, you know? Because, if the *Colonos* hadn't come ... there would have been no education.

This is also about the time that Tena Kichwa ethnohistories of colonization, told through the stories of the living grandparents and great-grandparents' generation, begin. The oral accounts that I have recorded among senior informants tend to paint a very different picture of development compared to Lucas's, in which "virgin forests" and the "***ruku kawsay***" ("old ways") of "ancient" Kichwa culture were suddenly pitted against hasty plans for economic development and the imposed ways of *Colonos*. Relationships between *Colonos* and the Napo Runa at this time tend to be described by older Tena Kichwas as strained and oppressive. Muratorio (1991) notes the especially autocratic new presence of evangelist missionaries and priests from the Josephine mission in Tena, who she, like other Napo Runa, refers to as the "patrons," who "became all powerful" (128). According to most of my elderly Tena Kichwa informants, this period was marked by tense interactions between appointed civil commanders and Kichwa community leaders in their attempts to plan the future of economic development. It is within this chronotope of struggle and transformation that Luis and Martin's stories begin, a time when Tena Kichwa community leaders were forced to carve out new roles for themselves as intercultural intermediaries and achieve agency within the social structures imposed on them by colonizers.

When the Missionaries Came

Luis's story, which I first recorded in 2009, begins during the first arrival of Catholic and Protestant missionaries to Lumullakta. These *Colonos* came with a grand vision to make the village a center of Amazonian missionizing operations, and, as Lucas explained earlier, saw the local Napo Runa residents as a readily available labor force. Having built relationships with missionaries since his boyhood, Luis eventually established himself as an Indigenous leader in the developing Kichwa community. I have included excerpts of Luis's portion of the narrative in Speech Sample 7, in its original Tena Kichwa form with English translations. Each line of text contains a single intonational unit, usually separated by a brief pause. Luis opens his story during his early childhood, when a Catholic missionary named Marqués became his family's first patron.

Speech Sample 7. Luis's oral history narrative

1	*Ñawpa punta*	Back then
2	***Lumullaktapi kawsakanchi, Lumullaktapi.***	We lived in Lumullakta.
3	*Ñuka,* **pagarinkak**	I, to earn money
4	**may** *pagarishkachu mana tiyawn*	there was no money anywhere
5	((…)) **Chy washa**	((…)) And so
6	*ñuka yaya, ñuka mama*	my father, my mother
7	*Llumullaktapi kawsakuna.*	they lived in Llumullakta.
8	*Marqués, ñukanchi* patrón	Marqués was our patron
9	((…)) *Ñukanchi ichilla*	((…)) We were little
10	casi unos, casi unos tres años	around, around three years
11	dos o cuatro años, por allí.	around two or four years old.
12	***Chy tupu ñukanchi ña.***	We were about that big.
13	***Kayma yaya***	My father
14	***wasikama kanchi, kaypi.***	we were here in this house.
15	*Marqués* patrón *ñuka yayara*	Marqués was my father's patron.
16	***Wasikamara apika***	He took us to his house
17	***wasikama, mama***	to his house, my mother
18	***wasikama ñukanchi churiuna.***	he took us as children.
19	*A Marqués,* mano *Marquésta* servió	He treated us like
20	como muchacho **kuinta ñukanchi**.	we were like his children.
21	… **Paywa misay karasha.**	… He fed us at his table.
22	***Paywa misay tukuyra servisha.***	He served us everything at his table.
23	… *Marqués***pa** *wasika kawsakanchi*	… We lived in Marqués' house
24	*kay* barancu Río **Napo**	on the shore of the Napo River
25	… **Chypi** *kawsawshka*	… He lived there
26	*ñukanchi tiyashka.*	And we stayed there.

Under the patronage of Marqués, Lumullakta was being made into a missionary post, which began with Marques' failed plan to build a Catholic Church.

27	**Shuk** iglesia católico **shamuk.**	A catholic church came.
28	Iglesia católico **shamusha.**	A catholic church was coming.
29	… **Atun** iglesiara.	… A grand chruch.

30	*Chy ichunawka.*	that was abandoned.
31	*Chy iglesiara*	That church
32	**ansa purisha, ansa purisha rawshka**	It was coming along little by little
33	*y ichunawka*	and they abandoned it
34	*ah, católico gente.*	uh, the catholic people.
35	*Mana shumunawka* padre.	The priest did not come.
36	*Mana shamusha.*	He did not come.
37	*Ña año, año*	A year
38	*casi unos tres años ya, ya pasó.*	almost three years passed.
39	*Chay washa, ña*	And so,
40	*católico* **mana** *shamukpi*	since the catholics never came
41	*Marqués, evangélicora* **randi**	Marqués, in his place, an evangelical
42	*amigo* **tukuka ña.**	friend took over.
43	*Dr. Cabrero,* **Tenamanta.**	Dr. Cabrero, from Tena.

Dr. Cabrero and his fellow evangelical missionaries, Luis recounted, ushered in a transformative period of growth of Lumullakta. Having developed close relationships with the missionaries, Luis was appointed as a Native assitant who accompanied them on trips to Tena to obtain permits for various construction projects.

44	*Chay washa* evangélico **shamuka**	Then the evangelicals came
45	misión**kuna shamunawka**	the misionaries came,
46	**visitanawka, visitanawka**	they visited
47	**shamunawka ña rawshka ña.**	they came too.
48	**Kikin Tena** misión**kuna shamunawka**	Misionaries from Tena came
49	**Kimsapurami ñawpa shamunawka**	Five of them came
50	… **Ñukanchi kimsalla yayawa kanchi.**	… We were with our five fathers
51	**Shina, ishkyra ñukanchi yayawa**	So, with two of our fathers
52	**ñukawa ishkyramas**	I, with those two
53	contacto **Ranciakuna**	((went)) to contact the White people
54	**apisha** permiso**kuna**	to get permits
55	**ñawpa punta tapunun**	to ask for them
56	orden**ta tapunun**	to ask for orders
57	**tukuy** derecho, **tukuy** razón	((to get)) everything straight and right.

Right away, Luis continued, the missionaries and their Napo Runa labor force began constructing a new evangelical church, a community school, and a carpentry workshop. Luis's new role was to mobilize large **minkas**, or work parties, who began clearing away virgin forest for the building of a runway that the missionaries could use for travel throughout the Ecuadorian *Oriente*, to Kichwa and Waorani communities deeper into the forest interior. At this point in his account, Luis became especially animated, as he detailed the massive gathering of troops of Kichwa and *Colono* workers and the laborious undertaking as if he was reliving the sensory awe of its grandeur and hardship.

58	*Tukuyra yaya*	Everything, father
59	*tukuyra* permiso*sha,* orden*ta,* maña*sha*	he asked, he ordered, he asked for
60	*tukuyra paskawasha.*	everything to be opened.
61	*Kayta* pista *rurangakmanta*	A runway was to be built
62	*kayta* pista*, ña,*	a runway
63	avión **urman**.	where planes land
64	*Kayta* pista *rurashka*	They built the runway
65	*kayta churakanchi.*	they put it here.
66	*Shina rashka washamari*	Like that, in the end
67	*yapa* corto *tukukpimari*	they succeeded very quickly
68	... Compañía **kuinta** shamuku*nama* gente.	... More people came, like a company
69	Compañía	A company
70	*shuk* compañía **kuinta** *tarabakuna.*	They worked like a company.
71	Pista **ranka** *shamun*	To build the runway they came
72	*may**MAN**ta*	from <u>EV</u>erywhere
73	*Tena* gente*, Archidona* gente	Tena people, Archidona people
74	*Lumullakta* gente ...	Lumullakta people
75	... <u>TUK</u>uy gente	... <u>ALL</u> the people
76	*kaypi kawsakuna.*	lived here.
77	*Chayta ñukaka kayta*	So I
78	<u>*TUK*</u>*uyra kasna*	to all of them
79	*ña* exegish*ka* kuinta,	urged them
80	*ña, ñuka shuk* derectiva **kuinta** *rasha.*	gave them an order.
81	... *Tukuy llacta rasha, ña.*	For the whole community to work.
82	... *Tukuy* eglesia*,* escuela *wasi*	On the church, the school house
83	misión*pa wasi.*	The missionaries' house.
84	*tukuyra rasha*	To build everything
85	<u>*TU*</u>*kuy* gente*.*	All of the people.

At this point, Victor interrupted Luis to ask him to describe the forest in Lumullakta at that time, how it used to look before it was cleared for the runway. Luis continued his animated narrative, describing the splendor of the dense forest and the exhausting work it took to level it. Luis's narrative, at times with the help of Marta and Victor, continued like this for another hour or so as family members came in and out of their home, just as they did on that subsequent retelling in 2015.

Through subtle semiotic moves throughout his story, Luis highlighted the theme of postcolonial Indigenous agency. As Victor explained during Luis's retelling of his narrative in 2015, the very act of speaking Tena Kichwa in a Kichwa home can be a form of resistance to domination and cultural erasure in the era of language shift and revitalization. The fact that Luis tells his story in Tena Kichwa dialect makes his history a symbolically "Indigenous" one. By reanimating his sensory experiences of colonization in Tena Kichwa, he restores a historical connection with Kichwa oratory traditions, a tropical forest territory, and a prior chronotope of "***ruku kawsay***," when "there was no money."

Meanwhile, Martín, the narrator of the next oral history of colonization, demonstrates that Spanish, while often dismissed as "poorly spoken" by Tena Kichwas as discussed in Chapter 3, can also be an artful and key vehicle for the expression of Indigenous identity and agency. Whereas Luis's demonstration of Tena Kichwa Indigeneity is conveyed largely through form (i.e., language choice), Martín's story is rich in iconic language and Indigenous indexes that are foregrounded through content.

Colono Officials and Indigenous Governors

While Luis's story detailed life under the patronage of missionaries, its central theme of working as an Indigenous agent of development within the power structures of White colonists was one I had become familiar with through various stories told by elders about this phase of Napo's colonization. In 2008 I recorded a tale of an elder Tena Kichwas' leadership role in the urbanizing of Tena under its newly appointed civil commanders. This story of working under the oppressive conditions of settler colonial rule was told as a third-person account by Martín, the protagonist's 55-year-old son, who was already a grandfather himself.

I was introduced to Martín by his son, Alonso, who worked as an office assistant in Tena's municipal government building, where I was a frequent visitor during my dissertation fieldwork. Alonso, like many Tena Kichwas I met early on in my fieldwork, was very interested in my research on Kichwa language and culture and generously offered to help me find some of my first informants. Soon after we had met, he offered to introduce me to his father, Martín, who he claimed was his family's expert on Kichwa culture and history. When I first visited Martín and Alonso's family home in the *barrio* of San José, just outside the city of Tena, our original plan was for me to audio record a conversational interview about Martín's reflections on San José's transformation from a Kichwa forest community to a peri-urban neighborhood. Apparently between my last meeting with Alonso and my visit to his house, he and his father had decided that, given the fact that I was planning to make a recording, Martín should instead tell a more important story. Martín's father, Juan, they told me, was in his time a San José community leader and one of the original Kichwa "governors" of Tena. With Alonso and two of his older sisters listening attentively by his side, Martín recounted a story of conflict between Juan and one of his first White bosses. As *Colono* officials were planning to arrive to Tena to begin their posts, the local *teniente politico* ("political lieutenant") directed Juan to assemble a work party to build homes for them.

Speech Sample 8. Martín's Oral History Narrative

1	*Con **churu**,* <u>TU-TU-TU-TU::::::::</u>	With a snail shell, <u>TU-TU-TU-TU::::::::</u>
2	*ya a las cinco de la mañana*	at five in the morning
3	*ya a llamar a la gente*	to call the people
4	*para que vengan para hacer **minka***	to come to assemble the work party
5	*para hacer la construcción de casa*	to begin constructing a house
6	*para el teniente político*	for the political lieutenant
7	*para la policía*	for the police
8	*y para los que vienen a visitar*	and for visitors
9	*así unas chozitas.*	some shacks.
10	*Entonces Juan tenía que animar.*	So Juan had to animate them.
11	*Juan tenía que coger del bolsillo*	Juan had to take from his pocket
12	*para dar de comer a la gente de la **minka**.*	to feed the people of the work party.
13	*No había plata nada.*	There was no money.
14	*Así es que, entonces, este*	So, uh,
15	*Juan tenía que dar de comer*	Juan had to feed them
16	*y dar de tomar **veintishinku***	and give them sugar cane liquor
17	*para hacer limpiar, o sea, la paja*	to clean the straw

18	*todo eso pues.*	all of that.
19	*Entonces Juan animaba así la gente*	So Juan motivated the people
20	*a hacer chicha*	to make *chicha*
21	*chicha de yuca para tomar.*	manioc brew to drink.
22	*Porque no había frescos*	Because there was nothing cold
23	*no había azúcar, nada.*	there was no sugar, nothing
24	*No conocían.*	they didn't know of those.
25	*Solo chicha de yuca.*	Only manioc *chicha*.
26	*En tiempo de chonta*	In the *chonta* season
27	*chicha de chonta.*	*chonta chicha*.
28	*Entonces, ellos tenían que preparar*	So, they had to prepare
29	*en una olla así, chicha.*	*chicha* in a pot like this.
30	*Así grande, olla grande*	Big like this, a big pot,
31	*chicha y brindar a la gente*	*chicha* and offer it to the people
32	*la **minka**, ya.*	the work party.
33	*Con eso trabajaban, ya.*	With that they worked.
34	*Al otro día, igual.*	The next day the same.
35	*Ya entonces allí es que venía poquito*	So, a few people arrived
36	*poquito gente, ya.*	few people.
37	*Y ya es que venía*	And they came
38	*ya hacer otra casita más*	to make another house
39	*otra casita más, ya.*	and another house.
40	*Ya, haciendo poquito poquito ya.*	Building little by little.
41	*… Entonces allí, un teniente político*	… And there, a political lieutenant
42	*ha dicho que tiene que cortar*	said they had to cut
43	*cincuenta guadúas*	fifty stalks of bamboo
44	*caña guadúa para hacer casa.*	bamboo stalks to make a house.
45	*Entonces Juan*	So Juan
46	*vuelto tenía que decir*	had to tell them
47	*"Ve*	"Look
48	*"usted me traen diez guadúa cada uno."*	"you bring me ten stalks each."
49	*Entonces, de arriba de Muyuna*	So, upriver from Muyuna
50	*por río que cartero pues*	via the riverway
51	*tenía que bajar por río*	they had to send downriver
52	*por, haciendo balsa*	by, making a raft
53	*llegar al puente donde es el Tena pues.*	to arrive at the bridge in Tena.
54	*Solo en vez de llegar cincuenta*	But instead of fifty
55	*ha llegado treinta.*	only thirty arrived.
56	*… Cuando contaba*	… When he counted

57	"¿Dónde esta? ¿Qué es?" dice.	"Where is it? What's this?" he said.
58	"Por qué no dijiste a la gente	"Why did you not tell the people
59	"que complete los cincuenta guadúas?	"to get fifty stalks?"
60	¡Esto no va a alcanzar!	"This is not enough!"
61	"Tú no sabe."	"You know nothing."
62	Es que le, le pega a Juan.	And so he, he hit Juan.
63	<u>PA PA</u>	<u>PAH PAH</u>
64	Le pega teniente político.	The lieutenant hit him.
65	Entonces, la mujer le dicho,	Then Juan's wife said to him
66	"¡Uy, no pegues!" que ha dicho.	"Uy, don't hit him!" she said.
67	"¡¿Por qué estás pegando a mi marido?!"	"Why are you hitting my husband?!"
68	"¡Calla!"	"Shut up!"
69	<u>AH</u>	<u>AH</u>
70	Le da a la mujer	He gave it to her
71	también le pega	he hit her too
72	por allá le bota.	He threw her over there.
73	Entonces, Juan ha querido pegar	So, Juan wanted to hit him back
74	pues dice ya	and ((the lieutentant)) said
75	"¡¿<u>CA</u>:rajo, vos me quieres pegar?!"	"<u>CA</u>:rajo, you want to hit me?!"
76	Es que dice.	He said.
77	<u>U:ta</u>	<u>U:ta</u>
78	<u>TA TA TA</u>	<u>TA TA TA</u>
79	Le pega, uta.	He hit ((Juan)), uta.
80	Saca sangre Juan.	Juan was bleeding.
81	Entonces Juan coge toda la sangre	So he gathered all of his blood
82	le chupa en la camisa así	he sucked it from his shirt like this
83	y esa camisa ha guardado.	and he saved that shirt.
84	Después de dos días Juan va a Quito	Two days later Juan went to Quito
85	cuando estado Presidente	when it was President
86	este, Galo Plaza.	uh, Galo Plaza.
87	Dentro de Galo Plaza.	During the time of Galo Plaza.
88	Así Juan no entró de ganas, pues.	Juan did not go there for fun, mind you.
89	Juan le nombraron de Quito	He was named by Quito
90	le nombraron que, como gobernador.	they named him governer.
91	Juan no entró de aquí como loco.	Juan did not go there like some crazy.
92	Así es que Juan, que eso	And so Juan
93	hace chichitas	made *chichas*
94	así **maitito, maitito**	and **maitito, maitito**
95	yuquita secando	drying manioc

96	*ahumando secando pescaditos*	smoking and drying fish
97	*ahumando haciendo **mait**itos así.*	smoking and making ***mait**itos* like that
98	***Shikra** carga a Quito.*	He carried a ***shikra*** to Quito.
99	*Para llegar en siete días a Quito*	To arrive in seven days in Quito
100	*en ocho días llegaban a Quito*	in eight days he arrived to Quito
101	*caminando de aquí del Tena.*	Walking from here in Tena.
102	*Allí, ha llegado a Quito*	There, he arrived to Quito
103	*para subir al palacio del gobierno.*	to go up to the government palace.
104	*Porque en tiempo*	Because at that time
105	*palacio de gobierno*	the government palace
106	*nadie sube allí, nadie.*	no one went up there, no one.
107	*Juan conversaba*	Juan told ((me))
108	*dice que bastante militares así*	there were many military guards
109	*con armamento*	with their guns
110	*en la puerta, en la escalera.*	at the entrance, in the stairs.
111	*Entonces, "Ellos vienen del Oriente.*	"They come from the Oriente.
112	*"Él es gobernador Juan Mamallacta*	"He is governor Juan Mamallacta
113	*"y tiene conversar con el señor presidente*	"he needs to speak with the president"
114	*"y tiene audiencia."*	"and have an audience with him."
115	*Y eso ya*	And so
116	*abrían las escaleras así*	they opened the stairs
117	*puro militares parado.*	Military men standing all over.
118	*Juan subía, **pata llucha** así*	Juan went up the slippery floor
119	*Nada de saco, zapato, nada.*	without his bag, shoes, nothing.
120	*Así, por el pie,*	By foot
121	*asisito, asisito Juan conversaba.*	little by Little Juan told ((me)).
122	<u>LA</u>*;stima por* <u>FLA</u>*co de hambre*	<u>PAIN</u>fully <u>SKIN</u>ny from hunger
123	*sin dormir, fr<u>Í</u>O.*	without sleep, <u>COLD.</u>
124	*Ay, es que llegaba*	Ay, and so he arrived
125	*es que al adentro donde vive el gobierno*	inside the ((President's)) residence
126	*pues, ya, arriba.*	up there.
127	*Decía, "Venga, venga Juan."*	((The president)) said, "Come in, Juan."
128	*Es qué, "¿Qué pasó? Toma asiento."*	"What happened? Take a seat," he said.
129	*Saludaba señor presidente*	The president greeted him
130	*"señor gobierno," es que daba.*	as "Mr. Governor."
131	*"Pues que, toma asiento*	"Well, take a seat
132	*"que me cuentas?" dice.*	"what do you have to tell me?" he said.
133	*Poco, poco es que sabía Kichwa.*	He spoke little, little Kichwa.
134	*"**Alli shamunki** Juan"*	"Welcome, Juan"

135	*es que dice.*	he said.
136	*"Sí, señor gobierno."*	"Yes, Mr. Governor"
137	*Pido el papel.*	He asked for the paper.
138	*"¡Chucha!" es que dice*	"Chucha!" he said
139	*"¡Carajo!*	"Carajo!
140	*Y por qué es que la policía," dice*	"And why did the pólice," he said
141	*"¡¿Por qué pega?!"*	"Why did he hit you?!"
142	*Juan saca la sangre que llevó*	"Juan brought out his ((bloody shirt))
143	*U::ta le sacará agua.*	U::ta it made him cry.
144	*Es que "El teniente*	He said, "The lieutenant
145	*"ocho días tiene que estar aquí en Quito.*	"must be here in Quito in eight days.
146	*"Aquí.*	"Here.
147	*"Nunca más va a volver al Tena.*	"He will never return to Tena.
148	*"Porque le ha sido malo*	"Because he has mistreated you
149	*"porque te ha pegado a usted autoridad.*	"Because he has hit you, an authority.
150	*"Vos eres gobernador.*	"You are governor.
151	*"Intocable usted.*	"You are untouchable.
152	*"Ya vamos a castigar, Juan.*	"And we will punish him, Juan.
153	*"No, no hay problema."*	"This will not be a problem."
154	*Y aquí va llevando Juan.*	And he took Juan.
155	*Ya es que regalaba terno*	He gave him a suit
156	*terno es que regalaba*	a suit he gave to him
157	*camisa blanco, manga larga*	a white long-sleeve shirt
158	*pantalones que le regalaba.*	he gave him pants.
159	*Zapatos que regalaba el gobierno, pues.*	The president gave him shoes.
160	*"Ya," dice*	"Okay," he said
161	*"Juan para que pongas."*	"Put these on, Juan."
162	*Ponía en **shikra** Juan traía.*	"He put them in his **shikra**."
163	*De allí ha dicho*	Then he said
164	*"Mañana venga" es que dicho*	"Come tomorrow," he said
165	*"para que lleves dos policías."*	"So that two policeman will escort you."
166	*Juan va vuelta*	Juan went there
167	*donde el gobierno manda dos policías.*	where the president sent two police.
168	*Ya con ellos viene siguiendo Juan.*	And Juan left with them.
169	*En caballo, sí, han venido*	On horses they went
170	*ellos, a'a hasta Papallacta.*	they, to Papallacta.
171	*De Papallacta otro caballo*	From Papallacta another horse
172	*hasta Baeza.*	To Baeza
173	*De Baeza otro caballo acá al Tena.*	From Baeza another horse to Tena.

174	*Llegaban policías.*	The police came.
175	*Ya llegado, orden del gobierno.*	At the order of the President.
176	*"A ver*	"Let's see
177	*"¿dónde está el teniente político?"*	"Where is the lieutenant?"
178	*"Aquí está, aquí está."*	"Here he is, here he is."
179	*"Ah, venga usted señor.*	"Ah, come forward sir.
180	*"¿Por qué le pegó al señor gobernador?*	"Why did you hit the governor?
181	*"¿Qué hizo de motivo?*	"What was your motive?
182	*"¿Por qué pegaste?"*	"Why did you hit him?"
183	*Es que nada.*	He said nothing.
184	*"¡Vamos!"*	"Let's go!"
185	*Así, amarando las manos a llevar.*	He tied his hands to take him away.
186	*Allí ha dicho en Quito*	Back there in Quito
187	*el Presidente Galo Plaza ha dicho*	President Galo Plaza said
188	*"No, Juan," ha dicho*	"No, Juan," he said
189	*"usted no vas a dejar.*	"you cannot quit.
190	*"Tú tienes que seguir*	"You have to carry on
191	*"más con ánimo para arriba.*	"and upward with courage.
192	*"Porque un día el Tena*	"Because one day Tena
193	*"va a ser como Quito," ha dicho*	"will be like Quito," he said
194	*"como Quito, un día.*	"like Quito one day.
195	*"U::, va a ser un pueblo grande.*	"U::, it will be a grand city.
196	*"Así acuerda," dijo.*	"Remember this," he said.
197	*"Siga usted trabajando con ánimo"*	"Carry on working with courage"
198	*ha dicho.*	he said.

Discourses of Indigenous Agency

Through sound-iconic language, striking performances of experiential perspectives, and pluralistic indexes and themes, Luis and Martín reanimate a chronotope of colonization that provides a historical ground for a contemporary Tena Kichwa intercultural identity. Being Tena Kichwa, as their stories show, has long meant being part of a tropical forest ecology and kin-based social organization while at the same time achieving agency within the "predominant power structures and processes" of colonization (Muratorio 1991: 3). Rendered as recorded performances of ethnohistory, both stories serve as forms of ritual activism. They are reanimations of history according to Indigenous experiential memory in Indigenous ways, in a time when both Indigenous histories and Indigenous communication forms are seen as under threat. Both stories, implicitly and explicitly, are about being Indigenous in a postcolonial world.

In her examination of Indigenous Amazonian engagements with the global public sphere, Graham (2002) shows how twenty-first-century Indigenous representatives are constantly confronted with important decisions about what to say and, just as important, how to say it. Their propositions, claims, protests, and cultural ideologies, just like their choices of language and modes of communication, can be used strategically to emphasize Indigeneity and uniquely Indigenous points of view. In private acts of ritual activism like those mentioned earlier, Tena Kichwas make similarly important choices about how best to engage in the political project of "rescuing and revaluing" their language, culture, and histories. Both of the aforementioned stories, contextually framed as ritual activist texts, objectify language and discourse as vehicles for asserting Indigenous identity and agency. In his retelling of life on the colonial frontier, Luis generally portrays his *Colono* patrons in a positive light, like fictive fathers who raised him and his siblings as their own children and helped build Lumullakta into a thriving community. Martín's story, on the other hand, resembles many other Kichwa accounts of *Colono* abuse, social subordination, and Indigenous resistance (cf. Muratorio 1991). But in neither story is the colonial project simply rebuked. Instead, both narrators recount tales of finding agentive roles within colonial power structures, where Indigenous actors could contribute to the economic and sociocultural remaking of the region.

In all three cases of ritual activism in this chapter—the Lumullakta storytelling event and Luis and Martín's oral histories—Tena Kichwa Indigeneity is expressed through pluralistic forms of discourse. The Lumullakta event included multiple languages, speech genres, and intellectual traditions, including Spanish-language political speechmaking and Kichwa autobiographical and mythological narrative. Victor opened the 2015 storytelling event with an invitation to his parents in their home language of Tena Kichwa. He closed it by looking directly into the camera and offering a politically charged speech in Spanish about "rescuing" the "ancient culture" of Amazonia and becoming "powerful." For this, he undoubtedly drew on his own experiences of working as a DIPEIB-N-trained scholar and community activist. He also voiced elements of the countless speeches given by DIPEIB-N administrators, Native beauty pageant emcees, and other cultural representatives about "rescuing and revaluing" Kichwa on the urban stages of Tena.

Luis's narrative in 2009 included themes of interethnic collaboration, religious conversion, economic development, and the transformation of geographic territory. Though speaking in Kichwa, his language contains frequent codeswitches and codemixes with Spanish, evidence of long historical contact between the two. In lines 58–85 of Speech Sample 7, Luis offers a spirited reanimation of the scope of labor required to remake Lumullakta by repeatedly raising his volume and drawing out of syllables (e.g., "*shamun mayMANta* . . . *TUKuy gente* . . ." "they came from EVerywhere . . . ALL the people . . ."). While the referent topic is *Colono* economic development, the semiotic effect of recreating his own first-hand experiences of sensorial awe is in line with long-documented Amazonian Kichwa storytelling traditions of using sound-iconic language.

Martín's narrative is likewise pluralistic in form and content. Also, in keeping with traditional Amazonian Kichwa storytelling strategies, Martín begins his reanimation of life on the colonial frontier with the evocative sound-iconic TU-TU-TU-TU::::::: —the call of Juan's *churu* snail shell (Speech Sample 8, line 1). He continues with sound-iconic language and direct quoting of his referent characters in lines 63–79, when he reenacts the political lieutenant's physical abuse of Juan. Though his narrative is delivered in Spanish (due largely to my presence), Martín foregrounds Juan's unquestionable Kichwa identity through indexical word choices, mostly referencing traditional material culture, throughout his tale. Juan assembles a ***minka*** (lines 4, 12), drinks *chicha* (lines 25–32), buys ***veintishinku*** (line 16), eats ***mait***itos (lines 94–98), carries a ***shikra*** and is welcomed by the president of Ecuador with an "***alli shamunki***" (line 134). Though recognized as a "governor" by the Ecuadorian president, Juan's authority is challenged by his *Colono* patron in Tena who treats him like a lowly Indigenous peon. In order to reaffirm his official status and seek legal restitution, he makes the long trek to Quito, the seat of *Colono* power, on foot. The *caminata*, or trek, has a long history in the social memory of Amazonian Kichwas, who periodically make high-profile treks up the Andean capital for transformative acts of political protest (see Whitten 2003; Whitten & Whitten 2008). Stories like this one, though rarely documented in official histories or necessarily based entirely on historical "facts," are often retold by Tena Kichwas as evidence of their claim to an original stake in the founding of the city. In part of her recounting of Native Napo oral histories, Muratorio (1987: 6) quotes a Kichwa woman who retold her father's account with a similar final message: "My father told us: 'That's how we began the town [of Tena]. You are descendants of the founders. For this reason I do not have fear, neither of the priests nor or of any authority figure.' My father said that when he dies, that is what we should teach to our children" (see also Hidrovo Castellanos 2000: 24–5).

Tena Kichwa Indigeneity and Interdiscursivity

Such direct linkages between Martín's story and those of other Tena Kichwas are evidence of interdiscursive accounts of Indigenous identity and agency that circulate in a variety of contexts, from my metalinguistic interviews to private and public acts of ritual activism, to intercultural urban media. The objectified use of Kichwa language, idiomatic phrases such as "drinking *chicha* and speaking Kichwa" and "rescuing and revaluing" language and culture, traditional practices, such as **minka**s and the *caminata*, and material culture references to **shikra**s and **maitu**s become circulated again and again through intercultural forms of discourse as defining features of Napo Runa Indigeneity in a postcolonial world. The themes of Indigenous adaptation, agency, and connections to ancestral Amazonian territory have similarly become defining historical motifs that emerge throughout Indigenous discourse genres, from everyday reflections on culture change to carefully orchestrated public performances. Linguistically and ideologically plural, the ritual activist events like those described in this chapter have become a key genre in contemporary Tena Kichwa discourse, where historical identity has become politicized, and activism has become part of everyday life. These stories of the elders serve as important historical ground for tracing links with deep Indigenous history. The semiotic references of the grandparents become important source matter for emerging linguistic and material emblems of identity that are presented to interethnic and global audiences, as we will see in Chapter 5.

5

Intercultural Futures
Urban Media and the Predicaments of Translation

Just after dawn on a spring day in Tena in 2015, I tuned in to the Spanish-language news hour on *Ally TV*, Napo Province's public television station. A *Colono* (White) anchor named Lorenzo had just brought into the newsroom four Kichwa women to promote the forty-seventh anniversary celebration of Tena's *barrio* of Yutsullakta. The guests included three young contestants for the annual Native beauty pageant, ***Ñusta Yutsullakta Warmi*** (Miss Yutsullakta Princess), the signature event of the four-day festival honoring Yutsullakta's Indigenous heritage. The girls arrived in their formal pageant wear of ***pachas***—long, blue, sleeveless tunics reserved for ceremonial occasions, along with necklaces, headbands, and ornamental belts made from native plant fibers and seeds commonly worn by Native performers (see Figure 14). The beauty pageant contestants were accompanied by an older female, Patricia, a Yutsullakta resident, former beauty queen, and member of the planning committee, who was asked to go over the four-day schedule of events for the *fiestas de Yutsullakta*.

The festivities were to open on a Wednesday with a ***minka* de *confraternidad***—a cooperative community work project. Thursday's events would include an offering of traditional food (*comida típica*) in the morning, followed by a formal opening ceremony in the afternoon, and then ***Ñusta Yutsullakta Warmi***, the Native beauty pageant, in the evening. While going over Friday and Saturday's schedule, Lorenzo ("Lor," in the following text) began prompting Patricia ("Pat," in the following text) for detailed descriptions of the events on behalf of his urban viewers, many of whom might be unfamiliar with traditional Kichwa community culture.

136   Remaking Kichwa

Figure 14 Screenshot of Patricia, Native beauty pageant contestants and Lorenzo on Telediario news, Ally TV Channel 34, Napo Province public television, 2015.

Speech Sample 9. Interview with Yutsullakta representatives on *Ally TV*. (In this chapter, select Kichwa and Spanish words remain untranslated in the transcript. Translations can be found in the footnotes.)

```
 1  Pat:   On Friday we begin with the traditional games and the *chaski*,¹ that we, as a
 2         barrio, we want to rescue our values, what our grandparents practiced, and
 3         we don't want to lose these [practices-]
 4  Lor:                             [And what] does that consist of, more or less? Tell
 5         us, what is this *chaski*?
 6  Pat:   Um, the *chaski* is one of the games that will be played. We have a map
 7         already made, where they will play- There are three players, uh, on each
 8         team, there are five teams that will participate. And in the traditional games it
 9         is, uh, it's mostly about the traps. The trap- the *pankua*, as we call it, uh, the
10         peeling of *pata*s,² like our grandparents did. And these, there are
11         [other activities]
12  Lor:   [The *pata* is    ] a type of cocoa.
13  Pat:   Uh huh, the white cocoa that we all know. And on Friday, well, continuing
14         with the program, we have the indoor ((soccer)) championship, the finals. And
15         at night we have a bit of the, uh, the local art[ists, which is the night-  ]
16  Lor:                                                  [*Noche de confraternidad*]³
```

¹ A traditional Amazonian Kichwa game.
² White cocoa.
³ "Night of brotherhood."

17	Pat:	*Noche de confraternidad*, which is at 8:00pm. And on Saturday, which ends
18		our program, at 2:00am we have the **wayusa upina**.[4] We will begin in the
19		barrios, with the oldest who have been collaborating. Uh, then the
20		authorities, uh, at 9:00 we have the-
21	Lor:	There will be some kind of [formal sitting or procession?]
22	Pat:	[Yes, the formal sitting] at 9:00am with
23		the invited authorities and directors and residents of the community of
24		Yutsullakta. ((...)) At night we have the dance.

Once Patricia had finished going over the schedule, Lorenzo suggested they get to know the pageant contestants, who were asked to state their names and the organization they represented in the contest. He also asked questions about their personal lives, such as where they went to school, what they studied, and how they got on with family and friends in Yutsullakta. Throughout the interview segment, Lorenzo made a show of inserting basic words and phrases from his limited Kichwa, including "good morning," "what is your name?" and "thank you very much." He opened the interview portion by turning to the first contestant, Luz, and inviting her to speak into a hand-held microphone.

25	Lor:	Good morning, ladies, how are you? **Alli puncha nisha. Alli puncha.**[5]
26	Luz:	((takes microphone)) *Buenos días*. **Alli puncha.**
27	Vic	Do you know how to speak Kichwa?
28	Luz:	Yes.
29	Lor:	Yes? Are you sure? Let's see, send a greeting to our dear viewers. Invite them
30		to the festival in Kichwa. Say to them **alli puncha**, good morning, to all of our
31		friends. Give them a cordial invitation.
32	Luz:	**Alli puncha tukuy mashikunata. Ñuka shutimi kan** Luz Andy. ####
33		**munani tukuy Napu marka rimakunata shamychi nisha ñukanchi raimima-**
34	Lor:	**Ashka pagarachu**.[6] You weren't lying to me, were you? That was very good,
35		right? Very good. **Ima shuti kan**?[7]
36	Luz:	Luz Andy.
37	Lor:	Luz Andy. And whom do you represent in the barrio?
38	Luz:	Barrio Yutsullakta.
39	Lor:	Barrio Yutsullakta, right? Very well. Who supports your candidacy there?

[4] Drinking of *wayusa*, a stimulant tea made from the leaves of *Ilex wayusa*.
[5] "Good morning."
[6] "Good morning, friends. My name is Luz Andy. I would like to say to all of you to please come to our festival. Thank you very much."
[7] "What is your name?"

40	Luz:	My family.
41	Lor:	Your whole family?
42	Luz:	Yes.
43	Lor:	Yes, they'll be there with trumpets, [drums,]
44	Luz:	[Yes.]
45	Lor:	flutes, right? They're prepared because many participants are known for
46		being happy, right? Funny and fun.

((...))

47	Lor:	And where do you go to school?
48	Luz:	At Colegio Yutsullakta
49	Lor:	Okay. And what do you do there?
50	Luz:	((shrugs and shakes head))
51	Lor:	Right? You have to study, right? Have you taken your university exams?
52	Luz:	I don't have the ####
53	Lor:	Yeah, okay. Here we go, with lots of enthusiasm, send an invitation to all local
54		people to participate in the festival.
55	Luz:	((In Spanish:)) I want to make a big invitation to all of the residents of Napo
56		Province, to our festival, which will happen on Thursday, Friday, and Saturday.
57		We will be waiting for you. Thank you very [much]
58	Lor:	[Thank] you very much. **Ashka**
59		**pagarachu**.[8]

During his interview with the second contestant, Vicki ("Vic," in the following text), Lorenzo made an abrupt segue from the beauty pageant to a leading question about urban development in Yutsullakta. After establishing that she was born and raised in the *barrio*, he asked Vicki if she thought Yutsullakta had changed.

60	Lor:	It has been growing. How has it changed? Has it been changing or has it not
61		been changing?
62	Vic:	Yes, it has changed a lot, our *barrio*. Yes, it's very beautiful.
63	Lor:	Very beautiful. I remember when it was much smaller. There was a *cancha*
64		*abierta*,[9] there was no *cancha cubierta*,[10] there was so much dust, the streets
65		were horrible. But now there is a *cancha cubierta*, right?

Sensing Vicki's hesitation to voice anything other than agreement, Lorenzo didn't wait for an answer. Instead, he awkwardly redirected, saying, "Invite the people to come and participate," which she did, in Spanish.

---

[8] "Thank you very much."
[9] An open-air ball court.
[10] A covered ball court with a roof.

During his conversation with the third contestant, Natali ("Nat," in the following text), Lorenzo quizzed her on the Kichwa names for elements of her outfit, some of which he seemed to already know, and then ended by asking about her relationship status.

66	Lor:	What is the name of the outfit you have on?
67	Nat:	Its called a **pacha**.
68	Lor:	Oh, it's a **pacha**. And it is decorated with?
69	Nat:	With native seeds from this area.
70	Lor:	Aha, San Pedro seeds-
71	Nat:	Uh huh.
72	Lor:	And we see a blouse also. ((Pointing to a bracelet)) What is this called?
73	Nat:	I think ###.
74	Lor:	**Maniya de muyu**,[11] they say.
75	Nat:	Uh huh, yeah.
76	Lor:	Oh, perfect. And those beautiful necklaces. Send out an invitation to
77		everyone to participate, to come to the festival.
78	Nat:	((In Spanish:)) I invite all of the residents of Napo Province to the festival of
79		our barrio which celebrates its 47th anniversary. Come, participate, and be
80		together with us. Thank you very much.
81	Lor:	Very nice! I thought she was just smiles, but instead she spoke very well,
82		right?
83	All:	((laughter))
84	Lor:	You have always been smiley, right? Always? Very nice. And do you have a
85		boyfriend?
86	Nat:	No.
87	Lor:	No? Are you sure? Oh, of course, Mom and Dad are watching.

Following this, Lorenzo wrapped up the segment by wishing the girls good luck in the beauty pageant and telling his audience that there would be a short break, followed by more news.

Revitalization Media and their Paradoxes

While this television interview hardly qualifies as an example of a "Native text" like some of those featured in previous chapters, it does foreground marked

---

[11] Literally "seed bracelet."

elements of Indigeneity, such as Kichwa language, material culture, and discursive content. It would also be imprecise to call this "Indigenous media," given that a Spanish-speaking, *Colono* host directs the interview and much of the spoken content. Performances of Indigeneity like this one, widespread on the airwaves in multicultural cities like Tena, form part of a larger corpus of what I term "intercultural media"—programming designed to boost the presence of minority cultures in the public domain, serving a similar role to folklore and folklife festivals in other countries. Intercultural media, like the television appearance above, are usually co-produced by members of minority communities and agents of the state, private organizations, and mainstream media. Forms of intercultural media like these are by definition pluralistic in that they are the product of coexisting visions of agents from disparate communities, who exhibit different material signs of identity, sets of values, forms of communication, and interpretive frameworks.

Indigenous revitalization activists have long recognized the power of broadcast media like television in projecting images of cultural legitimacy and linguistic prestige. Crystal (2000) puts access to communications media at the top of his influential list of prescriptions for successful language revitalization by an endangered community. However vital, mediation is also inevitably constraining for Indigenous agents, whose work, as Ginsburg (1994) affirms, is "a product of relations with governing bodies that are responsible for dire political circumstances" that motivated the use of new communication forms as a means of "cultural intervention" (366). Gaining media presence usually involves collaboration between minority peoples and other more politically and economically empowered agents of dominant culture. Thus, the intercultural media picture of Indigeneity is inherently contradictory, as Indigenous forms of self-expression become reliant on non-Indigenous agents and venues for their dissemination, the same agents and venues that have long histories of marginalizing Indigenous cultures.

Moreover, once this kind of mediation happens, it fundamentally changes the picture of the culture being represented. Achieving media presence for endangered practices, even in a highly supportive political environment like contemporary Ecuador, usually requires "enhancing" cultural activities and "consolidating" usage of a minority languages in order to make these practices appear significant, to grab the attention of media makers and their audiences (Crystal 2000). In so doing, Crystal reminds us, "decisions need to be made about which social activities to concentrate on: after all, people cannot revitalize everything at once" (131). In intercultural media, such decisions are made collaboratively by Indigenous representatives and non-Indigenous media producers, whose power relationship is asymmetrical. The features of language and culture that get revitalized through mainstream media tend to be the ones that appeal to mainstream audiences, ones they recognize and understand.

Communication is therefore also a collaborative process in intercultural media, where elements of Indigenous language and culture become subject to the simplifying and sometimes misleading processes of translation. All translation, as Hanks and Severi (2014) argue, can only ever be an act of "controlled equivocation" (see also Viveiros de Castro 2004), where accurate transfer between linguistic and cultural worlds is exceedingly difficult, if not impossible. Simply glossing between languages, they point out, requires constant selections, whereby features from an original utterance in an object language (like Kichwa) are omitted and features from a translating language (like Spanish) are added. Translating between languages like Kichwa and Spanish, as Uzendoski and Calapucha-Tapuy (2012) have demonstrated, involves incommensurate cultural categories and moving between language systems that are connected to "different philosophies of being in the world" (12). Even when single words are at stake, truly accurate translation requires what Manheim (2015) calls *analytic transduction*, a fully ethnographic account of the meanings of words, including a context-by-context explanation of their uses, indexical relationships, and semantic and philosophical complexities. And yet, even when such careful, contextualized interpretation is possible, as Gal (2015) argues, the process inevitably produces power differentials between different "knowledge practices" in contact (227).

Effective translation in intercultural media discourse depends on (1) the expressive abilities of self-appointed Indigenous spokespersons, (2) the interpretive abilities of likely uninitiated non-Indigenous hosts, and (3) the contrasting interests and interpretations of mainstream audience members. While analytic transduction (essentially, an ethnographic lecture) is usually dispreferred in nonacademic contexts, the intercultural media sphere is especially hostile to properly contextualized translations. In these media, translations of Kichwa words must be done quickly and sometimes without preparation by performers, in language that is approachable to uninitiated audiences, and in spectacles that are designed to be entertaining. Indigenous intercultural performers, who tend to be bilingual, try to mitigate the problems of translation by presenting Kichwa in small chunks, sometimes even introducing only a few isolatable words at a time, and often by foregrounding concrete and easily translatable nouns associated with material culture and a rainforest ecology. Furthermore, the intercultural code of performers tends to include elements of Unified Kichwa, which is more semantically and contextually equivalent with Spanish (cf. Limerick n.d., Manheim 2015) than the colloquial Tena Kichwa spoken by most local people.

The structure and style of intercultural media thus exert pressures on performers to avoid analytic transduction and adopt a strategy of what Manheim (2015) calls *appropriative transduction*. This is the process by which a language and culture become wholly recontextualized in another host language in an "alien configuration," where their appearance is presented as an "exotic semiotic turn." Language and culture are repurposed to serve the cultural and political interests of the representing "other." Even when signs of Kichwa-ness appear in intercultural media as untranslated material, they always occupy a subordinate position as exotic markers of Indigeneity. And, when translation does happen, Kichwa always occupies the role of the translated language, while Spanish is used as a language of translation, as is often the case for dominant and subordinated languages (Asad 1986).

In this chapter, I will show how Tena Kichwas creatively use intercultural media to adapt urban modernity to their own visions, co-creating pluralistic displays of language and culture and remaking urban Tena as Indigenous space. I also show how the main instrument of this Indigenous remaking, the intercultural translation process, is a potentially hazardous one. Performances of Indigeneity, like the aforementioned TV interview, allow Indigenous agents to call attention to endangered ancestral practices and potentially "rescue" them. Patricia and the beauty pageant contestants have a chance to show a broad audience that Indigenous culture is still alive in their urban *barrio*, where it can be experienced and celebrated by all local people. In so doing, Kichwas can use media like these to contest their own historical erasure, decolonize media, and possibly even secure new allies in their struggle for culture preservation. But, because these media occur in a dominant, historically non-Indigenous space of interaction, Indigenous media makers may end up inadvertently furthering their own discursive domination. Translators must accommodate to mainstream audiences' expectations about what Indigenous language and culture are supposed to look like. Foreign words and practices must be effectively explained in non-Indigenous terms. For these reasons, intercultural translation tends to promote enhanced versions of Indigeneity. It also privileges non-Indigenous ideologies of translation as a process based on *equivalency*, or a presumed correlation between signs from distinct semiotic systems and an egalitarian relationship between representative speakers (cf. Hanks 2010). Intercultural media thereby masks an uneven process of exchange that tends to reproduce simplified and romanticized versions of Amazonian Kichwa Indigeneity.

Intercultural Media

Intercultural media in Tena is both an innovative product of the multiculturalist era and a new iteration of decades-long trend in which Native Latin Americans have been "erupting onto the airwaves" after a long history of postcolonial invisibility (Castells-Tallens et al. 2009; see also Hartley 2004; Ramos Rodriguez 2005; Schiwy 2008). Indigenous Latin Americans have become adept at appropriating radio, video, and digital media in order to enact what Salazar (2009) calls a "reverse conquest," by reclaiming rights to self-representation and fostering community mobilization. This often involves taking advantage of new opportunities in state subsidization and legislation that make media access technologically and economically possible (Castells-Talens et al. 2009; Riggins 1992), thereby allowing Indigenous community members to become "critical" producers of content (Salazar 2009).

Kichwa-language radio in Napo Province has served the dual purposes of strengthening cohesion among separated Indigenous communities while transforming a dominant, Spanish-speaking "symbolic order" (cf. Ramos Rodriguez 2005) since the 1970s. The most popular Kichwa-language programming is the 3 a.m.–6 a.m. music slot when Kichwas throughout Napo engage in ***wayusa upina***, a time for drinking of ***wayusa*** tea, when women weave and families prepare for the day's horticultural work before the equatorial sun is high overhead. Music played during this time tends to be from the widely popular contemporary Kichwa pop genre called **Runa Paju**, Kichwa for "Indigenous Magic," in which, according to Uzendoski and Calapucha-Tapuy (2012), musicians tie together modern electronic instruments with traditional music, poetics, dance, and references to Amazonian ecology, creating a shared social connectedness to an ancient cultural and cosmological world. Meanwhile, radio DJs and their guests speak exclusively in Tena Kichwa dialect, with its frequent code-switching and codemixing with Spanish. Ennis (2019) documents recently introduced **wayusa upina** community radio programming in Napo aimed at cultural revival, remembering, and the use of dialect, or what her informants refer to as "our own language." Kichwa-language radio has thus long been a channel for language and culture maintenance that challenges both Spanish-language-dominated media and prescriptivist Kichwa-language planners' control over public discourse (cf. Urla 1995).

Other forms of intercultural media in Tena, such as Kichwa-language TV news, televised Native beauty pageants (Wroblewski 2014), scholastic oratory contests (Wroblewski 2019b), bilingual public signage (Wroblewski 2019a), traditional music and dance shows, and intercultural exhibitions like the TV interview in Speech Sample 9, tend to include politically oriented, self-conscious performances of revitalized culture. In these venues, media producers embrace hybridity, mixing Tena Kichwa dialect with Unified Kichwa, prescriptive and anti-prescriptive practices. Unlike monolingual Kichwa radio, these intercultural media are designed to appeal to multiethnic and Spanish-speaking audiences. They typically include self-reflective forms of commentary on the language and culture being displayed and bilingual translations.

As a case in point, in televised Native beauty pageants, Kichwa girls perform pluralistic roles as guardians of traditional gendered practices, custodians of the environment, and cosmopolitan speakers of Unified Kichwa. Like the girls in the TV interview, pageant contestants frequently make a show of speaking in Kichwa, sometimes without translations, dancing to traditional music in **pachas** and other Native clothing, and enacting pluralistic gender roles as modern Kichwa females who keep alive protected ancestral traditions. Meanwhile, emcees describe their performances through commentary in both Kichwa and Spanish.

Pluralism reaches its fullest expression during the *traje típico*, or traditional dress, portion of the pageants, in which contestants don vibrant costumes and handcrafted tiaras adorned with native seeds, fibers, and rainforest motifs (see Figure 15), and play-act "demonstrations" of conventional Kichwa female duties

Figure 15 A tiara for a Native beauty pageant designed by a Kichwa artisan in Tena.

while dancing to traditional music. In the 2015 ***Ñusta Yutsullakta Warmi*** pageant that followed the ***Ally*** *TV* interview in Speech Sample 9, Luz, one of the interviewees, used the *traje típico* presentation to demonstrate her horticultural skills—cutting plantains from a vine with a machete and pulling yuca roots out of a box of potted earth on stage. The emcee read aloud a Spanish-language message Luz had prepared prior to the presentation, in which she urged Kichwa youth to "not abandon ancestral traditions and continue enforcing our cultural identity." Meanwhile, Luz danced across the stage holding a dollar bill (Ecuador's official currency is the US dollar), showing that she was both a sustainable harvester and a self-sufficient wage earner. During her subsequent demonstration, Natali, another ***Ally*** *TV* interviewee, wove a ***shikra*** from plant fibers, traditionally Kichwa women's work, while the emcee read her preprepared invitation to "dear

Figure 16 Vicki demonstrates proper sorting of waste during her performance, the *Ñusta Yutsullakta Warmi* pageant.

tourists to visit our *cantón*." Vicki, the last of the three **Ally** *TV* interviewees, offered an especially innovative display of pluralism. She entered the stage in the orange uniform of a sanitation worker, with coveralls, rubber boots, and a yellow hardhat, and play-acted teaching a costumed Kichwa girl how to properly sort waste and recyclables into their appropriate disposal bins (see Figure 16).

Then, in an especially theatrical move, she removed her orange coveralls to reveal her *traje típico* underneath. A female assistant in a faux animal skin dress helped her slip on her tiara, and Vicki danced around the recycle bins while

Figures 17a and b Vicki reveals her *traje típico*.

the emcee listed the Kichwa names for native seeds adorning her costume, which, he noted, had been "offered by **Pachamama**" ("Earth Mother") (see Figures 17a and b). Vicki's was a masterful demonstration of pluralism, in which she played with her dual image as an educated Mother Earth figure, changing between costumes of two versions environmental stewardship—the first one literal and the second one implied.

Native beauty pageants have become widely popular among Kichwas and *Colonos* for these vibrant shows of intercultural Indigeneity, often

Figures 17a and b (Continued)

drawing large crowds that pack urban coliseums and also reaching a broad viewership via live local television. In these and other intercultural spectacles, performers combine traditional verbal art and global political rhetoric, traditional material culture and modern technologies, dialect and Unified Kichwa, and references to an idealized past in order to promote a utopian future of multiculturalism and social justice. Following a formula used by performers of Indigeneity throughout Latin America (e.g., Conklin

1997; Graham 2002, 2005; Graham & Penny 2014; Shackt 2005), Kichwa media makers package language and culture in recontextualized and enhanced forms. Signs of Indigeneity are strategically consolidated and ethnic homogeneity is projected for political effect (cf. Graham 2014). In so doing, they reinsert Napo Runa culture into a twenty-first-century urban media ecology and temporarily re-indigenize historically "non-Indigenous" urban space.

The Indigenous Interview and Discourses of Revitalization

The interview on *Ally TV* that preceded the Yutsullakta beauty pageant followed another formula I have seen repeatedly in Tena's intercultural media. Indigenous community representatives appear on Spanish-language radio and TV, usually in full ceremonial costume, and invite multiethnic audiences to visit and *"convivir"* ("co-live") with them as celebrants in multiday festivals. The marketing scheme usually includes instructional content, as Kichwa guests speak in untranslated Kichwa utterances and explain the meanings of preselected words and phrases for inquisitive *Colono* hosts. Like other intercultural media genres, the Indigenous interview is self-consciously pluralistic in terms of languages, discourses, material cultures, and philosophies. The interview genre is unique, though, in that it foregrounds collaborative translation by Indigenous representatives and *Colono* media hosts, who direct translation and act as proxies for mainstream, non-Indigenous audiences.

Throughout the encounter, Kichwa guests and *Colono* hosts use strategies of interdiscursivity to present colorful features of Indigenous identity and culture. They tend to use easily recognizable tokens of an Amazonian type, enregistered signs that I have pointed out in previous chapters, such as Kichwa words and cosmology (e.g., **Pachamama**), material culture (e.g., **shikra** bags and **wayusa** tea), revitalizationist phrases (e.g., "rescuing and revaluing" "ancient culture"), discourse topics and themes (e.g., "culture loss," Amazonian stewardship), and so on. The Indigenous interview in Speech Sample 9 incorporates many untranslated Kichwa words and familiar discourses surrounding cultural nostalgia, urban development, revitalization, and Amazonian environmentalism. It also appropriates rhetorical conventions from other genres of Kichwa oratory, such as the speaking portions of Native beauty pageants, in which contestants introduce themselves and address audiences in memorized Kichwa and Spanish speeches.

Patricia's sudden blurting in the beginning of Speech Sample 9, in lines 1–2, that "we, as a *barrio*, we want to rescue our values, what our grandparents practiced" in the middle of reading a schedule of events for a festival makes sense, given the interdiscursive patterns of this genre. Her language here echoes Ecuadorian constitutional policy of "respecting and stimulating conservation and use" of minority cultural practices, Kichwa-language activists' expressed goal of "rescuing" language and culture, and everyday Tena Kichwas' discourses of nostalgia for the idealized times of the "grandparents." The Yutsullakta anniversary celebration is especially symbolic of these themes, as it exemplifies the effects of urbanization on formerly rural forest communities. Once a rural Kichwa community is overtaken by urban sprawl, it becomes recast in legal and cultural terms as a *barrio*, which implies a loss of community autonomy over economic development and culture change. Kichwa community residents often express conflicted attitudes toward urbanization of this kind, welcoming certain signs of economic progress while denouncing the inevitable loss of traditional control.

Many members of urbanizing communities, like Patricia, bemoan urban absorption and the resulting loss of Kichwa community values. Many of my interviews on the topic of development included dramatic accounts of suddenly out-of-control ecological and cultural transformation. Gloria, a 38-year-old resident of Yutsullakta, wistfully recalled, "There used to be a river, the Yutsullakta river," and a bridge over it that "separated *indígenas* from the **Mishus**," the Kichwa word for *Colonos*. "On the Indigenous side," she recounted,

> It was pu::re vegetation ... there were no streets here. We used to go fishing ... And, some ten years later, they diverted the river far away. They made a culvert so that the street could pass through as if there had never been a river here ... Now there are buses, there is a *cancha cubierta*, the **Mishus** are mixed in, **Mishus** here- an Indigenous person here and a **Mishu** there, like that...Before there were trees, where ((children)) could play and hide, they could plant seeds, play games that a child of a community plays. But now the children only play soccer, people go by car, and early in the morning people are already drinking, since there are bars everywhere. But before, when it was a community, there was none of that.

"Even so," Gloria declared proudly in words that echo Patricia's in the interview,

> we continue speaking Kichwa. Despite this, every May we have a festival in Yutsullakta ... when we always have the election of the Kichwa beauty queen.

Yutsullakta is unique among Tena's *barrios* in that it still retains many of the properties of its former **ayllullakta** ("community"). Its population is predominantly Kichwa, it has a bilingual-intercultural school, and it has an annual folkloric festival. Patricia's comments about "rescuing" values "as a *barrio*" in this early part of the interview thus draws on interdiscursive discussions among Tena Kichwas about such communities-in-flux, where urban acculturation may still be kept in check. Lorenzo's, the *Colono* host's, related question to Vicki later in the interview, in lines 59–64, about how Yutsullakta has changed, draws on contrasting *Colono* discourses of urbanization as wholesale economic progress. Lorenzo notes that Yutsullakta has objectively improved, judging by the fact that it used to have only a *cancha abierta*, an open ball court typical of rural Napo forest communities and now it has a *cancha cubierta*, a ball court with a surrounding concrete enclosure, more typical of urban *barrios*. The reader will likely recall that the *cancha cubierta* also featured in Luis and Marta's story of the development of Lumullakta in Chapter 4. What's more, Lorenzo argued, the "horrible" streets have been paved and there is no more "dust," an icon of underdevelopment that Napo residents frequently contrast with "pavement" in conversations about urbanization.

Yutsullakta's showcasing of Kichwa heritage in its annual festival, in the **minka** *de confraternidad*, the offering of traditional food, the **chaski** and **pankua** games ("like children used to play"), the peeling of **patas** (white cocoa pods), and the **wayusa upina** (*wayusa* drinking time) that Patricia mentions in lines 6–19, harkens back to its days as a bona fide forest community. The festival, with its consolidated use of Kichwa language and traditional practices, continues in Yutsullakta as an act of defiance against urbanization and acculturation. The festival is now a key venue for showing off a revitalized Indigeneity that is designed to boost cultural pride among Kichwa youth as much as entertain non-Indigenous visitors. And the target audience appears to be responding positively. In my conversations with young Tena Kichwas I saw that they were easily animated by the topic of community festivals and beamed with optimism about the future of culture preservation. In one such

Spanish-language conversation, Carmen ("Carm") and Juan ("Juan"), two young Kichwa urbanites, rattled off a list of heritage practices that they go to community festivals to see on display.

Speech Sample 10. Recorded interview with Tena Kichwa youth

Carm:	I love it, for example, when they do the, uh, the, the **takinapuncha**[12] and all that. I mean, it's all in Kichwa and that they si[ing in Kichwa, dance-]
Juan:	[And it's the old tradition] that they practice.
Carm:	Dances in Kichwa, uh, everything in Kichwa. So it's very, very pleasing to be [there.]
Juan:	[Interesting.]
Carm:	Uh huh. Yeah, I have gone to those places and it's beautiful. For example, they have competitions of-
Juan:	Games of, of catching the **watusa**,[13] they play like, drink **wayusas**-[14]
Carm:	They drink **wayusa**, chicha de chonta,[15] uh, the typical foods, **chuntakuru**,[16] things like that ... it's great because it shows how, I mean, how one lives in-
Juan:	Communities.
Carm:	The communities. Mhm. How a **shikra**[17] is made, how they take, how a canoe is made, how **wayusa** is drunk, how they, they, how a **maitu**[18] is made of-
Juan:	**Karachama**.[19]
Carm:	of **karachama**, of **chuntakuru** and all that, and I eat them. And, and yeah, it's really interesting. I like it because we do that in our communities ... ((I hope)) we don't lose that because it's, it's beautiful, it's a very beautiful tradition.

Carmen and Juan's descriptions of community festivals perfectly parallel Patricia's in lines 1–24 of the TV interview. Again, we see speakers invoking untranslated Kichwa names for traditional practices and elements of forest ecology, re-enregistering these iconic elements of culture as important ones to save, the ones "we don't want to lose."

In a similar example from a bilingual speech at a widely publicized and well-attended interprovincial Amazonian folkloric dance competition in Tena in 2008, a member of the dance group **Inti Wayra** ("Wind of the Sun")

---

[12] Shaman's song.
[13] Agouti, a species of rodent of the genus *Dasyprocta*.
[14] A stimulant tea made from the leaves of *Ilex wayusa*.
[15] Beer made from the fruit of the *chonta* tree, also known as peach palm (*Bactris gasipaes*).
[16] Beetle larvae that feed on *chonta*.
[17] A woven handbag.
[18] A leaf-wrapped dish roasted over an open fire.
[19] Small species of Amazonian catfish.

described her group's performance of a dance titled "The Harvest" as an act of cultural preservation.

Speech Sample 11. Speech made by Kichwa performer during folkloric Amazonian dance competition in Tena

> *Alli chishi tukuy cantón mashikuna, rukuyayakuna, mamakuna, maltakuna. Ñukanchi shamushkanchi kaywan purishpa, Inti Wayra Rukullaktamanta. Kangunata kay chishipi gustanchinka ushkanchi, imasna, ñukanchi, ñawpa watamanta kuna uraspis, imasna ñukanchi chunta, chunta wañuka apayasha, aswata ranchi, upinchi ñukanchi, kaykunaman, chasna ñari imasna ñukanchi karikuna sachama paykuna lanzawa, ima tunus runakunata pishkukunata apinkak rinun, mikunkak wasima, mikunacha rinkak.*
> *Muy buenas tardes público presente. En esta tarde el grupo de danza **Inti Wayra** se presenta, con una danza titulada La Cosecha, en donde, representaremos que desde generación a generación, nuestra- las comunidades Kichwa cosechan lo que es la chonta, su elaboración a los esposos y familiares de la casa, y como nuestros maridos salen a la casería con sus lanzas, a ver animales, la **watusa**, el armadillo, y entre otros, y igual a las aves. Entonces, esta es una representación de nuestra danza autóctona como nosotros vivimos actualmente. Muchas gracias.*

((Kichwa:)) Good afternoon friends, grandfathers, grandmothers and youth of the *cantón*. We, **Inti Wayra** have come here from Rukullakta. We would like to demonstrate for you this afternoon our, as in the past as much as now, our ***chunta***[20] harvest, how we make and drink ***aswa***[21] and other things, like how our husbands still go to the forest with *lanzas*,[22] just like how we go to hunt birds to eat in the home, to look for food. ((Spanish:)) Good afternoon to those present. This afternoon the dance group Inti Wayra presents, with a dance entitled The Harvest, in which we will represent that, from generation to generation, our- the Kichwa communities harvest that which is the *chonta*,[23] its production, the married couples and relatives of the house, and how our husbands go hunting with their *lanzas*, to see animals, the ***watusa***,[24] the armadillo, among others, as well as the birds. Thus, this is a representation in our Native dance of how we presently live. Thank you very much.

This young female speaker frames the Indigenous symbols on display in the subsequent dance (see Figure 18) via material culture, music, and movement, as continuous with the ways Amazonian Kichwas "still" and "presently" live.

---

[20] Fruit of the *Chonta* tree, also known as peach palm (*Bactris gasipaes*).
[21] Aka *chicha*, or beer made from *yuca*, aka cassava root (*Manihot esculenta*).
[22] spears.
[23] Spanish pronunciation of *chunta*.
[24] Agouti, a species of rodent of the genus *Dasyprocta*.

Figure 18 Dance group *Inti Wayra* performs "The Harvest."

"The Harvest" is thus meant to present a picture of culture that challenges dominant historical narratives of acculturation and loss.

In this case, the speaker offers a self-reflective Kichwa-language description, complete with a nearly direct translation to Spanish, much like a bilingual emcee does at a Native beauty pageant. She incorporates both abstract references to rural Indigenous cultural practices often invoked in intercultural media—the forest, harvesting, hunting, etc.—and makes sure to include a list of specific Kichwa and Spanish nouns associated with them— spears (*lanzas* in Kichwa, borrowed from Spanish), birds (**pishkukuna** in Kichwa), armadillos, etc. Several of these same nouns were also mentioned by Patricia, Carmen, and Juan in the aforementioned speech samples—for example, *chicha* (**aswa** in Kichwa), *chonta* palm fruit (**chunta** in Kichwa), and **watusa**. Concrete nouns like these appear repeatedly in intercultural performance as hyper-salient linguistic markers of Indigeneity that have specific and easily translatable literal meanings. Like the other speakers quoted earlier, the dance performer selectively references these cultural and linguistic objects as showpieces of a threatened way of life that "we presently live," that the others asserted "we don't want to lose." And the show is packaged following an interdiscursive pattern in which hyper-salient Kichwa words circulate among the other enhanced and consolidated chunks of revitalized Indigenous identity. The lexicon of the forest has become an especially powerful semiotic resource for asserting Amazonian Kichwa identity in Tena, as its use in discourse at once references endangered ancestral land, knowledge, values, language, and an Amazonian steward image that multiethnic audiences instantly recognize.

Lexicalization, Translation, and Representation

It is this *lexicalization*, or reduction of Kichwa language to recognizable and easily translatable words, that allows intercultural translation to run smoothly before a multiethnic audience. Even though a fully contextualized, anthropological description is necessary to convey the complex and profound contextual meanings of all of these circulating signs, revitalization and translation happen without it. Kichwa media makers must find practical ways of communicating an Indigenous perspective in forms that are not too intellectually cumbersome for mainstream audiences, all while also keeping them entertained. Often, this means relying on select, recycled types of words such as easily translatable concrete nouns. It also means recirculating discourse types, philosophical references, and material culture elements that index a version of Indigeneity that Indigenous and non-Indigenous audiences recognize.

When they appear in intercultural media, Kichwa words and practices must then be translated for mainstream, predominantly Spanish-speaking audiences. Sometimes this happens in a prepackaged way, as in the case of memorized bilingual speeches. In Native beauty pageants, Indigenous actors perform, narrators narrate in two languages, and audiences are left to do the rest of the interpretive work on their own. In these cases, the audience simply watches translation happen. In the Indigenous interview, the *Colono* host becomes a key player in intercultural translation as a designated non-Indigenous interpreter. While Indigenous spokespersons come with an understandable inclination toward analytic transduction, or fully contextualized explanations of Kichwa words and practices, *Colono* hosts are inclined to stifle them in the interest of time, intelligibility, and entertainment. Together, *Colono* hosts and Indigenous guests thus reproduce a dominant ideology of translation as a simple and egalitarian process that assumes a correspondence between Kichwa and Spanish words, masking a reality of cultural complexity, incommensurability, and structural inequality.

To illustrate this process in action, I will return to the 2015 **Ally** *TV* news interview in Speech Sample 9, and compare it with an almost identical televised Indigenous interview I recorded in 2009. The interaction transcribed in Speech Sample 12 occurred during a segment of the evening news on *Líder Visión*, Tena's main private television station. During this event, the host, a former provincial politician and news reporter named Dr. Vargas ("Dr. V" in the following text) welcomes President Tapuy ("Pres," in the following text), the appointed Kichwa head of the forest community of Pano to publicly invite audiences to its fortieth-anniversary celebration. As in the previous example in Speech Sample 9, President Tapuy arrives accompanied by four female contestants for **Pano Warmi**, or the "Miss Pano" Native beauty competition. This time the interview begins with Dr. Vargas, the host, reading over the schedule of events.

Speech Sample 12. Interview with *Pano* representatives on *Líder Visión*, Tena, May 2009

1 Dr. V: Okay, so, uh, the festivities began yesterday, yesterday, uh, today,
2   today they began, right? with a radio program. It says, later, it says, **minka** de
3   confraternidad,[25] and later, tomorrow, we have the **wayusa upina**[26] and
4   **kamachina**.[27] That, **kamachina** is, uh, what is **kamachina**?

Like the *fiestas de Yutsullakta*, the *fiestas de Pano* open with a **minka de confraternidad**. Neither Lorenzo, the **Ally** *TV* host, nor Dr. Vargas, the *Líder Visión* host, asks for a translation of **minka**. Most Spanish-speaking viewers in Napo, though likely unaware of the rich cultural history behind this practice, have most likely heard of or participated in a **minka** themselves, as this term has been appropriated to denote a conventionalized activity in which Kichwas and *Colonos* engage in obligatory, cooperative work projects aimed at making improvements to community, or in this case *barrio*, infrastructures. The **wayusa upina**, or **wayusa** tea time, mentioned by both Patricia (Speech Sample 9, line 18) and Dr. Vargas (Speech Sample 12, line 3), also needs no translation as it has similarly been appropriated by the intercultural media sphere.

---

[25] "**Minka** of brotherhood," a cooperative community work party.
[26] A ceremonial toasting of *wayusa*, a stimulant tea made from the leaves of *Ilex wayusa*.
[27] Literally "to advise/counsel"; also refers to a ceremonial counseling of Kichwa youth by elders.

But when *Colono* hosts come across unappropriated Kichwa words and phrases, they must rely on their Indigenous guests for translation. This is where we see the contentious process of translation at work, where Indigenous speakers are forced to attempt on the spot, contextualized explanations of words, while their hosts pressure them to find simple equivalences in Spanish. In line 4 of Speech Sample 12, Dr. Vargas comes across an unfamiliar word in the schedule of events: ***kamachina.*** He appeals to President Tapuy for translation help, much like when Lorenzo, the ***Ally*** *TV* host from Speech Sample 9, interrupts Patricia to as what ***chaski*** means in lines 4–5. In that earlier case, suddenly put on the spot by Lorenzo, a visibly uncomfortable Patricia, tries to quickly summarize the ***chaski*** game and understandably stumbles a bit, since the game requires a lengthy and contextualized explanation. Similarly, President Tapuy attempts to offer an improvised response to Dr. Vargas's question about ***kamachina***, and he gets cut off.

5	Pres:	Well, we have scheduled that, precisely today in the morning, the young lady
6		candidates will be having ***wayusa*** with different families, local authorities, in
7		addition, I think, they will be going to the city of Tena [in order to]
8	Dr. V:	[***Kamachina*** is the,] to
9		advise, [right? To counsel, right?]
10	Pres:	[***Kamachina*** is to counsel.] Specifically, they are going to arrive with
11		***chicha, wayusa***, and the people [will-]
12	Dr. V:	[And what,] what will be the advice? That
13		they don't abandon their ancestral customs-
14	Pres:	It's, that [is-]
15	Dr. V:	[That's what] it should be, right?
16	Pres:	Yes, that-
17	Dr. V:	That is the ***kamachina***. Because many young women no longer like
18		to-
19	Pres:	They no longer like to [drink ***wayusa***-]
20	Dr. V:	[Nor even to speak Kichwa-]
21	Pres:	Right, to drink ***chicha***, they no longer want to rise at [dawn-]
22	Dr. V:	[Of course.]
23	Pres:	Already the are getting up to-
24	Dr. V:	What? they say, in the *chonta* season, they say, What is that? they
25		say.
26	Pres:	Yes, right. So-
27	Dr. V	So that is the ***kamachina***.

28 Pres:	That is the **kama**[**china-**]	
29 Dr. V	[Conser]ve the ancestral [cust-]	
30 Pres:	[Uh huh]	
31 Dr. V	-toms. Very well.	

Like Lorenzo, Dr. Vargas apparently has some knowledge of Kichwa, and he is eager to flaunt it. He first cedes the floor to President Tapuy, but when he suddenly recalls the Spanish gloss for **kamachina**, which is *aconsejar* ("to advise/counsel"), he blurts it out in lines 8–9, interrupting President Tapuy's description. President Tapuy affirms the Spanish translation and tries to resume his explanation in lines 10–11. But Dr. Vargas interrupts him again, redirecting the topic away from what **kamachina** means, since he has already found an appropriate Spanish gloss, toward a discussion of what the *consejo* ("advice") will be. He then even anticipates President Tapuy's expected answer to his question, suggesting the advice of not "abandoning ancestral customs" in line 17 and invoking that familiar refrain that youth "no longer drink **chicha** or speak Kichwa."

Dr. Vargas continued to seize control of translation throughout the TV interview, repeatedly interrupting President Tapuy's responses and flaunting his knowledge of Kichwa words, idioms, and discourse topics. While President Tapuy, the invited cultural representative, tries unsuccessfully to elaborate on the meaning of Kichwa words, Dr. Vargas works to find quick, reductionistic glosses that have easy prior meanings for his Spanish-speaking audience. And, in a seeming affront to President Tapuy, Dr. Vargas takes every opportunity to display his own expertise on Kichwa language and culture, presenting himself as a knowledgeable intercultural interviewer.

Lorenzo does this too in his interview with the women from Yutzullakta in Speech Sample 9. He interrupts Patricia's discussion of the peeling of **pata**s, reminding the audience that **pata** is the Kichwa word for white cocoa, which, as Patricia admits, is a food that "we all know" (lines 12–13). He greets the pageant contestants first in Spanish, with "*buenos días*," and then in Kichwa with "**alli puncha**" (line 25). When Luz, his first interviewee, takes the microphone and returns his **alli puncha**, he asks her if she speaks Kichwa, then if she is *sure* she speaks Kichwa, and then to *prove* that she speaks Kichwa by inviting the audience to the festival, in Kichwa (lines 27–31). She obliges, and he acts surprised, lavishing her with exaggerated praise (lines 32–35). Having established her fluency, Lorenzo tries out more of his beginner-Kichwa phrases with her, asking her name, "***Ima shuti kan?***" (line 35) even though she just told him her name a moment ago. This testing of the girls' Kichwa linguistic and cultural fluency happens again in lines 65–74, when he asks Natali, the third interviewee, what her outfit is called. She tells him it is a ***pacha***, though he appears to already know this. When he asks for the Kichwa name for her bracelet, she whispers something inaudible, and he helps her out, letting the audience know that it is called a ***maniya de muyu***, a fiber bracelet with seeds.

Dr. Vargas engages President Tapuy in a similar game. At one point in the interview, President Tapuy lists the various beauty pageants that take place in Pano parish, ***Pano Warmi*** among them, and tries to provide contextualized explanations of their Kichwa monikers. Dr. Vargas continues to interrupt him, submitting Spanish glosses as his own interpretations of their meanings.

32	Dr. V:	Let's see, ***Pano Warmi***.
33	Pres:	***Pano Warmi***.
34	Dr. V:	The first, right?
35	Pres:	The first.
36	Dr. V:	Okay, uh, later?
37	Pres:	***Purutu Warmi***.
38	Dr. V:	***Purutu Warmi*** is [the::]
39	Pres:	[***Purutu***] the, the, the bean.
40	Dr. V:	In other words, relating to [one of the-]
41	Pres:	[One of, uh, yes, yes-]
42	Dr. V:	-products.
43	Pres:	Uh huh.
44	Dr. V:	Okay, [important foods]
45	Pres:	[Because the women of Pano,] the women of Pano are accustomed to
46		planting, specifically in this month, they are planting-
47	Dr. V:	But everyone eats them, right?
48	Pres:	Yes.
49	Dr. V:	[Not only the-]
50	Pres:	[Everyone eats them]
51	Dr. V:	-women. ***Purutu Warmi***. Then comes-
52	Pres:	And then comes ***Chikta Warmi***. ***Chikta Warmi*** means, because not,
53		the custom of Pano, men as much as women, we are accustomed to,
54		including now, making the ***chikta***, uh, along the Pano river, in its
55		tributaries.

Hearing President Tapuy's reference to ***chikta***, a traditional fish-trapping technique, Dr. Vargas interrupts President Tapuy, and takes the opportunity to show off his knowledge of Kichwa names for local native species of river fish.

56	Dr. V:	Ah, to catch **karachamas**. What else is there?
57	Pres:	Uh, ***siklli***, most impor[tantly]
58	Dr. V:	[***Siklli***] is, [***siklli*** is-]
59	Pres:	[The largest]
60	Dr. V:	And what else is there? What other fish are there?
61	Pres:	There is another, uh, ***lupi***.
62	Dr. V:	***Lupi***.
63	Pres:	It's like the *barbudo*.
64	Dr. V:	Yes, the large *barbudo*, okay. Uh, other, other fish, what is there?
65	Pres:	Another is the-
66	Dr. V:	***HANDYA***, there are no more ***handya***, right?
67	Pres:	There are no more ***handya***.
68	Dr. V:	[They are gone?]
69	Pres:	[***Chinlus***,] *chinlus*, which is a small fish like a sardine.
70	Dr. V:	***Chiglus***.
71	Pres:	***Chinlus***.
72	Dr. V:	But that one is very small [still, right?]
73	Pres:	[Yes, small.] But th- [that-]
74	Dr. V:	[I] think that, I think that
75		many have disappeared-
76	Pres:	Yes.
77	Dr. V:	-many fish, right? The idea will also be, uh, to try to cultivate these
78		customs [of-]
79	Pres:	[Yes.]
80	Dr. V:	-that they are preserved.
81	Pres:	Uh huh.
82	Dr. V:	They are preserved.
83	Pres:	That's right.
84	Dr. V:	Or to repopulate, perhaps, the waters of the Pano River.

Using this discussion of fish as a springboard, Dr. Vargas then launches into a soliloquy about river contamination and species eradication in Napo. At the end of it, he pauses briefly to ask President Tapuy's advice, as the implied Amazonian steward, on how to better safeguard the aquatic environment. Suddenly put on the spot, and probably realizing the futility of trying to compose a well-developed position, President Tapuy lets Dr. Vargas offer his own suggestions.

In both of these interviews, we see translation happening via the collaborative work of a *Colono* director and Indigenous guests, in which the communication of content and meaning are largely controlled by the former. Though Lorenzo and Dr. Vargas's tactics may seem overbearing and impolite, they are formulaic for intercultural media in Tena, where quick, decontextualized translations are encouraged. Moreover, Dr. Vargas works to align himself, via an interdiscursive chain also exploited by Lorenzo, as an intercultural interviewer who is knowledgeable of Kichwa language, culture, and social issues, and who supports culture preservation, by invoking the styles and discourses of prior intercultural media performers.

Colono knowledge of Kichwa language and culture, even when it is obviously limited and superficial as in the above interviews, is often portrayed as a positive sign that non-Kichwas are taking an interest in intercultural learning. Kichwa spokespersons are expected to be fully bicultural and bilingual culture brokers. While presumably fluent in the lifeways of dominant culture, they must remain competent in their own heritage practices, even able to explain them on the spot in non-Indigenous terms. Meanwhile, only minimal recognition of Kichwa language and culture by *Colonos* is seen as a win for threatened Indigenous practices. This imbalance is continuously normalized through intercultural media, where the positive value of simply granting recognition to the presence of an Indigenous perspective tends to supersede the usually autocratic, ethnocentric, and reductionistic means by which this perspective is translated.

Intercultural Media and the Future of Revitalization

Through intercultural media, Kichwa performers are busy working to upend social inequality by challenging their own cultural marginalization. In so doing, they capitalize on the positive value of their native language and material signs of Indigeneity, thus appealing to romanticizing outsiders, as Graham (2002) has shown, as representing the "true" voice of the rainforest. What's more, Kichwa media spokespersons tend to be bilingual and can therefore potentially control the accurate translations of their messages to non-Indigenous, Spanish-speaking audiences. Taking advantage of the current climate of multiculturalism in Ecuador and Latin America and building on the legacy of DIPEIB-N, Kichwa activists see real potential to occupy mainstream media as channels for Indigenous empowerment.

Like members of revitalization movements elsewhere, however, Tena Kichwas must work within the constraints of a mainstream media sphere. They are forced to employ the contradictory logics and tactics of "cultural intervention" (Ginsburg 1994), whereby language and culture are strategically enhanced, consolidated, and co-translated by non-Indigenous agents who filter Indigenous language and culture through the interpretive lenses and interests of the romanticizing outsiders they serve. In other words, Kichwas are achieving "existential recognition" (Graham 2005), but it is an appropriated picture of existence, and recognition comes at a cost. Not only are Kichwas changing the picture of culture through its mediation, they also sometimes inadvertently reproduce their own semiotic domination. Through their participation in seemingly equivalent and egalitarian processes of intercultural translation, they mask enduring structural inequalities.

But, given a long history of erasure, this strategy may be the best available option. While educational settings may offer more suitable spaces for systematic revitalization and profound intercultural learning (ideally at least, if not in actual practice—see Limerick n.d.; Uzendoski 2009), Indigenous activists recognize the importance of popular media and urban stages in fostering public respect and self-pride for endangered languages and cultures. In an urban media sphere that disfavors contextualized, ethnographic depictions of language and culture, Kichwas must find practical ways to meet audiences in the middle, offering dynamic and appealing doses of Indigenous language and culture while trying to make sure they are responsibly presented. This means constantly carving out new media spaces, taking advantage of sympathetic agents of mainstream culture, forging new alliances with outsiders, and continuing to hone translation skills. Ideally, their efforts and growing expertise could have the eventual effect of forcing non-Indigenous allies, including *Colono* TV hosts, to reckon with their own limitations in translating Indigenous material and to be more open to letting Indigenous spokespersons translate for themselves.

While a revitalizing culture obviously cannot revitalize everything at once, experiments in high-profile mediation like those depicted here can potentially serve as critical first steps in a long process of reversing a history of Indigenous marginalization in the public sphere. Though the end products of this effort may include modified versions of Indigenous linguistic, cultural, and intellectual traditions, Tena Kichwas continue to expand their adaptive cultural practices while normalizing new and diverse visions of Indigeneity.

Conclusion

Discourse and the Remaking of Indigeneity in Amazonia

I have tried to paint a detailed ethnographic picture of the contemporary Tena Kichwa sociolinguistic world, defined by pluralism and polycentricity and driven by continuous innovation and adaptation. I have worked to show the necessity of deeply situated ethnographic research and contextualized linguistic anthropological analysis for making sense of how Indigenous pluralism is reflected through the dynamic words of Tena Kichwas. As I have demonstrated, explaining each experience, utterance, and text included in this book requires a full ethnographic account of its linguistic and semiotic make-up, as well as the social and historical conditions in which it is embedded. Meanwhile, in shedding some light on my data-gathering process, my task has been to "de-indexicalize" (Agar 2008) my rich and singular experiences among a people in a particular place, at a particular time. This challenging process involves tracing links between interactions and their conditions of occurrence, and deliberately exposing what has become unconscious "background knowledge" that allows me to successfully navigate the Tena Kichwa sociolinguistic world.

Let's return to the scene in the garden where this story began. Conveying what it is like to walk and talk through an Amazonian garden in a peri-urban *barrio* with two generations of Tena Kichwas, as we can now see, requires careful attention to the meaning of ancestral Amazonian forest territory, but also of the ongoing effects of urbanization. Speaking about Kichwa ancestral knowledge in Spanish requires understanding language shift and revitalization, cosmological adaptation, and political activism. Asking Tena Kichwas about their language practices requires an understanding of the available language choices, of the histories of use of these languages, and of the potential political consequences of saying things in different ways. Understanding what it means to be Tena Kichwa requires considering their perceived place in mythological space-time and living histories of colonialism, intercultural relations, and continued struggles for agency. Even watching TV in a multiculturalist nation like Ecuador requires an ethnographic sensibility. In order to make sense of Kichwa media makers' stylized versions of language within a Spanish-dominant environment, one has to know the players, their expectations and their ideological visions. In all of these cases, pluralism, the converging and juxtaposing of contrasting sources of knowledge and forms of expression, is openly embraced in a way that challenges outdated notions of Indigenous hybridity or "Indigenous modernity" (Halbmeyer 2018) as marked by problematic contradictions. Tena Kichwas' pluralistic lives and discourses present promising responses to the elders' lamentations of perceived culture "loss." Clearly, new generations are finding ways to use their experiences of navigating multiple, intersecting worlds to their advantage.

As I stated at the outset, this book serves as a documentation of my own experiences of Tena Kichwa life and discourse during a unique historical phase that I see as defined by language revitalization and a great intercultural experiment. This is an account of a historical era in which ideologies of language revitalization were central in private and public expressions of Indigeneity, including language standardization strategies, the mixed intercultural code of media performers and the oppositional words of those working to reclaim and revalue Tena Kichwa dialect. This is an account of Tena Kichwa life and language during a transformative historical shift, when language revitalization changed its locus from the work of a centralized Indigenous planning authority (DIPEIB-N) into more diffused sites of agency, including the hands of everyday Tena Kichwas like those featured throughout this book. While I have highlighted the transformational and enduring work of DIPEIB-N in the ongoing language revitalization process, it is, of course, important to recognize that language revitalization operates according to different logics and strategies now that the "Council of the Kichwa Language" has been dissolved.

In 2009, just after I completed my first fieldwork trip to Napo, the Ecuadorian Ministry of Education announced that it would take control of the BIE system, under the direction of the then president Rafael Correa. For over twenty years, BIE operated as a parallel education system run by Indigenous educators working in provincial offices with unparalleled autonomy among similar systems in Latin America (Martínez Novo & De la Torre 2010). In 2009, while these changes were taking place at the national level, DIPEIB-N's local authority over the "rescuing and revaluing" of Kichwa through Indigenous community education and public media was unmistakable. The move to merge the parallel Indigenous and state "Hispana" school systems into a singular "intercultural" one was hotly protested by Indigenous activists, who saw it as a seizing of their financial, administrative, and intellectual autonomy. According to Martínez Novo (2014), this action by the Correa administration signaled a larger state project of centralizing decision making in Ecuador while excluding Indigenous leaders from power, or an ongoing construction of Indigenous citizens as "passive recipients" of government projects. This is precisely how former DIPEIB-N administrators in Tena saw the change. During my visit to Ecuador in 2015, just under two years after the DIPEIB-N office in Tena was closed, I spent much of my time reconnecting with former administrators who once saw themselves as the vanguard of Amazonian Kichwa language and culture planning. While a few found roles within the new district offices of the Ecuadorian Ministry of Education, most were either laid off or forced into early retirement. The general consensus among those I talked to was that they were expelled by the government. One former administrator even described it as being thrown out, "like dogs in the street." "We worked in our own house for twenty-three years," another told me, "then, we were abandoned." The government apparently wanted "young, dynamic," people, and for the old ones to "go home."

Besides losing their autonomy in making financial decisions, hiring teachers, and creating curriculum, these former DIPEIB-N educators view the new unified education system as detrimental to the lives of students and their families and to Kichwas' abilities to maintain their heritage practices. "Children used to be taken by the hand," one educator explained, lamenting the disappearance of the formerly collaborative, community-based structure, "now they walk alone." Previous academic schedules allowed breaks for children to work on their families' *chakras* during harvest times, according to another teacher, now the new schedule conflicts with harvest time, and children are forced to miss classes. Most important, the state "named new guardians of the language," as one retired administrator put it, and forced out the "experienced chiefs" (Wroblewski 2019a). "The new teachers are like children," a former DIPEIB-N official complained to me, "and there is no one to lead them."

Hoping to regain some sense of direction, a small but motivated cadre of scattered DIPEIB-N educators is beginning to regroup. Working to keep the goals and models of the former Indigenous system alive, these leaders have taken on advisory roles in NGOs and private foundations, while others continue to publish educational guides in Unified Kichwa. In 2015, I attended an informal gathering of old guard educators in a rural community outside of Tena. The afternoon meeting began with a staged performance in the community ball court, including speeches in Unified Kichwa and Tena Kichwa dialect skits performed by community residents that reminded me of the oratory exhibitions DIPEIB-N hosted regularly back in the early 2000s. After the show, the elder teachers sat down to discuss tentative plans for the future over bowls of *chicha de yuca* and steaming **maitus** of white cocoa prepared by the village residents. Morale seemed remarkably high during the event. During a spirited conversation at mealtime, Carlos, a friend and former DIPEIB-N administrator, pulled me aside to make sure I took note of the scene, to record this evidence that the work he and his colleagues began in the late 1980s was still going.

While the "Council of the Kichwa Language" has been disbanded, and it remains uncertain how much direct influence the old guard will have in the new era of state-run language and curriculum planning, their legacies of language revitalization and standardization are unmistakably still intact. In fact, the contemporary era of language revitalization seems even more dynamic and innovative than it did at the height of DIPEIB-N's influence ten years ago, particularly now that it is back in the hands of everyday citizens. Eladio's Kichwa-language news show, **Rayu Shinalla**, discussed in Chapter 1, and the media performances highlighted in Chapter 5, are telling examples. Rather than following DIPEIB-N's strict model of top-down language standardization and linguistic prescriptivism, today's media makers openly mix Kichwa varieties and Spanish, adopting a more flexible approach to language choice in which they carefully weigh the interests of their diverse audiences and their polycentric social environment. Because it must now contend with Spanish and Unified Kichwa and its maintenance can no longer be taken for granted, Tena Kichwa dialect is being deliberately revived by some media makers and reclaimed as a source of pride by everyday speakers. Rejecting the model of wholesale language standardization that Tena Kichwas like Santiago, in Chapter 2, see as destined for "failure," these new grassroots language activists have decided that what Kichwas need is not elevated status but institutionalized normalization. They seek the opening of new public spaces where the use of Tena Kichwa dialect is "respected" and encouraged. Community radio programming, as discussed in Chapter 5, is one promising site where dialect has been able to flourish for several decades and where the mixing of Kichwa varieties is publicly embraced (cf. Ennis 2019). While the state has taken control over Indigenous education, without DIPEIB-N in charge, media formats like community television, radio, and staged urban events are now open forums. Media makers are free to stylize discourse in ways that draw on multiple logics and practices, including the selective use of markers of Indigeneity and Latin American modernity, Unified Kichwa and Tena Kichwa dialect. Language reclamation and bottom-up activism, rather than unchecked standardization, seem to be defining new trends among Kichwas throughout Ecuador, as other recent scholarship has shown (e.g. Ennis 2019; Limerick n.d., Martinez 2019).

Moving forward, there are some important lessons to be learned from my experiences of Tena Kichwa-language revitalization, relevant for both language activists and linguistic anthropologists working in Indigenous communities. As I have tried to show, in any situation of language revitalization, we must critically examine its main actors and their strategies. Ethnographers must continue to ask: Who are the drivers of language revitalization movements? What are their ideological orientations toward identity and language? How might their representations be partial? Who are their intended audiences? How are they received by those for whom they claim to speak? In Napo, we see a field of open contestation, marked by contrasting ideologies of language, divergent visions of Indigenous identity, and competing claims to representational sovereignty (Wroblewski 2019a). While efforts toward "revaluing" Kichwa receive unanimous support across generations of speakers, the so-far dominant strategies for "rescuing" the language—that is, standardization, purification, and the leveling of regional dialects—have been spurned by a large portion of the population, who see such moves as dismissive of their ancestral language practices and ignorant of the reality of linguistic diversity. While Unified Kichwa may have a place in select areas of education and media, what many people want, as Santiago put it in Chapter 2, is for local language to be "respected." Indigenous educators, media makers, activists, and everyday speakers, who hope to secure the future of their language, must therefore continue to weigh the pros and cons of potential revitalization and reclamation strategies.

On the one hand, these agents can choose to continue language revitalization logics of prescriptivism and the promotion of Indigenous language use in all contexts of interaction. Such work is predicated on the existence of centralized language planning bodies and top-down policies like the model created by DIPEIB-N. As its former activists have suggested, standardization, purification, and public mediation strategies have the potential to unify ethnic groups and empower Indigenous nationalities. Establishing shared sets of symbols can potentially put Indigenous languages on equal structural and symbolic footing with dominant ones. At the same time, the artificial restructuring of Indigenous languages may end up reproducing dominant-language ideologies and the dominance of non-Indigenous languages in the process. As the case of language revitalization in Napo has shown, such strategies run the risk of fostering social division between educated, socially mobile Indigenous leaders and everyday citizens, paradoxically leading to Indigenous language abandonment. As Santiago lamented in Chapter 2, when confronting the mixed signals of "rescuing" a heritage language by rendering it a "foreign" variety, "In the end," frustrated Kichwas may feel they are simply "better off learning Spanish."

On the other hand, Indigenous agents can choose to accept the realities of linguistic diversity and allow language contact, hybridization, and change to take their natural courses. This would mean tempering top-down language planning and wholesale language standardization strategies in favor of promoting language maintenance through family and community-based socialization practices. It may mean focusing energy on grassroots language media forms, like Indigenous language radio and television programming, that promote pride in local language, culture, and social issues. While this seems to be the direction favored by some opponents of language standardization, it is important to note that such strategies and conditions may have helped give rise to language shift and abandonment in the first place. Allowing natural language socialization practices to flourish means subjecting them to open competition with dominant languages, which can exert powerful pressures on communication and identity formation. If Spanish is allowed to operate unchecked as the dominant language of education, urban public interaction, and mainstream media, the functional range of Kichwa may become limited to the point of making its maintenance seem impractical or even detrimental. Such was the history of Kichwa in Napo before, and some would argue, even after the reign of DIPEIB-N.

What many of the Tena Kichwas in this book have shown, though, is that there may be a way to reach a middle ground in Indigenous language and culture maintenance by combining the above strategies. A middle-ground approach could mean creating spaces for co-management of language planning by educated community leaders and everyday speakers, or combining top-down and bottom-up language planning strategies by more effectively diffusing the work of language reclamation and language revitalization among members of Indigenous communities. Indigenous educators and linguists could retain the task of developing Indigenous "high" arts, literature, and sciences, while everyday community members, particularly youth, would be expected to control popular media, with sufficient economic and political support. Written standards like Unified Kichwa could continue to be advanced in educational and official contexts, but educators could send clearer messages about the context-dependent functions of distinct language varieties, like dialect and Unified Kichwa, and of the important differences between written standards and spoken norms. This is desperately needed in Indigenous language classrooms in Napo, where many community members see their home language practices as openly "disrespected" by those who blur the boundaries between written and spoken Unified Kichwa. The call to "write in Unified Kichwa and speak in dialect" could be more attentively regulated in the classroom, where students might speak and write as they see fit, except in contexts where written genre conventions call for the use of the standard variety.

Second, this middle-ground strategy would involve reconsidering how language activists "revalue" Kichwa. It would mean not only valuing Unified Kichwa literacy in all contexts but rather valuing and teaching multiliteracy in multiple varieties. Nonstandard and hybrid language forms that are, clearly, central to Tena Kichwas' linguistic identities should be embraced in speech *and* writing. Linguistic hybridity, which is far from unique to Kichwas, should be expected and embraced, not only in colloquial speech but in sanctioned sites of cultural expression like classrooms and public media. Grassroots media makers in Tena have already laid the groundwork for such an approach.

Finally, Indigenous leaders, including political representatives, teachers, and media makers, should promote critical understanding of dominant-language ideologies and their histories. This means calling attention to the negative effects of linguistic discrimination, such as the censoring of Kichwa-language use in "Spanish-language" contexts, the stifling of spoken dialect in "educated" or "official" spaces, the policing of Kichwa-Spanish codemixing, and the belittling of "poorly spoken Spanish." In her critique of linguistic discrimination in the United States, Lippi-Green (1997: 66) reminds us that, while it is commonly accepted to be wrong to ask people to change their race, gender, religion, or sexual identity, people still unashamedly "ask them to reject their own language practices, to drop allegiances to the people and places that define them." Indigenous language activists, too, must be critically aware of this double standard. If they are to succeed, language revitalization projects and the culturally sustaining pedagogies (Paris & Alim 2017) that Indigenous educators hope to create must include spaces for valuing and promoting non-normative language varieties and practices that define people, rather than continuing to racialize and dismiss them as barriers to progress.

Meanwhile, ethnographers of Indigenous cultures and language revitalization movements must continue to recognize pluralism and critical self-awareness as defining features of global Indigenous experiences and discourses. This book is my attempt to document the unique character of Tena Kichwa discourse while showing, like many authors before me, the complexity and inventiveness of Indigenous languages, identities, and cultures in a globalized world. Linguistic anthropology, as I hope to have shown, provides a powerful set of theoretical and methodological tools for illuminating this complexity in discourse. Given a comprehensive ethnographic grounding, we can unpack the semiotic moves through which Indigenous speakers reflect on and reconstitute their sociolinguistic worlds. By comparing expressions of discourse across spatial and temporal contexts, we can trace the interdiscursive patterns through which Indigenous Peoples assert their "relational autonomy" (Colloredo-Mansfeld 2003) and forge alternative modernities (Whitten & Whitten 2011). By zooming in on discourse, we can see concrete examples of Indigenous Peoples engaging critically with regional, national, and global processes, of Indigeneity as co-produced by colonialism and Western modernity without being dominated by their logics (Halbmayer 2018). The Tena Kichwa are but one example of an Indigenous people who engage regularly with these external forces, adapting them to their own logics and values, in a process of constant, radical reinvention of their language, identity, and social life.

That is to say, this book is intended as a case study for the ethnology of Indigenous discourse, in which pluralism, adaptation, and critical political awareness should be recognized as ordinary states of affairs. While the rescuing and revaluing of Indigenous languages and cultures are ultimately in the hands of Indigenous Peoples, outsider scholars and their readers also play a part in the revalorization process as links between Indigenous communities and dominant cultures (Grinevald 2007; Hill 2002; Rice 2009). If we are to take seriously the suggestions above for the future of Tena Kichwa language and identity, we must critically assess our own outsider expectations for what Indigenous languages and cultures are "supposed" to look like. We must recognize that, while Indigenous languages and identities are neither equivalent or commensurate with European ones, they are equally complex and equally subject to change, contestation, and remaking from within. The most convincing way to achieve this recognition, as I hope I have shown, is to provide spaces for peoples like the Tena Kichwa to speak for themselves, in their own words.

Notes

Introduction

1 Though official census data estimates the Kichwa population at 55 percent of that of Napo (SIISE 2009), local Indigenous organizations put the figure much higher, closer to 70 percent. Discrepancies in population statistics are common in Ecuador, particularly with regard to Indigenous populations, where ethnic and racial self-identification varies depending on the individual or organization soliciting demographic information, changing definitions of Indigeneity and shifting political climates. See King (2001: 35) for more on this.

Chapter 2

1 Contrary to popular conflations of Unified Kichwa with highland speech, Catta (1994) notes that voiced obstruents /b/, /d/, and /g/ have been part of the phonetic systems of Kichwa throughout all regions of Ecuador, highland as well as lowland, for at least two centuries.

Chapter 3

1 Because of the variability in pronunciation of *r* in these contexts and due to the very low frequency of such words in my recorded interviews, only intervocalic *rr* and word-initial *r* were considered for this study.
2 The designation of "fully bilingual" is based on speaker self-identification, a consideration of a speaker's personal educational history and the speaker's display of Spanish-Kichwa code-switching in interview and non-interview settings.
3 According to Aguirre (2000), palatal lateral /ʎ/ has been retained in Ecuador only in the extreme southern Andean province of Loja.[3] He notes that a distinction between the phonemes /j/ and /ʎ/ is also still maintained in the populous central and south-central highland regions of Ecuador, including the metropolises of

Quito and Cuenca, but the latter phoneme is realized not as a lateral, but rather a palatoalveolar fricative [ʒ], similar to the regional realization of /rr/ (Aguirre 2000: 29–30; see also Lipski 1994: 248).

4   The frequent lexeme *allí* was excluded from statistical analysis since it was not always clearly discernable in speech from the semantically similar *ahí,* which is common in conversational speech. Furthermore, the sound combination [ʎi] does not exist in Lowland Ecuadorian Kichwa and it appears to have fallen out of use in Ecuadorian Spanish. In Lowland Kichwa, /ll/ in <lli> orthographic environments is invariably pronounced as a palatal liquid [l] which actually occurred in very rare cases of Spanish <lli> in the recorded interviews here (e.g., "*allí*" > [ali], "*apellido*" > [apeliðo]). These scant palatal liquid realizations were the only /ll/ allophones coded as "other" in the data, and due to their infrequency (less than 1 percent), the "other" category was excluded from statistical analysis.

5   There is also an infrequent but increasing use of Spanish alveolar trilled [r] and a decreasing use of palatoalveolar fricative [ʒ] in Kichwa speech in Napo.

6   Due to the limited number of recorded interviews among *Colonos*, coding statistics from these interviews are not systematically compared to those from interviews with Kichwas in this study, as they are insufficient as a representative population of this ethnic group.

7   Two of the interviews used for /ll/ coding were excluded due to an insufficient number of /rr/ tokens (less than ten).

8   The "other" /rr/ variants were subsequently excluded from statistical analysis as they appeared to be anomalies, occurring in less than 1 percent of all tokens.

References

Acosta, A. (2012). *Buen Vivir Sumak Kawsay. Una oportunidad para imaginar nuevos mundos*. Quito: Abya Yala.

Agar, M. (2008). *The Professional Stranger: An Informal Introduction to Ethnography*, 2nd ed. Bingley, UK: Emerald.

Agha, A. (2005). "Voice, Footing, Enregisterment." *Journal of Linguistic Anthropology* 15(1): 38–59.

Agha, A. (2007). *Language and Social Relations*. Cambridge: Cambridge University Press.

Agha, A., & Wortham, S. (eds.) (2005). "Discourse Across Speech Events: Intertextuality and Interdiscursivity in Social Life." Special issue of *Journal of Linguistic Anthropology* 15(1).

Aguirre, F. (2000). *El Español del Ecuador*. Loja, Ecuador: Universidad Técnica Particular de Loja, Academia Ecuatoriana de la Lengua

Ahlers, J. (2006). "Framing Discourse: Creating Community through Native Language Use." *Journal of Linguistic Anthropology* 16(1): 58–75.

Ahlers, J. (2012). "Two Eights Make Sixteen Beads: Historical and Contemporary Ethnography in Language Revitalization." *International Journal of American Linguistics* 78(4): 533–55.

Alexiades, M., & Peluso, D. (2015). "Introduction: Indigenous Urbanization in Lowland South America." *Journal of Latin American and Caribbean Anthropology* 20(1): 1–12.

Alim, H. S. (2016). "Introducing Raciolinguistics: Racing Language and Languaging Race in Hyperracial Times." In H. S. Alim, J. Rickford, & A. Ball (eds.), *Raciolinguistics: How Language Shapes Our Ideas About Race,* 1–30. New York: Oxford University Press.

Alim, H. S., & Smitherman, G. (2012). *Articulate While Black: Barack Obama, Language, and Race in the US*. New York: Oxford University Press.

Armstrong-Fumero, F. (2009). "Old Jokes and New Multiculturalisms: Continuity and Change in Vernacular Discourse on the Yucatec Maya Language." *American Anthropologist* 111(3): 360–72.

Asad, T. (1986). "The Concept of Cultural Translation in British Social Anthropology." In J. Clifford & G. Marcus (eds.), *Writing Culture: The Poetics and Politics of Ethnography,* 141–64. Berkeley: University of California Press.

Asamblea Constituyente del Ecuador. (2008). *Constitución de la República del Ecuador*. Asamblea Constituyente. Available at http://www.asambleaconstituyente.gov.ec (accessed May 2010).

Austin, P., & Sallabank, J. (eds.) (2014). *Endangered Languages: Beliefs and Ideologies in Language Documentation and Revitalisation*. Oxford: Oxford University Press.

Avineri, N., & Kroskrity, P. (2014). "On the (Re-)Production and Representation of Endangered Language Communities: Social Boundaries and Temporal Borders." *Language and Communication* 38(1): 1–7.

Ayala Mora, E. (1992). "Estado nacional, soberanía, Estado plurinacional." In E. Ayala Mora (ed.), *Pueblos Andinos, Estado y Derecho,* 31–49. Quito, Ecuador: Abya Yala.

Babel, A. (2018). *Between the Andes and the Amazon: Language and Social Meaning in Bolivia*. Tucson: University of Arizona Press.

Bakhtin, M. M. (1973). *Problems of Dostoyevsky's Poetics* (C. Emerson, trans./ed.). Minneapolis: University of Minnesota Press.

Bakhtin, M. M. (1981). *The Dialogic Imagination*, Four Essays by M.M. Bakhtin (M. Holquist, ed., C. Emerson & M. Holquist, trans.) Austin: University of Texas Press.

Ball, C. (2018). *Exchanging Words: Language, Ritual, and Relationality in Brazil's Xingu Indigenous Park*. Santa Fe: University of New Mexico Press.

Bartesaghi, M., & Noy, C. (2015). "Interdiscursivity." In K. Tracey (ed.), *The Encyclopedia of Language and Social Interaction*, 1st ed., 1–6. Malden, MA: John Wiley and Sons.

Basso, E. (1987). *In Favor of Deceit: A Study of Tricksters in an Amazonian Society*. Tucson, AZ: University of Arizona Press.

Basso, E. (1995). *The Last Cannibals: A South American Oral History*. Austin, TX: University of Texas Press.

Bayley, R., Cameron, R., & Lucas, C. (eds.) (2013). *The Oxford Handbook of Sociolinguistics*. New York: Oxford University Press.

Becker, M. (2014). "Ecuador: Correa, Indigenous Movements, and the Writing of a New Constitution." In R. Stahler-Sholk, H. Vanden, & M. Becker (eds.), *Rethinking Latin American Social Movements: Radical Action from Below,* 267–84. Lanham, MD: Rowman & Littlefield.

Blommaert, J. (2007). "Sociolinguistics and Discourse Analysis: Orders of Indexicality and Polycentricity." *Journal of Multicultural Discourses* 2(2): 115–30.

Blommaert, J. (2010). *The Sociolinguistics of Globalization*. Cambridge: Cambridge University Press.

Blommaert, J. (2015). "Chronotopes, Scales, and Complexity in the Study of Language in Society." *Annual Review of Anthropology* 44: 105–16.

Blommaert, J., & Rampton, B. (2011). "Language and Superdiversity." *Diversities* 13(2): 1–21.

Bonfiglio, T. (2002). *Race and the Rise of Standard American*. New York: Mouton de Gruyter.

Bourdieu, P. (1991). *Language and Symbolic Power*. Cambridge: Harvard University Press.

Bucholtz, M. (1999). "Why Be Normal? Language and Identity Practice in a Community of Nerd Girls." *Language in Society* 28: 203–23.

Bucholtz, M. (2010). *White Kids: Language and White Youth Identities*. Cambridge, UK: Cambridge University Press.

Bucholtz, M., & Hall, K. (2004). "Language and Identity." In A. Duranti (ed.), *A Companion to Linguistic Anthropology*, 369–94. Malden, MA: Blackwell.

Bucholtz, M., & Hall, K. (2005). "Identity and Interaction: A Sociocultural Linguistic Approach." *Discourse Studies* 7: 585–614.

Cameron, M., & Hershberg, E. (2010). *Latin America's Left Turns: Politics, Policies, and Trajectories of Change*. Boulder, CO: Lynne Rienner.

Canclini, N. (2005). *Hybrid Cultures: Strategies for Entering and Leaving Modernity*. Minneapolis: University of Minnesota Press.

Canfield, D. (1979). "La identificación de dialectos del Español Americano a base de rasgos distintivos." In *Homenaje a Fernando Antonio Martínez*, 168–74. Bogotá: Instituto Caro y Cuervo.

Canessa, A. (2007). "Who Is INDIGENOUS? Self Identification, Indigeneity, and Claims to Justice in Contemporary Bolivia." *Urban Anthropology* 36(3): 195–237.

Castells-Tallens, A., Ramos Rodriguez, J., & Chan Concha, M. (2009). "Radio, Control and Indigenous Peoples: The Failure of State-Invented Citizens' Media in Mexico." *Development in Practice* 19(4/5): 525–37.

Catta, J. (1994). *Gramática del Quichua Ecuatoriano*, 3ra ed. Quito: Abya Yala.

Cavanaugh, J. (2012). "Entering into Politics: Interdiscursivity, Register, Stance, and Vernacular in Northern Italy." *Language in Society* 41(1): 73–95.

Cepek, M. (2016). "There Might Be Blood: Oil, Humility, and the Cosmopolitics of a Cofán Petro-Being." *American Ethnologist* 43(4): 623–35.

Chun, E., & Lo, A. (2016). "Language and Racialization." In N. Bonvillain (ed.), *The Routledge Handbook of Linguistic Anthropology*, 220–33. New York: Routledge.

Cojtí-Cuxil, D. (1996). "The Politics of Maya Revindication." In E. Fischer & R. M. Brown (eds.), *Maya Cultural Activism in Guatemala*, 19–50. Austin: University of Texas Press.

Collins, J. (2017). "Dilemmas of Race, Register, and Inequality in South Africa." *Language in Society* 46: 39–56.

Colloredo-Mansfield, R. (2003). "Tigua Migrant Communities and the Possibilities for Autonomy among Urban Indígenas." In N. Whitten (ed.), *Millennial Ecuador: Critical Essays on Cultural Transformations and Social Dynamics*, 275–95. Iowa City: University of Iowa Press.

CONAIE [Confederación de Nacionalidades Indígenas de Ecuador]. (1997). *Propuesta del Estado Plurinacional de la República del Ecuador*. Quito, Ecuador: CONAIE.

Conklin, B. (1997). "Body Paint, Feathers, and VCRs: Aesthetics and Authenticity in Amazonian Activism." *American Ethnologist* 24(4): 711–37.

Conklin, B., & Graham, L. (1995). "The Shifting Middle Ground: Amazonian Indians and Eco-Politics." *American Anthropologist* 97(4): 695–710.

Costa, J., Lane, P., & De Korne, H. (2017). "Standardizing Minority Languages." In P. Lane, J. Costa, & H. De Korne (eds.), *Standardizing Minority Languages: Competing Ideologies of Authority and Authenticity in the Global Periphery*, 1–23. New York: Routledge.

Crystal, D. (2000). *Language Death*. Cambridge: Cambridge University Press.

Davidov, V. (2013). "Mining versus Oil Extraction: Divergent and Differentiated Environmental Subjectivities in 'Post-Neoliberal' Ecuador." *Journal of Latin American and Caribbean Anthropology* 18(3): 485–504.

Davis, J. (2018). *Talking Indian: Identity and Language Revitalization in the Chickasaw Renaissance*. Tucson: University of Arizona Press.

De la Cadena, M. (2010). "Indigenous Cosmopolitics in the Andes: Conceptual Reflections Beyond 'Politics.'" *Cultural Anthropology* 25(2): 334–70.

De la Cadena, M., & Starn, O. (2007). "Introduction." In M. De la Cadena & O. Starn (eds.), *Indigenous Experience Today*, 1–32. New York: Berg.

De la Torre, C. (2010). *Populist Seduction in Latin America*. 2nd ed. Athens, OH: Ohio University Press.

Dick, H., & Wirtz, K. (2011). "Racializing Discourses." *Journal of Linguistic Anthropology* 21(s1): E2–E10.

DIPEIB-N [Dirección Provincial de Educación Intercultural Bilingüe de Napo]. (2009). Plan de desarrollo del DIPEIB-N. Tena, Ecuador: DIPEIB-N.

Dorian, N. C. (1994). "Purism vs. Compromise in Language Revitalization and Language Revival." *Language in Society* 23: 479–94.

Duchene, A., & Heller, M. (2012). *Language in Late Capitalism: Pride and Profit*. New York: Routledge.

Duranti, A. (2011). "Linguistic Anthropology: The Study of Language as a Non-Neutral Medium." In R. Mesthrie (ed.), *The Cambridge Handbook of Sociolinguistics*, 28–46. New York: Cambridge University Press.

Eckert, P. (2012). "Three Waves of Variation Study: The Emergence of Meaning in the Study of Sociolinguistic Variation." *Annual Review of Anthropology* 41: 87–100.

Eckert, P., & McConnell-Ginet, S. (1992). "Think Practically and Look Locally: Language and Gender as Community-Based Practice." *Annual Review of Anthropology* 21: 461–90.

Eisenlohr, P. (2004). "Language Revitalization and New Technologies: Cultures of Electronic Mediation and the Refiguring of Communities." *Annual Review of Anthropology* 33: 21–45.

Eloy, L., & Lasmar, C. (2012). "Urbanization and Transformation of Indigenous Resource Management: The Case of Upper Rio Negro." *International Journal of Sustainable Society* 4(4): 372–88.

England, N. (2003). "Mayan Language Revival and Revitalization Politics: Linguists and Linguistic Ideologies." *American Anthropologist* 105(4): 733–43.

Ennis, G. (2019). "Multimodal Chronotopes: Embodying Ancestral Time on Kichwa Morning Radio." *Signs in Society* 7(1): 6–37.

Errington, J. (2003). "Getting Language Rights: The Rhetorics of Language Endangerment and Loss." *American Anthropologist* 105(4): 723–32.

Espinosa, O. (2012). "To Be Shipibo Nowadays." *Journal of Latin American and Caribbean Anthropology* 17(3): 451–71.

Fasold, R. (1990). *The Sociolinguistics of Language*. Oxford: Basil Blackwell.

Fishman, J. (1991). *Reversing Language Shift: Theoretical and Empirical Foundations of Assistance to Threatened Languages*. Clevedon, UK: Multilingual Matters.

Flores, N., & Rosa, J. (2015). "Undoing Appropriateness: Raciolinguistic Ideologies and Language Diversity in Education." *Harvard Educational Review* 85: 149–71.

Fought, C. (2003). *Chicano English in Context*. New York: Palgrave Macmillan.

French, B. (2010). *Maya Ethnolinguistic Identity: Violence, Cultural Rights, and Modernity in Highland Guatemala*. Tucson: University of Arizona Press.

Gal, S. (2013). "Tastes of Talk: Qualia and the Moral Flavor of Signs." *Anthropological Theory* 13(1–2): 31–48.

Gal, S. (2015). "Politics of Translation." *Annual Review of Anthropology* 44: 225–40.

Gal, S. (2018). "Registers in Circulation: The Social Organization of Interdiscursivity." *Signs and Society* 6(1): 1–24.

Gal, S., & Irvine, J. (2019). *Signs of Difference: Language and Ideology in Social Life*. New York: Cambridge University Press.

García, M. (2005). *Making Indigenous Citizens: Identity, Development and Multicultural Activism in Perú*. Stanford: Stanford University Press.

Geertz, C. (1973). *The Interpretation of Cultures*. New York: Basic Books

Ginsburg, F. (1994). "Embedded Aesthetics: Creating a Discursive Space for Indigenous Media." *Cultural Anthropology* 9(3): 365–82.

Gobierno Municipal de Tena. (2000). "Plan Estratégico de Desarrollo Humano Sustentable del Cantón Tena." Tena, Ecuador: Gobierno Municipal de Tena.

Goffman, E. (1981). *Forms of Talk*. Philadelphia: University of Pennsylvania Press.

Goodfellow, A. M. (ed.) (2009). *Speaking of Endangered Languages: Issues in Revitalization*. Newcastle, UK: Cambridge Scholars Publishing.

Gow, P. (2007). ""Ex-Cocama": Transforming Identities in Peruvian Amazonia." In C. Fausto & M. Heckenberger (eds.), *Time and Memory in Indigenous Amazonia,* 194–214. Gainesville: University Press of Florida.

Gow, P., & Rappaport, J. (2002). "The Indigenous Public Voice: The Multiple Idioms of Modernity in Native Cauca." In K. Warren & J. Jackson (eds.), *Indigenous Movements, Self-Representation and the State in Latin America,* 47–80. Austin: University of Texas Press.

Graham, L. (1995). *Performing Dreams: Discourses of Immortality Among the Xavante of Central Brazil.* Austin: University of Texas Press.

Graham, L. (2002). "How Should an Indian Speak? Amazonian Indians and the Symbolic Politics of Language in the Global Public Sphere." In K. Warren & J. Jackson (eds.), *Indigenous Movements, Self-Representation and the State in Latin America,* 181–228. Austin, TX: University of Texas Press.

Graham, L. (2005). "Image and Instrumentality in a Xavante Politics of Existential Recognition." *American Ethnologist* 32(4): 622–41.

Graham, L. (2014). "Genders of Xavante Ethnographic Spectacle." In L. Graham & G. Penny (eds.), *Performing Indigeneity: Global Histories and Contemporary Experiences,* 305–50. Lincoln: University of Nebraska Press.

Graham, L., & Penny, G. (eds.) (2014). *Performing Indigeneity: Global Histories and Contemporary Experiences.* Lincoln: University of Nebraska Press.

Granadillo, T., & Orcutt-Gachiri, H. (eds.) (2011). *Ethnographic Contributions to the Study of Endangered Languages.* Tucson: University of Arizona Press.

Greene, S. (2006). "Getting over the Andes: The Geo-Eco-Politics of Indigenous Movements in Peru's Twenty-First Century Inca Empire." *Journal of Latin American Studies* 38: 327–54.

Greene, S. (2009). *Customizing Indigeneity: Paths to a Visionary Politics in Peru.* Stanford, CA: Stanford University Press.

Grenoble, L., & Whaley, L. (2006). *Saving Languages: An Introduction to Language Revitalization.* Cambridge: Cambridge University Press.

Grinevald, C. (2007). "Linguistic Fieldwork among Speakers of Endangered Languages." In O. Miyaoka, O. Sakiyama & M. E. Krauss (eds.), *The Vanishing Languages of the Pacific Rim,* 35–76. Oxford: Oxford University Press.

Guevara, D. (1972). *El Castellano y el Quichua en el Ecuador.* Quito, Ecuador: Casa de la Cultura Ecuatoriana.

Haboud, M. (1998). *Quichua y Castellano en los Andes ecuatorianos: Los efectos de un contacto prolongado.* Quito, Ecuador: Abya-Yala.

Halbmayer, E. (ed.) (2018). *Indigenous Modernities in South America.* Canon Pyon, UK: Sean Kingston.

Hale, C. (2005). "Neoliberal Multiculturalism: The Remaking of Cultural Rights and Racial Dominance in Central America." *PoLAR* 28(1): 10–28.

Hamilton, R. (2001). "The Insignificance of Learners' Errors: A Philosophical Investigation of the Interlanguage Hypothesis." *Language & Communication* 21: 73–88.

Hammond, R. (1999). "On the Non-occurrence of the Phone [r] in the Spanish Sound System." In J. Gutiérrez-Rexach & F. Martínez-Gil (eds.), *Advances in Hispanic Linguistics,* 135–51. Somerville, MA: Cascadilla Press.

Hanks, W. (2010). *Converting Words: Maya in the Age of the Cross.* Berkeley: University of California Press.

Hanks, W., & Severi, C. (2014). "Introduction: Translating Worlds: The Epistemological Space of Translation." *HAU: Journal of Ethnographic Theory* 4(2): 1–16.

Harkness, N. (2011). "Culture and Interdiscursivity in Korean Fricative Voice Gestures." *Journal of Linguistic Anthropology* 21(1): 99–123.

Hartley, J. (2004). "Television, Nation and Indigenous Media." *Television & New Media* 5(1): 7–25.

Heller, M., & Duchene, A. (2007). *Discourses of Endangerment: Ideology and Interest in Defence of Languages.* London: Continuum.

Hervik, P. (2001). "Narrations of Shifting Maya Identities." *Bulletin of Latin American Research* 20(3): 342–59.

Hidalgo-Capitán, A. L., & Cubillos-Guevara, A. P. (2013). "Seis debates abiertos sobre el Sumak Kawsay." *Iconos, Revista de Ciencias Sociales* 48: 25–40.

Hidrovo Castellanos, M. (2000). *Investigación Histórica del Tena*, Serie: Premios Regionales Jumandy. Tena, Ecuador: Gobierno Municipal de Tena.

High, C. (2015). *Victims and Warriors: Violence, History, and Memory in Amazonia.* Urbana, IL: University of Illinois Press.

Hill, J. (ed.) (1988). *Rethinking History and Myth: Indigenous South American Perspectives on the Past.* Urbana, IL: University of Illinois Press.

Hill, J. (1993). *Keepers of the Sacred Chants: The Poetics of Ritual Power in an Amazonian Society.* Tucson, AZ: University of Arizona Press.

Hill, J. (2019). "Music Within and About Myth / Myths About and Within Music: 30+ Years of Decentering Approaches to Discourse in Native Amazonia." *Journal of Linguistic Anthropology* 29(2): 161–7.

Hill, J. H. (1987). "Women's Speech in Modern Mexicano." In S. Phillips, S. Steele, & C. Tanz, (eds.), *Language, Gender, and Sex in comparative Perspective,* 121–60. Cambridge: Cambridge University Press.

Hill, J. H. (1995). "The Voices of Don Gabriel: Responsibility and Self in a Modern Mexicano Narrative." In D. Tedlock & B. Manheim (eds.), *The Dialogic Emergence of Culture,* 97–147. Champaign, IL: University of Illinois Press.

Hill, J. H. (2002). "Expert Rhetorics in Advocacy for Endangered Languages: Who Is Listening, and What Do They Hear?." *Journal of Linguistic Anthropology* 12(2): 119–23.

Hill, J. H. (2008). *The Everyday Language of White Racism*. Malden, MA: Wiley-Blackwell.

Hill, J. H., & Hill, K. (1986). *Speaking Mexicano, Dynamics of Syncretic Language in Central Mexico*. Tucson, AZ: University of Arizona Press.

Hinton, L., & Hale, K. (2001). *The Green Book of Language Revitalization in Practice*. San Diego: Academic Press.

Hinton, L., Huss, L., & Roche, G. (2018). *The Routledge Handbook of Language Revitalization*. New York: Routledge.

Holquist, M. (1981). "Glossary." In M. Holquist (ed.), *The Dialogic Imagination, Four Essays by M. M. Bakhtin*, 423–34. Austin, TX: University of Texas Press.

Hornberger, N. (2008). *Can Schools Save Indigenous Languages? Policy and Practice on Four Continents*. New York: Palgrave Macmillan.

Hornberger, N., & King, K. (1996) "Language Revitilisation in the Andes: Can Schools Reverse Language Shift?." *Journal of Multilingual and Multicultural Development* 17: 427–41.

Hymes, D. H. (1974). "Ways of Speaking." In R. Bauman & J. Sherzer (eds.), *Explorations in the Ethnography of Speaking*, 433–52. Cambridge: Cambridge University Press.

Imilán, W. (2010). *Warriache: Urban Indigenous*. Berlin: Verlag.

Irvine, J., & Gal, S. (2000). "Language Ideology and Linguistic Differentiation." In P. Kroskrity (ed.), *Regimes of Language*, 35–84. Santa Fe, New Mexico: School of American Research.

Jackson, J. (1991). "Being and Becoming and Indian in the Vaupés." In G. Urban & J. Sherzer (eds.), *Nation-States and Indians in Latin America*, 131–55. Austin: University of Texas Press.

Jackson, J. (2019). *Managing Multiculturalism: Indigeneity and the Struggle for Rights in Colombia*. Stanford: Stanford University Press.

Jacobs-Huey, L. (2006). *From the Kitchen to the Parlor: Language and Becoming in African American Women's Hair Care*. New York: Oxford University Press.

Jaffe, A. (1999). *Ideologies in Action: Language Politics on Corsica*. New York: Mouton de Gruyter.

Jameson, K. P. (2011). "'The Indigenous Movement in Ecuador.' The Struggle for a Plurinational State." *Latin American Perspectives* 38(1): 63–73.

Jerez, B. C. 2008. *Gramática Básica de la Lengua Kichwa*. Quito, Ecuador: DINEIB.

Johnson, E., & Zentella, A. (2017). "Introducing the Language Gap." *International Multilingual Research Journal* 11(1): 1–4.

Keane, W. (2001). "Voice." In A. Duranti (ed.), *Key Terms in Language and Culture*, 268–71. Malden, MA: Wiley-Blackwell.

Kiesling, S. (2001). "Stances of Whiteness and Hegemony in Fraternity Men's Discourse." *Journal of Linguistic Anthropology* 11: 101–15.

King, K. (2001). *Language Revitalization Processes and Prospects: Quichua in the Ecuadorian Andes*. Cambridge, UK: Multilingual Matters.

Kohn, E. (2005). "Runa Realism: Upper Amazonian Attitudes to Nature Knowing." *Ethnos* 70(2): 171–96.

Kohn, E. (2007). "How Dogs Dream: Amazonian Natures and the Policies of Transspecies Engagement." *American Ethnologist* 34(1): 3–24.

Kohn, E. (2013). *How Forests Think: Toward an Anthropology beyond the Human*. Berkeley: University of California Press.

Kroskrity, P. (ed.) (2000). *Regimes of Language: Ideologies, Polities, and Identities*. Santa Fe: School of American Research Press.

Kroskrity, P. (ed.) (2012). *Telling Stories in the Face of Danger: Language Renewal in Native American Communities*. Norman, OK: University of Oklahoma Press.

Kroskrity, P., & Field, M. (eds.) (2009). *Native American Language Ideologies: Beliefs, Practices, and Struggles in Indian Country*. Tucson: University of Arizona Press.

Kubota, R. (2014). "Race and Language Learning in Multicultural Canada: Toward Critical Anti-Racism." *Journal of Multilingual and Multicultural Development* 36(1): 3–12.

Lave, J., & Wenger, E. (1991). *Situated Learning: Legitimate Peripheral Participation*. New York: Cambridge University Press.

Lemon, A. (2002). "Without a "Concept": Race as Discursive Practice." *Slavic Review* 61(1): 54–61.

Leonard, W. (2012). "Reframing Language Reclamation Programmes for Everybody's Empowerment." *Gender and Language* 6(2): 339–67.

Lewis, M. Paul (ed.) (2009). *Ethnologue: Languages of the World*, 6th ed. Dallas: SIL International.

Limerick, N. (n.d). "Recognizing Indigenous Languages: Kichwa and the Double Binds of Intercultural Bilingual Education in Ecuador." Unpublished Manuscript.

Lippi-Green, R. (1997). *English with an Accent: Language, Ideology, and Discrimination in the United States*. New York: Routledge.

Lipski, J. (1994). *Latin American Spanish*. New York: Longman.

Lloyd, P. (1987). *From Latin to Spanish: Historical Phonology and Morphology of the Spanish Language*. Philadelphia: American Philosophical Society.

Macas, L. (2010). "Sumak Kawsay: Vida en plenitud." *America Latina en Movimiento* 452: 14–16.

Manheim, B. (2015). "All Translation Is Radical Translation." In C. Severi & W. Hanks (eds.), *Translating Worlds: The Epistemological Space of Translation*, 199–220. Chicago: HAU Books.

Marr, T. (2011). "'Ya no podemos regresar al Quechua': Modernity, identity, and language choice among migrants in urban Peru." In P. Heggarty & A. Pearce (eds.), *History and language in the Andes*, 215–38. New York: Palgrave Macmillan.

Martinez, R. (Patlán, Q) (2019). "The Verbal Art of Kichwa Reclamation." *Anthropology News* website, September 19, 2019. Available at https://www.anthropology-news.org/index.php/2019/09/19/the-verbal-art-of-kichwa-reclamation/ (accessed January 13, 2020).

Martinez Novo, C. (2014). "Managing Diversity in Postneoliberal Ecuador." *Journal of Latin American and Caribbean Anthropology* 19(1): 103–25.

Martínez Novo, C., & de la Torre, C. (2010). "Racial Discrimination and Citizenship in Ecuador's Educational System." *Latin American and Caribbean Ethnic Studies* 5(1): 1–26.

McSweeney, K., & Arps, S. (2005). "A "Demographic Turnaround": The Rapid Growth of the Indigenous Populations in Lowland Latin America." *Latin American Research Review* 40(1): 3–29.

Meek, B. (2006). "And the Injun Goes "How!": Representations of American Indian English in White Public Space." *Language in Society* 35(1): 93–128.

Meek, B. (2010). *We Are Our Language: An Ethnography of Language Revitalization in a Northern Athabaskan Community*. Tucson: University of Arizona Press.

Meek, B. (2011). "Failing American Indian Languages." *American Indian Culture and Research Journal* 35(2): 43–60.

Meek, B. (2014). "Gender, Endangered Languages, and Revitalization." In S. Ehrlich, M. Meyerhoff, & J. Holmes (eds.), *The Handbook of Language, Gender, and Sexuality*, 2nd ed, 549–66. Hoboken, NJ: Wiley Blackwell.

Mendoza-Denton, N. (2008). *Homegirls: Language and Social Practice among Latina Youth Gangs*. Malden: Blakwell.

Ministerio de Educación y Cultura. (1993). *Modelo del Sistema de Educación Intercultural Bilingüe* [MOSEIB]. Quito: Ministerio de Educación y Cultura.

Ministerio de Educación. (2009). *Kichwa Yachakkunapa Shimiyuk Kamu*. Quito: Ministerio de Educación.

Mithun, M. (1979). "The Consciousness of Levels of Phonological Structure." *International Journal of American Linguistics* 45(4): 343–8.

Montejo, V. (2002). "The Multiplicity of Mayan Voices: Mayan Leadership and the Politics of Self-Representation." In K. Warren & J. Jackson (eds.), *Indigenous Movements, Self-Representation and the State in Latin America*, 123–48. Austin: University of Texas Press.

Muratorio, B. (1987). Lanzado. *Semanario Nosotros* 103(21).

Muratorio, B. (1991). *The Life and Times of Grandfather Alonso, Culture and History in the Upper Amazon*. New Brunswick, NJ: Rutgers University Press.

Muratorio, B. (1998). "Indigenous Women's Identities and the Politics of Cultural Reproduction in the Ecuadorian Amazon." *American Anthropologist* 100(2): 409–20.

Muysken, P. (1979). "La mezcla de Quechua y Castellano. El caso de la 'Media Lengua' en el Ecuador." *Lexis* 3: 41–56.

Muysken, P. (2000). "Semantic Transparency in Lowland Ecuadorian Quechua Morphosyntax." *Linguistics* 38(5): 973–88.

Muysken, P. (2011). "Change, Contact, and Ethnogenesis in Northern Quechua: Structural Phylogenetic Approaches to Clause-Embedded Predicates." In A. Hornborg & J. Hill (eds.), *Ethnicity in Ancient Amazonia: Reconstructing Past Identities from Archaeology, Linguistics and Ethnohistory*, 225–36. Boulder: University Press of Colorado.

Nagel, J. (1996). *American Indian Ethnic Renewal: Red Power and the Resurgence of Identity and Culture*. New York: Oxford University Press.

Nettle, D., & Romaine, S. (2000). *Vanishing Voices: The Extinction of the World's Languages*. New York: Oxford University Press.

Nevins, M. E. (2013). *Lessons from Fort Apache: Beyond Language Endangerment and Maintenance*. New York: John Wiley and Sons.

Nuckolls, J. (1996). *Sounds Like Life: Sound-Symbolic Grammar, Performance, and Cognition in Pastaza Quechua*. New York: Oxford University Press.

Nuckolls, J. (2010). *Lessons from a Quechua Strongwoman: Ideophony, Dialogue and Perspective*. Tucson, AZ: University of Arizona Press.

Nuckolls, J., & Swanson, T. (2014). "Earthy Concreteness and Anti-Hypotheticalism in Amazonian Quichua Discourse." *Tipití* 12(1): 48–59.

Oakdale, S. (2005). *I Foresee My Life: The Ritual Performance of Autobiography in an Amazonian Community*. Lincoln, NB: University of Nebraska Press.

Oakdale, S., & Course, M. (eds.) (2014a). *Fluent Selves: Autobiography, Person, and History in Lowland South America*. Lincoln, NB: University of Nebraska Press.

Oakdale, S., & Course, M. (2014b). "Introduction." In S. Oakdale & M. Course (eds.), *Fluent Selves: Autobiography, Person, and History in Lowland South America*, 1–34. Lincoln, NB: University of Nebraska Press.

Oberem, U. (1980). *Los Quijos: Historia de la transculturación de un grupo indígena en el oriente ecuatoriano* (1538–1956). Madrid: Facultad de Filosofía y Letras de la Universiadad de Madrid.

Ochs, E. (1992). "Indexing Gender." In A. Duranti & C. Goodwin (eds.), *Rethinking Context: Language as an Interactive Phenomenon*, 335–58. Cambridge: Cambridge University Press.

O'Rourke, E., & Swanson, T. (2013). "Tena Quichua." *Journal of the International Phonetic Association* 43(1): 107–20.

Orr, C., & Wrisely, B. (1965). *Vocabulario Quichua del Oriente del Ecuador*. Quito, Ecuador: Instituto Lingüístico de Verano.

Paris, D., & Alim, H. S. (eds.) (2017). *Culturally Sustaining Pedagogies: Teaching and Learning for Justice in a Changing World*. New York: Teachers College Press.

Park, R. (1928). "Human Migration and the Marginal Man." *American Journal of Sociology* 33(6): 881–93.

Philips, S. (2013). "Method in Anthropological Discourse Analysis: The Comparison of Units of Interaction." *Journal of Linguistic Anthropology* 23(1): 82–95.

Radcliffe, S. (2012). "Development for a Postneoliberal Era? Sumak Kawsay, Living Well and the Limits to Decolonisation in Ecuador." *Geoforum* 43(2): 240–9.

Ramírez, A. (2008). *Cultura, Interculturalidad y Dimensión Política de la Interculturalidad*. Quito, Ecuador: DINEIB.

Ramos, A. (1995). *Sanumá Memories: Yanomami Ethnography in Times of Crisis*. Madison: University of Wisconsin Press.

Ramos, A. (1998). *Indigenism: Ethnic Politics in Brazil*. Madison: University of Wisconsin Press.

Ramos Rodríguez, J. (2005). "Indigenous Radio Stations in Mexico: A Catalyst for Social Cohesion and Cultural Strength." *The Radio Journal – International Studies in Broadcast and Audio Media* 3(3): 155–69.

Rappaport, J. (2005). *Intercultural Utopias: Public Intellectuals, Cultural Experimentation, and Ethnic Pluralism in Colombia*. Durham: Duke University Press.

Reyhner, J., & Lockard, L. (eds.) (2009). *Indigenous Language Revitalization: Encouragement, Guidance, and Lessons Learned*. Flagstaff: Northern Arizona University Press.

Reeve, M. E. (1985). "Identity as Process: The Meaning of Runapura for Quichua Speakers of the Curaray River, Eastern Ecuador." PhD diss., University of Illinois-Urbana.

Rice, K. (2009). "Must There Be Two Solitudes? Language Activists and Linguists Working Together." In J. Reyhner & L. Lockard (eds.), *Indigenous Language Revitalization: Encouragement, Guidance, and Lessons Learned*, 37–59. Flagstaff: Northern Arizona University Press.

Rickford, J. (1999). *African American Vernacular English: Features, Evolution, Educational Implications*. Malden: Blackwell.

Riggins, S. (ed.) (1992). *Ethnic Minority Media: An International Perspective*. Newbury Park, CA: Sage.

Rindstet, C., & Aronsson, K. (2002). "Growing Up Monolingual in a Bilingual Community: The Quichua Revitalization Paradox." *Language in Society* 31: 721–42.

Romaine, S. (2002). "The Impact of Language Policy on Endangered Languages." *International Journal of Multilingual Societies* 4(2): 1–28.

Rosa, J. (2016). "Standardization, Racialization, Languagelessness: Raciolinguistic Ideologies Across Communicative Contexts." *Journal of Linguistic Anthropology* 26(2): 162–83.

Rosa, J. (2018). *Looking like a Language, Sounding Like a Race: Raciolinguistic Ideologies and the Learning of Latinidad*. New York: Oxford University Press.

Rosa, J., & Flores, N. (2017). "Unsettling Race and Language: Toward a Raciolinguistic Perspective." *Language in Society* 46: 621–47.

Rubenstein, S. (2002). *Alejandro Tsakimp: A Shuar Healer on the Margins of History*. Omaha: University of Nebraska Press.

Roth-Gordon, J. (2016). *Race and the Brazilian Body: Blackness, Whiteness, and Everyday Language in Rio de Janeiro*. Oakland: University of California Press.

Salazar, J. (2009). "Self-Determination in Practice: The Critical Making of Indigenous Media." *Development in Practice* 19(4/5): 504–13.

Santos-Granero, F. (2009). "Hybrid Bodyscapes." *Current Anthropology* 50(4): 477–512.

Schieffelin, B., Woolard, K., & Kroskrity, P. (eds.) (1998). *Language Ideologies: Practice and Theory*. New York: Oxford University Press.

Schiwy, F. (2008). "Indigenous Media and the End of the Lettered City." *Journal of Latin American Cultural Studies* 17(1): 23–40.

Selinker, L. (1972). "Interlanguage." *International Review of Applied Linguistics in Language Teaching* 10(3): 209–31.

Shackt, J. (2005). "Mayahood through Beauty: Indian Beauty Pageants in Guatemala." *Bulletin of Latin American Research* 24(3): 269–87.

Sherzer, J. (1983). *Kuna Ways of Speaking: An Ethnographic Perspective*. Austin: University of Texas Press.

Sherzer, J. (1987). "Discourse-Centered Approach to Language and Culture." *American Anthropologist* 89(2): 295–309.

Sherzer, J. (1990). *Verbal Art in San Blas: Kuna Culture Through Its Discourse*. Cambridge: Cambridge University Press.

Shulist, S. (2018). *Transforming Indigeneity: Urbanization and Language Revitalization in the Brazilian Amazon*. Toronto: University of Toronto Press.

Sieder, R. (ed.) (2002). *Multiculturalism in Latin America: Indigenous Rights, Diversity, and Democracy*. New York: Palgrave Macmillan.

Silverstein, M. (1979). "Language Structure and Linguistic Ideology." In R. Clyne, W. Hanks, & C. Hofbauer (eds.), *The Elements: A Parasession on Linguistic Units and Levels,* 193–247. Chicago: Chicago Linguistic Society.

Silverstein, M. (1996). "Monoglot "Standard" in America: Standardization and Metaphors of Linguistic Hegemony." In D. Brenneis & R. Macaulay (eds.), *The Matrix of Language: Contemporary Linguistic Anthropology,* 284–306. Boulder: University of Colorado Press.

Silverstein, M. (2003). "Indexical Order and the Dialectics of Sociolinguistic Life." *Language and Communication* 23: 193–229.

Silverstein, M. (2005). "Axes of Evals: Token versus Type Interdiscursivity." *Journal of Linguistic Anthropology* 15(1): 6–22.

Silverstein, M. (2017). "The Fieldwork Encounter and the Colonized Voice of Indigeneity." *Representations* 137: 23–43.

Spitulnik, D. (1999). "Mediated Modernities: Encounters with the Electronic in Zambia." *Visual Anthropology Review* 14(2): 63–84.

Stahler-Sholk, R., Vanden, H., & Becker, M. (eds.) (2014). *Rethinking Latin American Social Movements: Radical Action from Below*. Lanham, MD: Rowman & Littlefield.

Tetreault, C. (2019). "Sherzer's Discourse-Centered Approach Applied Across Generations of Speakers." *Journal of Linguistic Anthropology* 29(2): 149–54.

Thomas, M. (2016). *The Challenge of Legal Pluralism: Local Dispute Settlement and the Indian-State Relationship in Ecuador*. New York: Routledge.

Torero, A. (1984). "El comercio y la difusión del quechua: El caso de Ecuador." *Revista Andina* 2: 367–89.

Toscano Mateus, H. (1953). *El Español en el Ecuador*. Madrid: Consejo Superior de Investigación Científica.

Trechter, S. (1999). "Contextualizing the Exotic Few: Gender Dichotomies in Lakhota." In M. Bucholtz, A. Liang, & L. Sutton (eds.), *Reinventing Identities: The Gendered Self in Discourse*, 101–22. Oxford: Oxford University Press.

Trechter, S. (2003). "The Marked Man: Language, Gender, and Ethnicity." In J. Holmes & M. Meyerhoff (eds.), *The Language and Gender Handbook*, 478–501. Oxford: Blackwell.

Turner, T. (1991). "Representing, Resisting, Rethinking: Historical Transformations of Kayapo Culture and Anthropological Consciousness." In G. Stocking (ed.), *Colonial Situations: Essays on the Contextualization of Ethnographic Knowledge*, 285–313. Madison: University of Wisconsin Press.

Urban, G. (1989). "The 'I' of Discourse in Shokleng." In B. Lee & G. Urban (eds.), *Semiotics, Self and Society*, 27–51. Berlin: Mouton de Gruyter.

Urban, G. (1991). *A Discourse-Centered Approach to Culture: Native South American Myths and Rituals*. Austin, TX: University of Texas Press.

Urban, G., & Sherzer, J. (eds.) (1986). *Native South American Discourse*. New York: Mouton de Gruyter.

Urciuoli, B. (1996). *Exposing Prejudice: Puerto Rican Experiences of Language, Race, and Class*. Boulder, CO: Westview Press.

Urla, J. (1995). "Outlaw Language: Creating Alternative Public Spheres in Basque Free Radio." *Pragmatics* 5(2): 245–61.

Urla, J. (2015). *Reclaiming Basque: Language, Nation, and Cultural Activism*. Reno: University of Nevada Press.

Uzendoski, M. (2004). "The Horizontal Archipelago: The Quijos/Upper Napo Regional System." *Ethnohistory* 51(2): 317–57.

Uzendoski, M. (2005). *The Napo Runa of Amazonian Ecuador*. Chicago: University of Illinois Press.

Uzendoski, M. (2009). "La Textualidad Oral Napo Kichwa y Las Paradojas de la Educación Intercultural Bilingüe." In C. Martinez Novo (ed.), *Repensando Los Movimientos Indígenas*, 147–92. Quito: FLACSO.

Uzendoski, M., & Calapucha-Tapuy, E. (2012). *The Ecology of the Spoken Word: Amazonian Storytelling and Shamanism among the Napo Runa*. Urbana: University of Illinois Press.

Uzendoski, M., & Whitten, N. (2014). "From "Acculturated Indians" to "Dynamic Amazonian Quichua-Speaking Peoples."" *Tipití* 12(1): 1–13.

Van Cott, D. (2005). *From Movements to Parties in Latin America: The Evolution of Ethnic Politics*. Cambridge, UK: Cambridge University Press.

Vásquez, H. (1980). *El Quichua en Nuestro Lenguaje Popular*. Cuenca, Ecuador: Departamento de Difusión Cultural de la Universidad de Cuenca.

Veronelli, G. (2015). "The Coloniality of Language: Race, Expressivity, Power and the Darker Side of Modernity." *Wagadu* 13: 108–34.

Vigoroux, C. (2017). "The Discursive Pathway of Two Centuries of Raciolinguistic Stereotyping: 'Africans as Incapable of Speaking French.'" *Language in Society* 46(1): 5–21.

Vilaça, A. (2007). "Culture Change as Body Metamorphosis." In C. Fausto & M. Heckenberger (eds.), *Time and Memory in Indigenous Amazonia*, 194–215. Gainesville: Florida University Press.

Vilaça, A. (2015). "Do Animists Become Naturalists When Converting to Christianity? Discussing an Ontological Turn." *The Cambridge Journal of Anthropology* 33(2): 3–19.

Virtanen, P. (2010). "Amazonian Native Youths and Notions of Indigeneity in Urban Areas." *Identities: Global Studies in Culture and Power* 17(2–3): 154–75.

Viveiros de Castro, E. (1998). "Cosmological Deixis and Amerindian Perspectivism." *Journal of the Royal Anthropological Institute* 4(3): 469–88.

Viveiros de Castro, E. (2004). "Perspectival Anthropology and the Method of Controlled Equivocation." *Tipití: Journal of the Society for the Anthropology of Lowland South America* 2(1): 1–22.

Walsh, C. (2009). *Interculturalidad, estado, sociedad, Luchas (de)coloniales de nuestra época*. Quito, Ecuador: Abya Yala.

Warren, K. (1998). *Indigenous Movements and Their Critics: Pan-Maya Activism in Guatemala*. Princeton: Princeton University Press.

Warren, K. (2001). "Indigenous Activism across Generations: An Intimate Social History of Antiracism Organizing in Guatemala." In D. Holland & J. Lave (eds.),

History in Person: Enduring Struggles, Contentious Practice, Intimate Identities, 63–92. Santa Fe: School of American Research Press.

Warren, K., & Jackson, J. (2002). "Introduction." In K. Warren & J. Jackson (eds.), *Indigenous Movements, Self-Representation and the State in Latin America*, 1–46. Austin: University of Texas Press.

Warren, K., & Jackson, J. (2005). "Indigenous Movements in Latin America, 1992–2004: Controversies, Ironies, New Directions." *Annual Review of Anthropology* 34: 549–73.

Webster, A., & Barrett, R. (2019). "Joel Sherzer and the Importance of Staying Discourse-Centered." *Journal of Linguistic Anthropology* 29(2): 146–8.

Whitely, P. (2003). "Do "Language Rights" Serve Indigenous Interests? Some Hopi and Other Queries." *American Anthropologist* 105(4): 712–22.

Whitten, N. (1976). *Sacha Runa: Ethnicity and Adaptation of Ecuadorian Jungle Quichua*. Urbana: University of Illinois Press.

Whitten, N. (1985). *Sicuanga Runa: The Other Side of Development in Amazonian Ecuador*. Urbana: University of Illinois Press.

Whitten, N. (2003). "Preface." In N. Whitten (ed.), *Millenial Ecuador: Critical Essays on Cultural Transformations and Social Dynamics*, ix–xvii. Iowa City: University of Iowa Press.

Whitten, N., & Whitten, D. (2008). *Puyo Runa, Imagery and Power in Modern Amazonia*. Chicago: University of Illinois Press.

Whitten, N., & Whitten, D. (2011). *Histories of the Present: People and Power in Ecuador*. Urbana, IL: University of Illinois Press.

Willis, E., & Bradley, T. (2008). "Contrast Maintenance of Taps and Trills in Dominican Spanish: Data and Analysis." In L. Colantoni & J. Steele (eds.), *Selected Proceedings of the 3rd Conference on Laboratory Approaches to Spanish Phonology*, 87–100. Somerville, MA: Cascadilla Proceedings Project.

Wolfram, W. (1969). *A Sociolinguistic Description of Detroit Negro Speech*. Washington, DC: Center for Applied Linguistics.

Wong, P. (2019). "Biographies of a Sociological Type: 'Marginal Men' and the Establishment of 'Middle American' Anthropology." *Journal of Latin American and Caribbean Anthropology*, Early View. DOI: 10.1111/jlca.12430.

Woolard, K. (2008). "Why *Dat* Now?: Linguistic-Anthropological Contributions to the Explanation of Sociolinguistic Icons and Change." *Journal of Sociolinguistics* 12(4): 432–52.

Woolard, K., & Schieffelin, B. (1994). "Language Ideology." *Annual Review of Anthropology* 23: 55–82.

Wortham, S., & Reyes, A. (2015). *Discourse Analysis Beyond the Speech Event*, 1st ed. New York: Routledge.

Wroblewski, M. (2010). "Voices of Contact: Politics of Language in Urban Amazonian Ecuador." PhD diss., University of Arizona.

Wroblewski, M. (2014). "Public Indigeneity, Language Revitalization, and Intercultural Planning in an Amazonian Beauty Pageant." *American Anthropologist* 116(1): 65–80.

Wroblewski, M. (2019a). "Inscribing Indigeneity: Ethnolinguistic Authority in the Linguistic Landscape of Amazonian Ecuador." *Multilingua*, early view. DOI: https://doi.org/10.1515/multi-2018-0127

Wroblewski, M. (2019b). "Performing Pluralism: Language, Indigeneity, and Ritual Activism in Amazonia." *Journal of Latin American and Caribbean Anthropology* 24(1): 181–202.

Zentella, A. (2007). *Growing Up Bilingual: Puerto Rican Children in New York*. Malden: Blackwell.

Zentella, A. (2014). "TWB (Talking While Bilingual): Linguistic Profiling of Latina/os, and Other Linguistic Torquemadas." *Latino Studies* 12: 620–35.

Zhang, Q. (2008). "Rhotacization and the "Beijing Smooth Operator": The Social Meaning of a Linguistic Variable." *Journal of Sociolinguistics* 12: 201–22.

Index

acculturation   11, 12, 18, 63, 154
  implications of   53
  urban   25, 151
Agha, A.   65
Aguirre, F.   92, 102, 175–6 n.3
allophones   98, 102–3, 176 n.4
  ll frequency   98, *99, 101*
  palatoalveolar fricative   100, 102, 106, 108
  Spanish *rr*   102–8, 103, *104, 105*
  voiced and voiceless   72
Ally TV   35, 49, *136*, 149, 156
alternative modernity   11, 30, 50, 172
alveolar tap [ɾ]   102–3, 106–8
Amarunkachi myth   114, 117
Amazonia   30, 54. *See also individual entries*
  discourse-centred research in   116
  Native/Indigenous   13, 20, 31, 132, 165–73
  significance of   58, 120
Amazonian Kichwa speech community   46–7
analytic transduction   141, 142
Andean highland region (*sierra*)   66
anthropological studies, of Indigenous activism   30–1
appropriative transduction   142
aswa (beer)   6, 25
auca (savage)   19
"authentic Kichwa"   65
ayawaska (*Banisteriopsis caapi*)   5, 6
ayllullakta (kin-based community)   1, 20, 48, 151

Babel, A.   42
Bakhtin, M. M.   56, 57, 118
Barrett, R.   115
barrio, significance of   150, 151
Becker, M.   14
Bilingual and Intercultural Education (BIE)   7, 15, 24–5, 54, 62, 166

bilingual-intercultural education, critique of   54–5
bilingualism   83–6, 117, 119, 175 n.2. *See also* "poorly spoken Spanish" (*Castellano mal hablado*)
  ethnography and   95, 107–10
  Indigenous   90
  intercultural media and   142, 144, 151, 152, 154, 155, 161
  language revitalization and   53, *54*, 56, 57, 60, 62–5, 70, 72
  pluralism and   16, 28, 32–3
  semiotics and   81, 87, 110
  sociolinguistics and   36, 38, 45, 83, 87, 92, 94–6, 102, 107–10
Blommaert, J.   43, 45
Bradley, T.   103
Bucholtz, M.   47

Calapucha-Tapuy, E.   117, 141, 143
cancha abierta (open ball court)   151
cancha cubierta (covered ball court)   113, 151
Castellano mal hablado   84–6. *See also* "poorly spoken Spanish" (*Castellano mal hablado*)
Catta, J.   175 n.1 (Ch 2)
chakra/chakrakuna (family garden plots)   1–3, *2*, 23, 27, 28, 167
chaski game   136, 151, 157
chronotopes   118, 121, 125, 131
chunta aswa (beer)   6
"Citizens' Revolution"   14
codemix   37, 117, 144
codes   32, 57, 59–60, 79
  definition of   37
  multiple   37, 38, 46–9
codeswitch   37, 45, 46, 117, 133, 144
Colloredo-Mansfield, R.   26, 50
Colonos (Whites and Mestizos)   19, 25–6, 92, 101, 106, 161, 176 n.6
  late colonial frontier and   120–1

media hosts 149, 155, 157
missionaries and 121–5
officials, and indigenous governors 125–31
communities of practice 46
significance of 47
Confederation of Indigenous Nationalities of Ecuador (CONAIE) 14–15
consonant devoicing 73
"continuum of ways of speaking", notion of 95, 110
Correa, R. 14, 64, 166
"Council of the Kichwa Language" 8
Course, M. 119
Crystal, D. 140
cultural intervention 140, 162
cultural legitimacy 61, 140
cultural marginalization 58, 161
cultural patrimony 90
Napo's Indigenous communities as 21
cultural vulnerability 21
city as 25
culture preservation 142, 151, 153, 161

"de-quotative I" 57
devoicing 72–3
dialect 11, 33. *See also* Tena Kichwa dialect
Directorate of Bilingual and Intercultural Education (DINEIB) 62–3
duties and functions of 63
Directorate of Provincial Bilingual and Intercultural Education of Napo (DIPEIB-N) 15–16, 63–4, 115, 166–8
language and culture revitalization by 16, 62
direct reported speech 57
discourse
definition of 9
double-voiced 57
ethnography and 115–19
Indigenous 9, 12
Indigenous agency 131–4
language ideologies in 87
of linguistic difference 59
of loss and revitalization 25–8
metalinguistic, of purity and power 65
pluralistic 12–13, 48–51

prescriptivist 92–6
racializing 88–92
remaking 28–31
of revitalization and Indigenous interview 149–55
significance of 9
voices in 56

Ecuador
Andean highland region (*sierra*) and 66–7
Article 1 of constitution (2008) 14
bilingual education in 62
"Citizens' Revolution" of 14
Kichwa speaking as iconic sign in 42
map of 18
as multicultural 15
pink tide in 14
regional accents in 83–4
Ecuadorian Ministry of Education 77
Eladio Tapuy (interviewee) 35–8
indexing diversity of 40–2
metalinguistic interview with 39–40
pluralism in discourse of 48
polycentricity and 46
as transculturite 49
Ennis, G. 144
enregisterment 65, 71, 91, 94, 95, 149
ethnography 13, 46–7, 141, 162
bilingualism and 95, 107–10
discourse and 115–19
language revitalization and 53, 60–1, 75
significance of 8, 17–20, 22, 29–30, 32–4, 87, 165–6, 169, 172
ethnolinguistic authority 32, 47, 49
ethnolinguistic domain 58

fincas (farms). See *chakra/chakrakuna* (family garden plots)
Flores, N. 89

Gal, S. 141
Ginsburg, F. 140
Goffman, E. 56
GoldVarb software 98, 103
Graham, L. 31, 44, 132, 161

Hamilton, R. 94
Hammond, R. 103

Hanks, W. 141
heritage speaker 2, 19, 48
heteroglossia 56
Hidrovo Castellanos, M. 120
highland Kichwas 73
Hill, J. 116
Hill, J. H. 37, 56, 94, 107–8
Hill, K. 37, 94
"Hispanophone" population 94
hybridity, Indigenous 110, 116, 144, 166, 170, 171
   pluralism and 10–13, 29, 30

iconization process 42, 44
   sounds and 71–4
index 46
   lexicon/vocabulary and 74–7
   order 73, 74
      and language 43–5
      multiple 45–6
   significance of 40–1
   signs and 42
Indigeneity. *See also individual entries*
   plural 9–13, 44, 116–18, 132, 144, 146, 147, 149, 165, 166, 172, 173
   remaking 13–17
indigenous [ɾ] 102–8
Indigenous agency discourses 131–4
indirect index. *See* non-referential index
intercultural code 32, 142, 166
   language revitalization and 59, 70–2, 74–6,78, 80, 82
interculturality
   in Napo 15–16
   significance of 13, 15
intercultural media 135
   on contextualized translations 141–2
   Indigenous interview and revitalization discourses and 149–55
   Kichwa-language radio in Napo Province and 143–4
   lexicalization, translation, and representation and 155–61
   Ñusta Yutsullakta Warmi (Miss Yutsullakta Princess) contest 135–9, 145–8, 151
   oral narratives and 136–9, 150–3, 156, 158–60
   pluralism and 144
   revitalization future and 161–3
   revitalization media and paradoxes and 139–43
   significance of 140, 143–9
intercultural memories 111
   chronotopes and 118
   Colono officials and Indigenous governors and 125–31
   Indigenous agency discourses and 131–4
   missionaries and 121–5
   oral history narratives and 112–14, 117, 118–19, 122–4, 126–31
   Tena Kichwa Indigeneity and interdiscursivity and 134
   verbal art and 115–16
   White colonization and 120–1
intercultural translation 142, 143, 155, 162
interdiscursivity 31, 33, 119, 134, 149–51, 154, 161, 172
interlanguage 94, 102, 110
Inti Wayra ("Wind of the Sun") dance group 152–4
isogloss 66

Jackson, J. 67

kalulu (wood ear mushroom) (*Auriculara auricula*) 3, 4
kamachina (advise/counsel), significance of 157–8
Kichwa, ethnic identity 16–17
Kichwa-language radio, in Napo Province 143–4
Kichwa lexicon, purification of 62
Kichwa nation-building/nationality 32, 45, 58–61, 64, 70
   opponents of 67
Kichwa-ness 17, 20, 142
King, K. 62, 65, 175 n.1 (Ch 1)
kumpalina (Kichwa ethnic dress) 26

language ideologies 33, 60, 170, 172
   poorly spoken Spanish and 87, 94, 100, 110
   power of 108–9
languagelessness 89, 90
language revitalization 25–8, 49, 115, 166
   communications media and 140
   iconic sounds and 71–4
   indexical words and 74–7

Index

language politics and 55–8
language standardization
    and 61, 65, 67
linguistic context and 66–7
new ethnolinguistic
    consciousness and 58–60
new ethnolinguistic
    identity and 79–80
new indigenous order and 60–5
proprietary code and intercultural
    code and 67–71
significance of 81–2, 168–70
symbolic morphemes and 77–9
language shift 8, 26, 93, 125, 165, 170
    language revitalization and 53–5, 58,
        61, 62, 65, 67
Lider Vision (private television
    station) 156
linguistic anthropology 95, 118, 119
linguistic deficiency 85, 91, 92, 110
    of racialized speakers 89
linguistic disorder 91
linguistic drift 68, 70
linguistic prescriptivism 92
Lippi-Green, R. 172
Lipski, J. 92, 94, 96–8, 102
lisanpapa (*Carludovica palmata*) 3
literacy planning, significance of 77
makikutuna (Kichwa ethnic dress) 26
maltakuna (young people) 36
mamakuna (mothers) 36
Manheim, B. 141, 142
Marr, T. 90
Martínez Novo 167
mashi (friend/companion) 36, 43, 48, 75
    distinction with *wawki* 75–6
mestizaje 120
minka (cooperative community work
    party) 123, 133–5, 151, 156
Mishus. *See* Colonos (Whites
    and Mestizos)
Model of Bilingual and Intercultural
    Education (MOSEIB) 63
Moreno, L. 14
morphemes 37, 62, 74
    symbolic 77–9
multilingualism 10, 17, 46, 93,
    109, 110, 116
    global ideologies of 90
    language revitalization and 55–7, 63

significance of 89–90
Muratorio, B. 93, 121, 134
Napeños and multiculturalism 90
Napo Runa 18–19, 92–3, 134
    allophone in contemporary 106
    essentialized 80
    ethnic reconfiguration 67–8, 79
    ethnogenesis 58, 59, 70
    Unified Kichwa as menace
        to 53, 64–5, 77
    view of contemporary life 93
Napu Marka (Napo Province) 36
Native Certificate 7
Native texts, significance of 28–9,
    32, 49, 139
neutralization 96–7
    rejection of 103
non-referential index 41, 42
Ñusta Yutsullakta Warmi (Miss
    Yutsullakta Princess)
    contest 135, 145–8
oral narratives and 136–9, 151
performance demonstration
    during 146, 147, 148
Oakdale, S. 119
oral history narratives 112–14,
    117, 118–19
Oriente 1, 5, 120, 124
    poorly spoken Spanish and 83–8,
        91–4, 100, 106, 109–10
    significance and implications
        of 96–102, 110
    overlooking 92
orthographic conventions *xi*
pachakutik 59, 68
Pachamama (Earth Mother) 147, 149
pacha (ceremonial dress) 135
pagarachu (thank you) 76
palatoalveolar fricative allophone 100,
    102, 106, 108, 176 n.5
pan-indigenism 59, 61, 62, 64, 67–9, 79
    critique of 69
pankua 136, 151
Pano Warmi, significance of 156, 159
pata (white cocoa) peeling
    game 136, 151, 158
Peirce, C. S. 40, 42
performances 28, 70, 168
    collective 43
    of dialogue 56

"double voiced" discourse and   57
  ethnic   88
  before global public sphere   44
  of Indigeneity   116, 117,
       140, 142
  interdiscursive   119
  of linguistic differentiation   81
  as linguistic markers of
       Indigeneity   154
  public   72, 115, 116, 134
  of revitalized culture   144
  of ritual activism   119
  significance of   31, 117, 131,
       144, *146*, 153
  signs and   119
  speech   53
  storytelling   114
  on television   39, 49
phonemes   33, 72, 74, 86, 96–102, 109,
       110, 175–6 n.3
phonology   71, 73, 74, 86–7
"pink tide"   13, 14
pluralism   15, 22, 34, 44, 133, 140
  in discourse   48–51
  identity of   25
  Indigenous   9–13, 44, 116–18,
       132, 144, 146, 147, 149, 165,
       166, 172, 173
  linguistic   32
  sociolinguistic   56
plurinationality   13
  significance of   14–15, 63
  Spanish and   60
polycentricity   9, 32, 38, 48,
       49, 165, 168
  and communities of practice   45–7
"poorly spoken Spanish" (*Castellano mal
       hablado*)   85–7, 94
  indigenous [r] and   102–8
  language ideologies and   108–9
  Oriente [ʎ] and   96–102
  prescriptivist discourse and   92–6
  racializing discourses and   88–92
  social stratification of [ʎ] and
       [r] and   96
postcolonial Indigenous agency   125
Praat phonetic analysis software   98

raciolinguistics, significance of   33, 89
Rancia (white foreigner)   5

Rayu Shinalla (TV show)   35–8, 48, 168
  greeting on   36–7
  icons usage in   44
  opening credits of   35
  significance of   49
Real Academia Española   103
reanimation, of past   118
referential index   41
relational autonomy   50, 172
reverse conquest   143
rhematization   42
ritual activism   115, 132, 134. *See also*
       intercultural memories
Rosa, J.   89
Runa. *See also* Napo Runa
  and Kichwa compared   17
  significance of   11, 16–17
Runa-ness   20
Runa Paju (Kichwa pop genre)   143–4
Runapura (humans among themselves)   19
Runa Shimi (human speech) language
       17, 48, 69

Salazar, J.   143
samay (empowering forces)   23
Santos-Granero, F.   11, 12
self-identification, as Kichwa   17
semiotics   65, 165, 172
  bilingualism and   81, 87, 110
  intercultural media and   142,
       143, 154, 162
  intercultural memories and   116, 119,
       125, 133, 134
  significance of   10, 30–3, 42–4,
       46, 47, 49
Severi, C.   141
shikra   145, 149
signs   10, 44, 119, 140, 143, 155
  of diversity   88
  enregistered   149
  index and   40, 42
  of Indigeneity   30, 149, 161
  of Kichwa-ness   142
  making sense of   47
Silverstein, M.   28, 43
social index. *See* non-referential index
social stratification, of [ʎ] and [r]   96
sociolinguistics   35, 38–40, 165, 172
  bilingualism and   83, 87, 92, 94–6,
       102, 107–10

indexing diversity and 40–2
language and indexical
 order and 43–5
language revitalization and 55, 56, 81
and pluralism 9, 10, 32–4
 in discourse and 48–51
 polycentricity and Tena
  Kichwa communities of
  practice and 45–7
Rayu Shinalla (TV show) and 35–8
sociolinguistic variants,
 significance of 87
Spanish. *See also individual entries*
 as foreign language for Kichwas 91
 as language of intercultural relations 63
 significance of 60
Spanish *rr* allophone 102–8, 176 nn.7–8
 frequency
  according to education level 104
  according to gender 105
  according to generation 104
  according to residence history 105
speech community, Amazonian Kichwa
 46–7
stigmatization 12, 84, 89–90, 101, 108
storytelling 114, 117–18, 132–3
substrate languages 97
Sumak Kawsay (good living) 15

Tena Kichwa. *See also individual entries*
 bilingualism and 90–1
 communities of practice, and
  polycentricity 45–7
 contemporary lifestyles and identity
  practices of 27–8
 existential recognition for 162
 home concept for 22
 Indigeneity and interdiscursivity 134
 intercultural media forms and 143–4
 on language and culture loss 26
 lo propio and 58, 59
 loss and revitalization discourses and
  25–8
 multicultural sensibility of 29–30
 significance of 17–20
 social stratification of [ʌ] and
  [ɾ] and 96
 on Spanish of Kichwa bilinguals
  84–5
 storytelling practices of 117–18

urban acculturation and 25
urban living and 23–4
visit to rural heritage communities
 22–3
weekend *macheteros* and urban
 intellectuals and 20–5
Tena Kichwa dialect
 language revitalization and 59–60,
  64–5, 67, 70, 82
 significance of 19, 27, 32, 42,
  48, 73–4, 77, 80, 82, 117,
  125, 168–9
 and Unified Kichwa compared
  lexical differences 75
  morphological differences 78
  phonological differences 71
Thomas, M. 15
Toscano Mateus, H. 92, 102
traje típico (traditional dress)
 144–6, *147*
transculturation 11, 31

unay (mythical space-time) 23, 116
Unified Kichwa 32, 36, 54
 as altered 69
 as foreign language variety 67
 as hallmark of pan-indigenist
  activism 64
 as intercultural code 70
 introduction into BIE in Napo 65
 as invented 80, 81
 literacy advancement in 62–3
 as menace to Tena Kichwa and Napo
  Runa 53, 64–5, 77
 morphemes 78–9
 morphology, critique of 77–8
 neologisms 75, 76, 81
 opponents of 70, 74–6, 79–81
 significance of 16, 39–40, 45,
  48, 60, 171
 standardization of 62
 and Tena Kichwa Dialect
  lexical differences 75
  morphological differences 78
  phonological differences 71
 as *Unificado* 69
 writing in 72
Upper Napo Kichwa dialect. *See* Tena
 Kichwa dialect
Urban, G. 57

Urciuoli, B. 88, 91
Uzendoski, M. 11, 17, 19, 117, 141, 143

verbal art 115–16, 148
Vigoroux, C. 91
Vilaça, A. 11
voice *xi*, 12, 34, 47, 54, 81,
      175 n.1 (Ch 2)
  definition of 56
  in discourse 56
  double, and discourse 57
  multiple 56–7
  shifts in 56
  system 56
voiced allophones 72
voiceless allophones 72

Walsh, C. 15
Wayra Apamushkas (wind-bearers) 68
wayusa upina (*wayusa* tea drinking time) 143, 144, 151, 156
Webster, A. 115
Whitten, D. 11
Whitten, N. 11
Willis, E. 103
Woolard, K. 95

yayakuna (fathers) 36
yeísmo 97, 100, 101
yupaychani (I am grateful) idiom 36, 76
yura (tree) 40

www.ingramcontent.com/pod-product-compliance
Lightning Source LLC
Chambersburg PA
CBHW072236290426
44111CB00012B/2122